LITERATURE OF AFRICA

**Recent Titles in
Literature as Windows to World Cultures**

Modern South Asian Literature in English
Paul Brians
Latino Literature in America
Bridget Kevane
Literature of Latin America
Rafael Ocasio

LITERATURE OF AFRICA

Douglas Killam

Literature as Windows to World Cultures

GREENWOOD PRESS
Westport, Connecticut • London

Library of Congress Cataloging-in-Publication Data
Killam, G. D.
   Literature of Africa / Douglas Killam.
      p. cm. — (Literature as windows to world cultures, ISSN 1543–9968)
   Includes bibliographical references and index.
   ISBN 0–313–31901–4
   1. African literature—History and criticism. I. Title. II. Series.
   PL8010.K53   2004
   809′.896—dc22   2004013212

British Library Cataloguing in Publication Data is available.

Library of Congress Catalog Card Number: 2004013212
ISBN: 0–313–31901–4
ISSN: 1543–9968

First published in 2004

Greenwood Press, 88 Post Road West, Westport, CT 06881
An imprint of Greenwood Publishing Group, Inc.
www.greenwood.com

Printed in the United States of America

The paper used in this book complies with the
Permanent Paper Standard issued by the National
Information Standards Organization (Z39.48–1984).

10 9 8 7 6 5 4 3 2 1

Contents

Acknowledgments

I have shared the excitement of African literature with many people since I first read Chinua Achebe's *Things Fall Apart* in 1960. Eldred Jones, John Ramsaran, Ayo Banjo, Sam Asein, Wole Soyinka, J. P.Clark, Bruce King, Keith Sambrook, James Currey, Chinua Achebe, Margaret Laurence, Bernth Lindfors, John Reed, Stephen Arnold, Rowland Smith, Bernard Fonlon, and Johan van Wyk are colleagues and friends who have shared and shaped my interest and opinions on African literature over the years. To them I owe a special debt of gratitude and friendship.

I also want to thank Marie M. Davis for her monumental help with this book.

Introduction

Because the work of African writers is known and read throughout the
English-speaking world and well beyond, this book, a guide to
African literature, is also a guide to a part of world literature.
Indeed, in virtually all countries of the world, selections of African writing
are found on outlines in literature courses in secondary schools, colleges,
and universities. One need only search the web for courses in modern literature to see the extent to which African writing is required or recommended
reading. I have seen African literature taught in the United States, England,
Canada, South East Asia, Australia, New Zealand, the Pacific Islands,
Western and Eastern Europe, and Russia. For some readers, the writing
brings news of foreign parts of the world; for others, it elaborates and deep-
ens whatever understanding they have of Africa, its peoples, and their cultures.

The African writers discussed in this guide are known internationally for
their work. This guide is meant to help students to gain understanding of
the issues these writers' books raise and a fuller appreciation of the richness
of African writing. The novels discussed here are selected from a wide range
of titles by African authors. These books are ones that are found most frequently on courses of study and the ones most frequently mentioned in critical commentaries on the writing.

It can be noted that in the brief span of 40 years, beginning with the publication of Amos Tutuola's *Palm-Wine Drinkard*, 215 writers have published more than 2,000 books (exclusive of South Africa, a special case), an
unprecedented publishing achievement. The celebrated Heinemann African

Writers Series published 270 titles between 1962 and 1984, and though the series has been discontinued, many of the original titles are still in print. Since Heinemann's publication boom, other publishers have entered the field of African writing.

This guide is arranged by geographic region—West, East, South-Central, and South Africa. For reasons of geography, the use to which Europeans put the land once they had annexed it from African peoples varies from region to region. Accordingly, the literary response to this historical fact varies among writers from different regions. In the Introduction to this guide and in the individual entries on authors, I have described briefly the history of European association, including initial contacts and responses to the land; the responses of Europeans to African peoples and their cultures; and the subsequent responses of African peoples as they are recorded in the novels under review.

I have also indicated the major preoccupations of the authors in this guide, with special treatment of the writings of Chinua Achebe, Buchi Emecheta, Ayi Kwei Armah, Miriama Ba, Sembene Ousmane, Ngugi wa Thiong'o, Nadine Gordimer, Alex La Guma, Alan Paton, and Bessie Head. Their writing is discussed in the context of a survey of the literatures in each of the geographic regions, organized by date of the first publication of individual authors. This arrangement is a means of tracing the development of the literary tradition of countries within each region. Individual author entries include literary and, where relevant, extra-literary careers; a comment on the major preoccupations that inform each author's writing, a description of the writer's literary output, and detailed commentary on his or her most prominent works. Discussion of the historical and cultural issues in the novels is integrated into the literary commentary.

The biographical notes on authors are arranged alphabetically by African author within each of the four regional sections.

Despite the differences in themes among works of African literature, all of the literature has a common starting point: it develops out of a colonizing experience, an experience based on racial imperatives. Thus, the writing is, in the first instance, a response to the colonizing experience—how it affected colonial subjects, what responses African peoples made to it, and in what ways the experience of being colonized has spilled over into the post-colonial and independent period. Because it is a literature about race, culture, and power, African literature is considered a political literature.

Chinua Achebe is the dominating voice in African literature. Achebe set a literary standard with his first novel, *Things Fall Apart* (1958), a book that is as widely read and discussed as any literary work in the second half of the twentieth century and the early years of the twenty-first. In 2002 the novel was placed in the top 12 books in a listing of "Africa's 100 Best Books of the Twentieth Century." Two other of his books appear in the full list from this survey. Eight of the 18 books in the major sections of this guide are placed on the same list, a measure of their secure place in African publishing.

Ignited by the publication of *Things Fall Apart,* an unprecedented literary explosion reverberated throughout Africa south of the Sahara and north of South Africa (a special case to be noted below). As has been shown in this brief and selective history of West African fiction writing, authors in West Africa—Sierra Leone, Ghana, and Nigeria—have published at least one work and, in most cases many more. Nigeria by virtue of its larger population leads the way.

In East Africa—Kenya, Uganda, and Tanzania—where publication in English begins later than in West Africa—a literary tradition began in 1964 with the publication of *Weep Not, Child* by Ngugi wa Thiong'o (at that time called James Ngugi). *Weep Not, Child* was the catalyst in East Africa that *Things Fall Apart* was in West Africa. Since 1964 the pattern of growth in East Africa has been similar to that of West Africa, with 42 authors going into print in English.

And the pattern repeats itself in South Central Africa—Zambia, Malawi, and Zimbabwe—with the publication in 1967 of David Rubadiri's *No Bride Price.* Since 1967 some 37 writers have appeared in print in English. Writing from Zambia, Malawi, or Zimbabwe is not represented in this book largely because none of the writers from these countries has achieved the prominence of the writers from West, East, and South Africa, whose books are discussed in this study. But their writing reveals the same concerns as that of their peers from other parts of Sub-Saharan Africa.

The publication history of South Africa's literature is longer and more complex than that of the other three regions. It is more complex because of the country's evolution from colonization through independence in 1903 to the present, and especially because of the fact that apartheid permeated the culture for much of that time. Olive Schreiner's *The Story of an African Farm* (1883) is generally agreed to mark the beginning of publication in English. The first novels were written by white settlers whose interest, like Schreiner's, is in conveying the complexities of settler life, of expansion into the interior, and of encounters with indigenous African nations.

Writing by black writers from South Africa begins in the mid- to late 1920s. From then on, writing by black and white writers developed along parallel lines. And from 1948—the year in which racial discrimination began to be established in law—much of that writing was focused on the consequences of apartheid in human terms for the majority of the South African population.

While our predominant interest here is in writing in English, two of the novels to be discussed are from a substantial tradition of writing in French in Africa. I have selected Sembene Ousmane's *God's Bits of Wood* (1962) and Miriama Ba's *So Long a Letter* (1981) from a long list of French novels in English translations because they have received as much acclaim by English readers as the books by the other authors included in this guide.

African literature in French began to be published at about the same as African writing in English and has developed at about the same pace. There are probably one thousand examples of poetry, drama, and fiction in French, more or less the same amount as in English. Some have been translated into English. The writing of Mongo Beti and Ferdinand Oyono from Cameroon are widely read in English translations. None, however, has received critical acclaim nor are more widely read than the two novels which follow in this discussion—*God's Bits of Wood* by Sembene Ousmane and *So Long a Letter* by Miriama Ba.

African literature is attracting an increasing world readership because it gives to readers an understanding of places, peoples and cultures that have a vital and influential place in a global context. Literature as much as, perhaps more than other forms of communication—newscasts, documentaries, travelogues—presents the lives of people in living cultures, evokes the whole range of emotions, opinion, and sentiments of these peoples in describing the most pressing problems that face them. It is a cliché to say that the best literature breaks down prejudice and promotes understanding. But like many clichés it contains a truth.

ADDITIONAL READINGS

Ba, Miriama. 1981. *So Long a Letter.* Translated by Modupe Bode-Thomas. London: Heinemann.

Booker, M. Keith. 1998. *The African Novel in English: An Introduction.* Portsmouth, N.H.: Heinemann; Oxford: James Currey.

Gakwandi, Shatto Arthur. 1977. *The Novel and Contemporary Experience in Africa.* London: Heinemann.

Gikandi, Simon. 1987. *Reading the African Novel.* London: James Currey.

Ousmane, Sembene *God's Bits of Wood.* Translated by Francis price. 1962. N.Y. Doubleday.

Rubadiri, David. 1967. *No Bride Price.* Nairobi: East African Publishing House.

Schreiner, Olive. 1883. *The Story of an African Farm.* 2 vols. London: Chapman and Hall.

Africa and Europe

U ntil the closing years of the eighteenth century, contacts between
Europeans and Africans south of the Sahara were limited for the
most part to the operation of slavers—West Africa was the source of
the human cargo transported in the hundreds of thousands to the Caribbean
Islands and North America—to the cursory development of trade, and the
activities of missionaries along the coastal areas. There had been some
exploring expeditions, principally along the great rivers—the Congo, the
Niger, and the Benue—but knowledge of the way of life of the inhabitants
of the African interior was cursory.

But about 1780, European interest in Africa changed dramatically. A
number of related facts of history account for this change. The growth of
industrial societies in Europe coincided, more or less, with the abolition of
the slave trade. Legitimate trade replaced the slave trade as European countries competed for markets for their goods and sought, in return, supplies of
raw materials for their manufacturing needs. A regular commerce between
Europe and Africa developed quickly. Because the slave trade had been
based in West Africa, it was natural that this is where the British should turn
their attention and they began to consider possible ways in which Africa
might be developed.

Missionary activity increased alongside the development of trade. An
embryonic colonization took place. Coupled with these facts was the application of the social Darwinism of the nineteenth century, the belief held by
Europeans that they were at the top of the evolutionary scale, themselves
and their societies superior to what they viewed as the primitive and anar-

chic cultures they encountered as they progressively penetrated the interior of the continent.

Out of this belief in their superior status came the conviction on the part of Europeans that they had a moral duty to "civilize" and "enlighten" Africans, to take up what poet Rudyard Kipling termed "the white mans' burden." Kipling was one of the most popular poets of his day, an ardent supporter of imperialism and a firm believer in the humanitarian potential of British expansion overseas.

The stereotypes about Africans and African societies embodied in these beliefs were used to justify colonial expansion in Africa. These patronizing sentiments were enunciated and consolidated in the principal of the "dual mandate," a policy whereby the European powers would provide the benefits of civilization—education, commerce, medical services, the construction of roads and railways—in exchange for full rights to exploit the potential of the continent for trade.

So competition among European powers for territories in Africa escalated as the nineteenth century progressed and it became a matter of national pride to have territory in Africa. The intense rivalry among European powers—principally Britain, France, Germany, Belgium, and Portugal—as it played out in Africa reached the point where it was feared that hostile engagements in Africa would prompt wars in Europe.

To forestall this possibility—indeed likelihood—the German chancellor, Otto von Bismarck, organized the Conference of Berlin for the purpose of reconciling national differences and antagonisms. The conference opened in Berlin on November 15, 1884. Nations represented were Germany, Great Britain, Portugal, Austria-Hungary, the Netherlands, Italy, Russia, Spain, Sweden, Norway, Turkey, and the United States.

The conference lasted for three months, ending on February 26, 1885. The conference brought to a formal end what had come to be known as "the Scramble for Africa" and put in its place the partition of Africa. The conference produced the Treaty of Berlin. Under the terms of the treaty, almost 90 percent of Africa came under European control. Only Freetown in Sierra Leone and Liberia, established as havens for repatriated slaves at the close of the eighteenth century, were exempted from the process of partition. No Africans were consulted about European action.

Through this process of annexation, Great Britain was ceded Egypt, the Sudan, Uganda, Kenya, what came to be known as Zambia, and South and Southern Africa—Southern Rhodesia (Zimbabwe) and Botswana on the East Coast of Africa, and the Gold Coast (now Ghana) and Nigeria in West Africa. This book focuses on the British legacy in the colonization of Africa but it should be noted that other European powers were treated equally generously.

From 1885, the formal colonization of Africa began in earnest—countries were created, cutting across ethnic, social, political, and linguistic barriers.

The two principal ways in which colonization proceeded were by striking treaties with the chiefs and/or elders of African nations and communities, and, when this failed, by the use of superior military force, for example, the infamous "punitive expeditions" of the British.

Colonization was consolidated by 1914 and once territories were secured, various forms of government were implemented by the European powers. The British introduced a system of "indirect rule" into their colonial administration. This meant that colonial administrators ruled, as much as possible, through existing African political institutions. The policy assumed that African governing systems were hierarchical. When this was so, indirect rule worked reasonably well. When this was not so, as was often the case, the policy bred divisions and confusion that had not hitherto existed. (Chinua Achebe shows, in *Things Fall Apart* and *Arrow of God,* the disastrous consequences of imposing indirect rule on communities not based on hierarchical practices.)

Colonial government, trade, and commerce remained intact in British possessions until 1957 when the Gold Coast, renamed Ghana, was granted independence. The decolonization process proceeded swiftly after that and the right to self-determination was granted to the rest of Britain's colonies. By 1963, this decolonization process was complete.

The rise of African literature in English coincides with the transfer of colonial power to individual African countries. Given this political context, it seems natural that African literature in English is a wide and varied response to the general social, political, and cultural needs of the peoples of the countries of Africa. When talking and writing about this large and growing body of literature, it is customary to think of it in four general groups—West Africa, East Africa, South-Central Africa, and South Africa. These are categories that reflect differences in the literatures as shaped by each group's colonial and postcolonial experiences.

The first concern of African writers was to examine the consequences of colonial rule, to choose what was useful from the years of colonial control and governance, years during which established political institutions were altered and new political systems derived from Europe were imposed. In considering the legacy of the colonial experience, African writers ask a basic question: what can be taken from this experience and made useful in the independence period? Writing thus has an educative as well as artistic purpose. As Achebe has said, art matters, but, at least in the initial stages of the development of an African literary tradition, the educational potential of the writing takes precedence.

The primary purpose of writing for Achebe was to help African people retrieve what they had lost because of years of foreign rule. This means reexamining all aspects of their culture—political, social, economic, and religious—with a view to reconstituting African communities and nations so that their peoples may regain and assert a sense of individual and collective dignity.

Achebe, who became the major exponent of this educative purpose of writing, sums up this need:

I had to tell Europe that the arrogance on which she sought to excuse her pillage of Africa, i.e. that Africa was a Primordial Void, was sheer humbug; that Africa had a history, a religion and civilization. We reconstructed this history and civilization to challenge the stereotype and the cliché. Actually it was not Europe alone that I spoke to, I spoke also to that part of ourselves that had come to accept Europe's opinion of us. (Achebe 1964, 160)

A second concern of writers has been to examine the achievements and abuses of postcolonial African governments. Here, again, the responses of writers is determined by the nature of the legacy left by foreign powers and domination. Specific attention to this general point is made in discussions of the individual writers and their works.

A third major concern of writers has been to defend their choice of language. The writers who interest us here are those who have chosen to write in English. And while there is much debate about whether or not the authenticity of African experience can be conveyed in a non-African language, and while there is more and more literature being written and published in African languages, writing in English continues to increase. The reason authors choose English or French (the latter language is used in two of the books under review here) is obvious. It allows them to communicate with a readership in African countries whose people speak many different languages. Thus, as Achebe says: "There are not many countries in Africa today where you could abolish the language of the erstwhile colonial powers and still retain the facility for mutual communication" (Achebe 1966, 19–20). It is also important to note that many writers draw extensively on oral literary materials. Writing in English does not replace the folktales, the proverbial materials, the legends, praise poems, and epic poems that convey the accumulated heritage of various nations and reveal their accumulated wisdom. Rather, it is enhanced by the use writers make of their cultural inheritance as embodied in proverbial materials. Indeed, Achebe insists that using the language of the colonizer does not necessarily mean that the African cannot convey his or her experience: "The price a world language must be prepared to pay is submission to many kinds of different use. The African writer should aim to use English in a way that brings out his message best without altering the language to the extent that its value as a medium for international exchange will be lost." The Kenyan writer Ngugi wa Thiong'o disagrees with Achebe and has turned to writing in his African language, Kikuyu, after first publishing in English. The Senegalese writer Sembene Ousmane, while wishing that he could communicate with all of his people by using an African language, takes Achebe's position that only by using the colonial language can he convey his convictions to a wide audience.

ADDITIONAL READINGS

Achebe, Chinua. 1964. *Arrow of God*. London: Heinemann.
———. 1966. *A Man of the People*. London: Heinemann.
Curtin, Philip D. 1964. *The Image of Africa: British Ideas and Actions*. Madison: University of Wisconsin Press.
Pakenham, Thomas. 1991. *The Scramble for Africa: The White Man's Conquest of the Dark Continent from 1876 to 1912*. New York: Random House.

PART I
A SELECTED HISTORY OF WEST AFRICAN LITERATURE

African literature achieved what one critic has called "sudden maturity" with the publication in English of *Things Fall Apart* in 1958 wherein Chinua Achebe set the pattern and standard for literary inquiry and achievement.

There were earlier examples of writing in English in West Africa: Amos Tutuola's *The Palm-Wine Drinkard* (1952) and Cyprian Ekwensi's *People of the City* (1956) were the first examples of African writing published overseas. But the former defied classification at first and was not highly regarded by the author's fellow Nigerians, even though it achieved considerable acclaim in England.

Amos Tutuola was born in 1930 in Abeokuta in the then Western Region of Nigeria. He had little formal education and worked at various jobs, eventually entering the colonial service as a messenger in 1948. He had the habit of recording Yoruba folktales. Eventually he produced the full-length *Palm-Wine Drinkard*.

The book tells the story of a young man whose only responsibility is to drink palm wine. When his favorite palm wine tapster is killed in a fall, the young man sets off to find the now-dead tapster. The young man has many dangerous encounters in his search, which leads him through the Deads Land. He survives all of these dangers through luck, the help of magic, and various beneficent agents. Eventually, he arrives at the Deads Town where he finds the dead tapster. The tapster cannot return to the land of the living, but he gives the young man a magic egg that will supply all his needs. When the young man returns to his town, he finds it in the grip of famine. Fortunately, the egg is helpful in restoring the health of the town.

Tutuola went on to publish seven more novels. All follow the same pattern. They are episodic and picaresque in form. They have heroes or heroines who have supernatural powers or are in league with someone who does. They involve a journey and a search for something important. Along the way the hero or heroine experiences severe hardships, often passing through the netherworlds. He or she must perform demanding tasks, combat various monsters, and sometimes even endure torture. In the end, these characters survive their ordeals and become better people, wiser, happier, and often wealthy. As has been noted by various commentators, Tutuola owes a debt in terms of subject matter, literary form, and moral purpose to Bunyan's *Pilgrim's Progress.*

Tutuola's other seven novels are *My Life in the Bush of Ghosts* (1954), *Simba and the Satyr of the Dark Jungle* (1955), *The Brave African Huntress* (1958), *Feather Woman of the Jungle* (1962), *Ajaiyi and His Inherited Poverty* (1967), and *The Witch-Herbalist of the Remote Town* (1981). *Pauper, Brawler and Slanderer* (1987) comprises as a series of episodes with many of the same characters and situations as in the earlier books. Tutuola's place in the canon of modern African literature is secure and his work is now defined as falling in the class known as magic realism.

Cyprian Ekwensi's novel *People of the City* fits into the class of popular literature, important in the way that all such literature becomes a record of the values and predilections of a people, time, and place , but not possessing the qualities of style and expression that distinguish serious literary achievement. Ekwensi was the second Nigerian to have a novel published outside Nigeria. Hutchinson of London published his *People of the City,* a realistic rendering of life in the Nigerian capital city, Lagos, in 1954. Prior to this, Ekwensi published *When Love Whispers* (1948) in Nigeria. And he continued to publish inside Nigeria with such titles as *Murder at the Yaba Roundabout* (1962) and *Samankwe and the Highway Robbers* (1975), both crime thrillers aimed at a wide popular audience.

With *People of the City,* Ekwensi introduces characters, concerns, and a style and format that is typical of all of his writing for adult audiences. His plots are episodic and deal with social themes at the forefront of Nigerian experience—politics, crime, business practices—usually set in the underside of city life. His language is colloquial and contemporary Nigerian. He is concerned with events that prompt action without examining at great depth the sources of action. Like his characters, his novels live vividly on the surfaces of life in Nigeria, mostly in the city. Ekwensi knows well the tensions and fears of his characters as they strive to overcome the fear of failure and poverty that characterizes modern Nigerian life in the ever-changing social scene of Lagos.

People of the City tells the story of Amusa Sango, born in the "Eastern Greens" of Nigeria and now a crime reporter for the *West African Sensation* by day and the leader of a dance band in various Lagos nightclubs at night.

Ekwensi places Sango where life in the capital city is at its most volatile. Through Sango's work as a crime reporter, Ekwensi is able to comment on a wide range of events and issues of public, political, social, and national importance. For example, Sango reports on the frightening activities of the Ufemfe Society, which deals in crime, coercion, and sometimes murder; on the causes and consequences of a coal strike; and on a national election campaign. Ekwensi offers implicit comment on the quality of Nigeria life. And by having Sango travel to various parts of the country, Ekwensi is able to show that his concerns about a wide range of social issues are not confined to the capital city. Indeed, Ekwensi is able to show the contrast between urban and rural life, the former always suffering by contrast with the latter.

Ekwensi continues his use of the novel as a vehicle for serious social criticism in *Jagua Nana* (1961), perhaps his best known novel. This book deals with problems of burgeoning urbanization, as well as corruption and violence in politics. It foreshadows postcolonial disillusionment. The novel, in other words, resembles *People of the City*—spotlighting the poverty and squalor that exist side by side with riches and glamour; and replete with pimps, prostitutes, and politicians with all their lust and greed.

Jagua Nana is the heroine of the novel. "They call her Jagua . . . Jagua after the famous British prestige car" (1)—an independent woman from Eastern Nigeria. Not young when we meet her, Jagua indulges her love of fine clothes, dancing, and drinking. She is a woman of easy virtue and engages in a series of causal sexual affairs, living on the "dashes" (tips or gratuities) of the men she sleeps with. But her real love is Freddie, an idealistic, young, and impecunious student. Freddie returns to Nigeria after a period of study overseas, becomes involved in an election campaign, and is murdered. Jagua is overcome with grief—and coincidentally and improbably, loses a child born of an affair with a taxi driver. She eventually finds peace (and fifty thousand pounds stolen from party funds and given to her by a politician who is eventually murdered but who was responsible for Freddie's death).

As is evident from this brief plot description there is a good deal of melodrama in Ekwensi's story, a melodrama balanced against his serious concern about the political life in his country. Ekwensi was taken to task for presenting Nigeria in a bad light, with critics seeing mere sensationalism as the dominant quality in his first two adult novels. But events in Nigeria subsequent to the publication of these books bear out in quite clear ways his implicit forecasts of the way corrupt politics would eventually compromise the country.

His interest in politics continues in his next book. *Beautiful Feathers* (1963) has the same strengths and weaknesses of the earlier writing—a strong sense of place, an abundance of event and incident, the same moral earnestness balanced against careless plotting and uncertain use of language. The novel tells the story of Wilson Iyari, the proprietor of the Independence

Pharmacy. Iyari is also the leader of the Nigerian Movement for African and Malagasy Solidarity, a movement formed because of Iyari's conviction that the political parties in Nigeria—the NCNC, the Action Group, and the National Peoples' Congress—could not reconcile their differences and forge a unified state. Iyari is respected by the masses—even though he is without respect in his own home: his wife scorns him, indulges in a number of affairs, and eventually leaves him. But when Iyari attends a meeting of the Pan-African Congress on self-determination, a meeting attended by both Africans and non-Africans, a meeting at which the complexities of international affairs and finance are exposed, Iyari realizes that his political convictions are naive and that politics is a much more complicated business than he had thought. In the end, after reconciling himself with his family, Iyari settles for the modest life of a successful pharmacist, husband, and father. The ending is perhaps too facile, perhaps even a cop-out, but the novel does show that Ekwensi's concern here was to raise the level of political awareness of his fellow Nigerians.

Iska (1966) is Ekwensi's fourth full-length novel and tells the story of five vaguely connected parts of the life of Filia Enu, the Iska of the book's title. Iska is "a child of the wind [Iska] . . . the wind which blows strongly through Africa, destroying the old, preparing the way for the new" (1). Filia's experiences provide Ekwensi with the opportunity to present a kind of panoramic view of contemporary Nigeria.

Filia, a young Igbo girl born in Northern Nigeria, experiences the horror of the pogroms that eventually lead to the Nigerian civil war. She sees her father and her lover killed in rioting. Eventually she escapes to Lagos and there becomes involved in the fashionable and vacuous political and literary life of the capital. In due course, she becomes a fashion model, attracts a number of lovers, and eventually dies, overwhelmed and defeated by the city.

The limitations of the novel are several. Ekwensi is concerned with the external features of Nigerian life, especially the life of the city. Characters are less important to him than events. He does not penetrate the inner workings of their minds. Nevertheless, Ekwensi offers a compelling account of the tensions in Northern Nigeria that erupted in a devastating civil war. The first two parts of the novel are the most compelling—and enduring—flawed as they are by the author's moralizing intrusions.

Ekwensi's continuing interest in the Nigerian civil war and its aftermath inform *Survive the Peace* (1976) and *Divided We Stand* (1980). *Survive the Peace,* as the title suggests, dramatizes the condition of near-anarchy that characterized Nigerian life after the civil war. Ekwensi uses a series of flashbacks in a present-time narrative to juxtapose the horrors of the war and humiliations and fears of civilians who are as hard pressed to survive the peace as they were the war.

Divided We Stand treats the same materials as the first parts of *Iska:* how the harmony that existed over two and sometimes three generations between Northerners and Northern Igbos was shattered when the war broke out. Ekwensi had given the novel the provisional title *Africhaos,* suggesting perhaps that what was happening in Nigeria in the immediate post-colonial period was typical of what was happening in other parts of the continent.

Ekwensi mixes history and fiction in describing the 1966 coup and countercoup that fragmented Nigeria and in exposing the complicity and duplicity of international interests in the war that followed the coups. He exposes as well the ineffectuality of the Organization of African Unity as an agency attempting to negotiate peace. The novel emphasizes the self-serving actions of the politicians who provoke the holocaust in which ordinary people die in the thousands for reasons they never understand.

Despite lapses in technical control, Ekwensi is a serious writer in revealing his concerns for the quality of life in Nigeria, in particular, how Nigerian potential was abused by the postindependence leaders out of motives of greed. In this respect his themes and implicit judgments are typical of the first generation of Nigerian writers and find their counterparts in writers from other African states.

Timothy Mofolorunsa (T. M.) Aluko displays the same social concerns and writes in the same realistic manner as his contemporaries in the first wave of Nigerian writers. He is concerned with the social, political, and religious morality of society and with the tensions that exist between tradition and modernity. Aluko trained as a professional engineer, a background reflected in his concern with practical problems associated with modernization, a concern that he links to the quest of his characters for power—economic and political.

Aluko's seven novels deal with events that overlap the late colonial and immediate postcolonial periods. He is a satirist who sees the disparity between talk and action and, as with all satirists, he exposes the duplicity of his central characters to point the way to right conduct.

One Man, One Wife (1959) as the title suggests, deals with the conflict between traditional polygamous religion and the Christian concept of monogamy. Aluko uses this disparity to reveal the wider gulf between African conservatism and adventurous Western modernizing processes. The conflict in the novel is centered on the responses of a community to a smallpox epidemic. The traditionalists believe a cure is to be found in propitiating the deity Shopona. The modernist Christians believe the cure will be found in western medicine. Aluko is impartial in his fictional and satiric examination of the motives and conduct of both sides. His most severe irony is aimed at the zealots in either camp, the intransigence of the traditionalists, and the narrow-mindedness and rigidity of the mission-trained Christians. While he sees benefits in modernization—in this case the healing power of medications for the relief of the epidemic—he shows equally the validity of traditional practices.

The title of Aluko's second novel, *One Man, One Matchet* (1964), is a satirical parody of the political slogan "One Man, One Vote." Here, as in the first book, Aluko deals with problems arising from the imposition of modern, secular administrative practices on a traditional community. He mingles a series of beliefs and actions which cause confusion in the community—the ineptitude of the newly educated political elite in governmental administration, the increasing resistance of traditionalists, and the disruptive intervention of Christian teachings, to name but the most prominent.

The novel's action follows the attempt of the first African district officer—called a "black whiteman"—to wipe out a disease that is ravaging a cocoa crop by destroying the infected farms. Opposition to his plan is vested in Benjamin Benjamin, a local zealot, who uses the district officer's campaign to stir up the community for personal gain. Here again Aluko is impartial and his satire and humor are directed at every influential member of the community. The book implicitly advocates moderation in conduct, through which useful solutions to local problems will be found.

In *Kinsman and Foreman* (1966) the theme again is the clash between tradition and modernity. Titus Otis is posted to his home town as Director of Public Works. Simeon, his kinsman, is foreman in the Public Works Department. Titus discovers that Simeon is using his position to achieve personal gain. Here the antagonism is between public duty and the ties of kinship. Aluko treats the subject satirically, in commenting through the action of characters on a variety of related topics—the incompetence of modern governments and the naivety of overseas benefactors. As well, Aluko explores the psychological problems that arise when someone like Titus is torn between personal and professional commitments within the context of kinship and community.

Aluko's fourth novel, *Chief, the Honorable Minister* (1970), is a political novel set in a fictional but representative African country, which Aluko calls Afromacroland. It deals with the historical experiences of many African countries where the breakdown of civilian rule—seen here as inevitable given the motives that inspire its practitioners—brings about (again, for motives that are mixed), inevitably, military coups d'etat and rule.

Wrong One in the Dock (1982) is about inequality in the judicial process. In the novel, two characters, Jonathan and his son, Paul, become victims of a judicial system that is meant to render impartial verdicts. Aluko points out the disparity between what the law proposes and what it provides. In revealing the duplicity and self-serving motives that inform the characters' actions in the novel, Aluko implicitly points toward a positive social vision.

Gabriel Okara is best known as one of Africa's finest poets but he earns a prominent place in the development of modern African fiction for his experimental novel, *The Voice* (1964). The novel is an attempt to reconcile a syntax and literary form adapted from his Ijaw language and culture with English vocabulary and grammar. *The Voice* is an allegory of the search by

the principal character, known simply as "the man," for "it." "It" is inter-
preted in various ways—as "truth" or "faith" or "meaning"—in a world
becoming more and more politically corrupt. The man's quest upsets and
frightens the leaders of his village as well as his peers and he is sent into exile.
A sense of moral duty prompts him to return to his village. He is put to
death after he has confronted the leaders with their moral, ethical, and political abnegation, with their abuses of the trust placed in them. But his spirit
lives on in the moral revolution of villagers inspired by his example. Hence,
despite the experimental nature of the form and language of the book,
Okara shares with his fellow writers of the period a similar concern—to
expose peoples whose motives and actions are destructive of society.

Chukwumeka Ike has held a number of educational administrative posts
in Nigeria and has been an influential figure in secondary and postsecondary
education in his country. Even so, he has found time to publish nine novels,
making him Nigeria's most prolific novelist after Cyprian Ekwensi. His first
novel, *Toads for Supper* (1965), takes its title from the Igbo proverb that says
that when a child eats a toad, it destroys his appetite for meat. Ike uses the
proverb to reveal the complexities of a romantic encounter between two
university students from different ethnic cultures. Embedded in the plot is
commentary, satirically offered, on a variety of topics relevant to the students' affair—intertribal marriage, polygamy, education, and village and
national politics. Reform is not, as it is with some of his peers, his primary
intention. Ike is content to exploit the comic potential of the situation he
evokes

Ike's second novel, *The Naked Gods* (1970), is also about university life, a
scene Ike knows well. Here he exposes the disparity between the public rev-
erence in which learned academics are held and the moral and ethical weakness of their personal behavior. Ike also aims satire at the misdirected
meddling of visiting American and British academics in the affairs of an
African university. It is not just postsecondary academia that Ike targets.
Indeed, his next novel, *The Potter's Wheel* (1974), is a satire on Nigeria's secondary school system. The significance of the title is found in the metaphor
that the training of a child is like molding clay into a pot.

Sunset at Dawn (1976) is much more serious in tone than the earlier novels. It is about the Nigeria-Biafra civil war and tells of its effects on Dr. Kanu,
who becomes an official in the Biafran political organization, and his
Northern-born wife, Fatima; the couple's personal lives are devastated by
the sudden collapse of Biafra.

The Chicken Chasers (1980), as with *Toads for Supper,* takes its title from
an Igbo proverb that says that a person who chases a chicken quite often falls
while the chicken escapes capture. The proverb is a metaphor for Ike's revelations about the pettiness, jealousies, and mendacity of members of a fictitious African Cultural Organization, who try to unseat their
secretary-general, the only honest member of the organization.

Ike becomes increasingly reform-minded with each successive novel. *Expo '77* (1980), Ike's sixth novel, deals with corruption in the administration of the Certificate of Secondary Education, a fictitious name for the West African school certificate, where through underhanded practices various people try to attain false credentials. *The Bottled Leopard* (1985) is a retroactive view of life in a boys' school in the 1940s in Igboland. It traces the lives of Amobi and Chuk as they work their way through the school's various demands and confront the ambiguities of growing into adolescence.

In *Our Children Are Coming* (1990), Ike again uses his professional experience in education. He tells the story of young Nigerian students who are denied representation on a Presidential Commission on Juveniles under Twenty-One. The students know the commission to be corrupt and so they set up their own investigative body, the satirically named National Commission on Parents over Twenty-One. Through their activities they are able to expose corruption on a vast scale. It is in this way that Ike indicts the corrupt practices of political figures, military rulers, and fraudulent education officers. The tone here is unlike the earlier satirical novels. Ike is serious—and angry—as he points out the unrestrained corruption in his country. The novel reads in part like a political tract. And there is no doubting its author's moral earnestness.

The Search (1991) opens with a military coup and ends, twenty-two hours later, with a second coup. Within this framework, Ike examines a number of issues as put forward by a group of Nigerian academics. Comment is made on how the high hopes of the immediate independence period have dissipated in a very short space of time. In a country where all systems—political, educational, monetary, and religious—have collapsed, where self-serving motives and personal acquisitiveness have replaced any sense of collective public duty and responsibility, the only (faint) hope is to keep searching and pressing for solutions that will serve the public good.

Ike's early novels are distinguished by the warmth and humor that inform his irony and by a use of dialogue that catches the social and cultural background of his various characters. These are compassionate and serious commentaries on contemporary Nigerian life and, by implication, on African communities in general. The good humor and tolerance of the early novels gives way to a more mordant tone as Ike exposes the worsening lot of most Nigerians.

Ike believes with his fellow Nigerian and African writers that literature has an important central place, particularly in its potential to prompt to action those who may be able to effect reform.

Ike is not the only Nigerian novelist to combine a writer's life with that of a busy professional. Flora Nwapa, Nigeria's first woman novelist, found time to produce five novels, three volumes of short stories, and four books for children and young adults. Nwapa is best known for her first two novels, *Efuru* (1966) and *Idu* (1969). Both books tell the story of strong women living in traditional societies who through strength and courage overcome the adversities that place heavy social and psychological demands on women. In the first novel, Efuru is abandoned by two husbands. She returns to her father's home and devotes her life to celebrating the goddess of the lake and helping her neighbors, thus achieving a kind of spiritual and psychological fulfillment. *Idu* explores the nature of a love so selfless that Idu wills her own death when her husband dies. Both novels contain a good deal of information about precolonial Nigerian life and society where traditional customs and traditions are solidly interpolated into the text, a practice which, to some extent, interrupts the narrative flow of the novels and compromises the drama of the human tragedies, which is their principal concern.

In *One Is Enough* (1981), *Women Are Different* (1986), and *Never Again* (1992), Nwapa turns to contemporary settings to explore a variety of circumstances, domestic and public, that curtail the lives of women in Nigerian society. *Never Again,* although only 80 pages in length, is a powerful indictment of Biafran leadership during the civil war. The novel is written from the point of view of an ordinary citizen who sees the self-serving treachery of the military leadership and of civilian entrepreneurs whose apostasy they are unable to resist. Nwapa also implicitly puts forward the view that Biafra's separation from the Federation of Nigeria was ill conceived and that internal conditions of the sort she dramatizes in the book would likely have crippled the Biafran state even if the Nigerian government had not mounted the war. *Never Again* is a bitter book the title of which suggests frightening ambiguities.

Like Nwapa, Elechi Amadi offers us an interesting portrait of communities before contact with colonialism. Amadi has published four novels—*The Concubine* (1966), *The Great Ponds* (1969), *The Slave* (1978), and *Estrangement* (1986). The first three novels are set in African communities in the precolonial period. Amadi works to reveal the values and attitudes—in family relations, commerce, religion, and superstition—that produced a wide range of emotions and responses typical of close-knit communities. Ihumo, the heroine of *The Concubine,* is the earthly avatar of the water spirit who has a tragic destiny, as have all the men who have sought her hand in marriage: they are doomed to die for the unintentional affront they have offered the spirit.

The Great Ponds also explores the nature and influence of the supernatural in precolonial society. Two villages are at war over who owns fishing rights in the great pond. The priest, Iguni, ponders the question of how far he can intervene in the dispute. Though he unleashes a plague that all but destroys his community, nothing is resolved. Amadi is a discreet author, content to show the force, both spiritual and psychological, of religion on a traditional society characterized as much by ambiguity as by certainty.

In *The Slave* Amadi shows the destructive force of traditional beliefs on well-intentioned people as he portrays the reception and experiences of

Olumati, who returns after a long absence to reclaim his inheritance and to rebuild his life in his village

Estrangement deals with the experiences, both social and personal, of four characters who have participated in the Nigeria-Biafra war and with the destructive consequences of the war on them as they strive to adjust to the peace.

Clearly, Amadi is primarily interested in human relations in communal contexts. He creates strong and intelligent characters, both female and male, and examines without authorial intrusion the dynamics of various kinds of human relations. Overriding the specific actions and resolutions of events in the novels is a sense of the power of the supernatural in controlling the actions of human beings. Irony is thus his most characteristic mode.

John Munonye, who published six novels between 1966 and 1978, also examines religion and tradition, but from a different perspective. Specifically, Munonye displays the alienating and traumatizing effects of Christianity on his traditional Igbo community. *The Only Son* (1966), his first novel, tells the story of a widowed mother who is devastated by her only son's abandonment. The son leaves home and travels to a distant village to take up employment in a Catholic mission. Custom dictates that a widow with a male child to continue the family lineage should not remarry. The widow violates custom, hoping, despite this, that by remarrying she can nevertheless honor tradition. But happiness eludes her. The irony is that in seeking to honor tradition she betrays it.

In *Obi* (1969) and *Bridge to the Wedding* (1978), Munonye continues his exploration of the alienating effects of Christianity by dramatizing the difficulties that an ideal (and idealized) young Christian couple experience when, having achieved financial success in the city, they return to their village to reestablish their lives there. The wife finds she is sterile and the tension in the novel arises from the conflict between the Christian ideal of monogamy and the traditional practice of polygamy. Custom has it that the husband should take a second wife in order to ensure the succession of the family. Munonye's approach in displaying this dilemma is disinterested: each side gets a chance to present its position. And this, however compelling as a description of the contending forces, makes for a certain flatness of effect.

Oil Man of Obanje (1971) is the story of Jeremiah. He is a Christian who earns a hard living in the palm oil trade. His life is a constant struggle, made the more so when he loses his wife through illness. He is determined to keep his children in school. But he is beset by hardship: he is seriously in injured in a road accident and then his bicycle (his sole and vital means of transport) and the equipment by which he earns his living are stolen. Throughout all of this Jeremiah maintains his dignity until the end, when he succumbs to madness and death. In this novel, Munonye's compassion for human suffering and his admiration of the traits of determination and moral rectitude, are deeply moving.

Munonye deals with more pressing issues in *A Wreath for the Maidens* (1973) and *A Dancer of Fortune* (1974). The first novel offers the author's assessment of why Nigeria descended into genocide and social chaos so soon after achieving independence. *A Dancer of Fortune* also treats the moral and political anarchy that overtakes Nigeria, leading to a series of military coups and, eventually, to the secession of Biafra. The novel is distinguished by its creation of compelling women characters.

Taken together, Munonye's novels, whatever their specific themes and treatments, trace a history of Nigeria from colonial times forward. We see how Nigeria achieved nationhood after a long period of colonial rule. We learn about the causes and prosecution of the Nigerian civil war beginning with the independence period, through the burgeoning ethnic rivalries that almost immediately emerged and that resulted in the political impasses of the First Republic, and the military coups that bred further antagonism, the ultimate consequence of which is civil war. For Munonye, greed is the ultimate motivating factor. His deep concern is that through the abnegation of responsibility on the part of the first wave of independent politicians, the young of the country are being robbed of their just inheritance. Munonye's tone ranges from serious to ironic as he uses his writing to prompt discussion and possible action.

In contrast to Nigeria, Ghana has produced only a few novelists, but two are prominent on the world literary stage. The first is Ayi Kwei Armah, whose work is discussed at length later in this book. The second is Ama Ata Aidoo, Ghana's and West Africa's most protean woman writer. She has published fiction, plays, poetry, short stories, and books for children. *Our Sister Killjoy; or Reflections from a Black-Eyed Squint* (1969) is a four-part novel in epistolary form, the first part of which is a prologue. It is an innovative book in that it blends poetry and prose. The book describes the problems that women, particularly African women, encounter in studying abroad, problems that derive from the perception that Africans are still colonized, that traditional forms of bondage still obtain even in postindependence countries, and, particularly, from the reality that women are still an exploited group, particularly women of color. Aidoo is harsh as she dramatizes the exploitation of women under the guise of racial stereotypes.

Changes (1991), Aidoo's next novel, is a work about sexual relations that won the Commonwealth Writers Prize in 1992. Modern marriages and questions raised about the possibility for women to achieve professional parity with men are the principal concerns of the book; related topics are monogamy versus polygamy, love, marital rape, and the need for compromise.

No other novelist from Ghana has emerged to join Armah and Aidoo. But in Nigeria, with its vast population, new writers publish works regularly. Prominent among the second generation of Nigerian writers is Festus Iyayi. Iyayi has published three novels and a collection of short stories. He is a writer who believes that fiction has a social function and should be used for the purpose of liberating the oppressed. His fiction deals with what he determines to be the most pressing social and political issues of his time within a broader examination of class relationships and class struggles in postindependence Nigeria. His stories portray oppressed characters who, initially naive and trusting, achieve political awareness through distressing public and personal experiences that cause them to take action to alleviate their conditions.

Violence (1979) dramatizes the experiences of a group of casual laborers who are exploited and demeaned by entrepreneurs in Benin City. *The Contract* (1982), also set in Benin City, exposes the economics of the Nigerian oil boom and the decadence of the entrepreneurial class that made huge personal gains at the expense of the workers in the oil fields. Iyayi dramatizes the violence that can arise from exploitation and social inequality once the exploited recognize their own oppression.

Heroes (1986) won the Commonwealth Writers Prize in 1988 and is therefore Iyayi's best known novel. The novel examines the causes and prosecution of the Nigeria-Biafra war from the perspective of a newspaper reporter who is not aligned in any way with the principal participants in the war, neither Yoruba, Igbo, nor Hausa-Fulani. As a journalist he has access to all of the participants in the conflict—from soldiers at the front lines to generals at their cocktail parties in Lagos, far away from the battle. The most compelling and alarming scenes in the novel are those replaying the battle at Ore, the turning point in the civil war, and the utterly wasteful battle of Asaba-Onitsha.

Iyayi's conviction, dramatized here, is that both sides in the war were equally barbaric and that the real casualties were soldiers, workers, and peasants whose suffering continues long after the conclusion of fighting. Iyayi reserves a special scorn for the officers, traditional rulers, and business tycoons who benefited from the war.

Heroes is more than a war novel. Produced 20 years after hostilities ended, its subtext is an examination of class structures and interests in contemporary Nigeria. For Iyayi, the army represents in microcosm the exploiters of the country's wealth. He numbers among this group generals, politicians, businessmen, traditional rulers, religious leaders, and professors. His condemnation of their self-interest at the expense of the exploited and innocent makes Iyayi one of the few Nigerian writers who deploys his art directly to write radical history from the exploited peoples' point of view and to prompt those peoples to action.

Iyayi is but one of a number of writers who may be said to form the second generation of Nigerian writers. Unlike the first generation of African writers whose two main concerns were to display the consequences of colonial rule and to interpret their societies for a non-African audience, what these writers have in common is a concern with contemporary Africa. Their avowed audience is their fellow citizens. Names associated with this group of writers are the poets Niyi Osundare, Tanure Ojaide, and Tayo Olafioye and novelists Kole Omotoso and Ken Saro-Wiwa, to name the most prominent.

Of this group, Omotoso is the most substantial in terms of how much he has published, the range of forms that he uses, the issues he deals with in his writing, and the audience at whom he directs his work. He looks for a popular audience—in addition to adult works, he has written books for children and is active in promoting writing in both English and Yoruba. Omotoso, like his peers, believes that literature can be effective at the grassroots level.

Whatever the subject matter of his fiction and plays, his writing is committed to making society better than it is by castigating the comprador bourgeoisie class of capitalist entrepreneurs operating in conjunction with international finance agents who abscond with the nation's wealth. For Omotoso, redress is found in following the classic Marxist pattern of eventually destroying the means of producing wealth. His analysis of the way in which this works to create a population of victims is best shown in the novel *Just Before Dawn* (1988), but it is adumbrated in earlier novels—*The Sacrifice* (1974) and *The Scales* (1976) (and in the plays *The Curse* [1976] and *Shadows in the Horizon* [1977]).

Even *Fella's Choice* (1974), sometimes described (probably wrongly) as the first Nigerian detective novel, takes up a serious economic theme—the attempt by South African agents to undermine the Nigerian economy by flooding the country with counterfeit *naira,* the country's currency. In *The Combat* (1972) Omotoso deals with the Nigerian civil war in allegorical terms, using a plot in which two friends fight over the paternity rights to a child born of a market girl mistress they have both "known."

Kenule (Ken) Saro-Wiwa was murdered by agents of General Sani Abacha's military dictatorship in Port Harcourt, Nigeria, on November 9, 1995. Saro-Wiwa, writer, publisher, acknowledged leader of the Ogoni people, and nominee for the Nobel Peace Prize, had been held in confinement for 18 months prior to the closed trial, which found him guilty of complicity in the murders of four Ogoni elders. He had incurred the displeasure of Abacha's military junta through his advocacy of human and civil rights for his people, whose ancestral land was being destroyed for agricultural purposes by exploitative oil companies, their callous enterprise supported by a military presence.

Saro-Wiwa was a writer with a serious purpose, but his means of expressing this was through comedy and satire. His interest was in society's victims, the downtrodden who are without the opportunity to make a better lives for themselves but who have the resilience to prevail. His writing—particularly for the television series *Basi and Company*—shows the infinite number of ways in which victims find the way to survive. He also shows an interest in the lives of the dispossessed and the criminal classes in modern Nigerian cities.

This interest in the downtrodden and dispossessed informs all of Saro-Wiwa's works, from *Sozaboy: A Novel in Rotten English* (1985), the first

Nigerian novel written entirely in pidgin English, the lingua franca of the West African coast, through *Songs in a Time of War* (1985), *On a Darkling Plain: An Account of the Nigerian Civil War* (1989), the short story collections *A Forest of Flowers* (1987) and *Adaku and Other Stories* (1989), to *Prisoner of Jebs* (1988) and possibly the most widely watched series in the history of television (an estimated 55 millions viewers each week), the plays forming the Basi series—*Basi and Company: A Modern African Folktale* (1987) and *Basi and Company: Four Television Plays* (1988). Saro-Wiwa also published a number of books for children featuring Basi—*Mr. B. Goes to Lagos* (1989), *Mr. B. Again* (1989), and *The Transistor Radio* (1989).

Sierra Leone has produced even fewer novelists than Ghana, and Syl Cheney-Coker is the country's best-known writer. He is a poet who has published three volumes of verse in which he deals with a multitude of themes and subject matter—the slave trade, the creation of Freetown in Sierra Leone as a homeland for repatriated slaves, creoledom, political animosities leading to violence, and the betrayal of the country's independence leading to one of the ugliest civil wars in history.

All of the themes found in the poetry are brought together in his one novel to date, *The Last Harmattan of Allusine Dunbar* (1990). The novel won the 1990 Commonwealth Writers Prize. The novel is epic in length and scope, dealing with Africa and Africans over a long historical period. African relations with Britain, America, and Canada figure in Cheney-Coker's renderings. Like so many of his fellow African writers, Cheney-Coker is on the side of the masses of Africa's dispossessed. His approach is inventive, called by some "magic realism," a genre in which the natural/realistic world combines with the supernatural. Cheney-Coker hopes that through his writing he may restore freedom to those who have had it wrongfully usurped.

From Nigeria (although brought up in London where he currently lives), Ben Okri has written four novels, two collections of short stories, and a collection of poems. His first novel was *Flowers and Shadows* (1980), followed by *The Landscapes Within* (1981), *The Famished Road* (1991), and *Songs of Enchantment: A Novel* (1993). *The Famished Road* won the prestigious Booker Prize and thus drew international attention to Okri's work.

Like his peers in what we might call the second generation of Nigerian writers, Okri is concerned with the quality of contemporary life in his country and, by implication, other countries living within the same constraints as those he draws attention to in his writing. *The Famished Road* adapts the Yoruba belief that there is no distinction between the living and the dead; hence, the supernatural is a sustaining element in his writing. Within the framework of a magical realism treatment, Okri displays the brutalizing of people under oppressive leaders. He exposes the brutality of the Nigerian civil war and the callous apostasy of the succession of post–civil war leaders. And he is concerned with the abuses of power in the hands of both the populace and politicians who act solely out of self-interest. Okri depicts an African state—of which for him Nigeria is the epitome—without responsible leadership, a lack that denies civilians the possibility of full participation in daily living. Fear, violence, terror, greed, mistrust, and brutality, amplified by images of disease, dying, death, and deformity characterize Okri's fictional world, a world that is clearly a metaphor for the real state of his nation.

The central figure in *The Famished Road* is an *abiku* child, which means a child doomed forever to perpetuate a cycle of birth, growth, and death. Okri uses this character to suggest that the social conditions he places his characters in are doomed, like the *abiku* child, to a continuing cycle of misadministration and misery.

Songs of Enchantment is a sequel to *The Famished Road* and conforms to Okri's conviction that there is no change in the vicious circumstances he dramatizes in the earlier novel, that things may indeed have gotten worse.

ADDITIONAL READINGS

Achebe, Chinua. 1958. *Things Fall Apart*. London: Heinemann.

Aidoo, Ama Ata. 1969. *Our Sister Killjoy; or Reflections from a Black-Eyed Squint*. London: Nok Publishers.

———. 1991. *Changes*. London: Women's Press.

Aluko, T. M. 1959. *One Man, One Wife*. Lagos, Nigeria: Nigerian Printing and Publishing.

———. 1964. *One Man, One Matchet*. London: Heinemann.

———. 1966. *Kinsman and Foreman*. London: Heinemann.

———. 1970. *Chief the Honourable Minister*. London: Heinemann; New York: Humanities Press.

———. 1982. *Wrong One in the Dock*. London: Heinemann.

Amadi, Elechi. 1966. *The Concubine*. London: Heinemann Educational.

———. 1969. *The Great Ponds*. London: Heinemann Educational.

———. 1978. *The Slave*. London: Heinemann Educational.

———. 1986. *Estrangment*. London: Heinemann Educational.

Cheney-Coker, Syl. 1990. *The Last Harmattan of Alusine Dunbar*. Portsmouth, N.H.: Oxford.

Ekwensi, Cyprian. 1948. *When Love Whispers*. Lagos, Nigeria: Chuks Bookshop; Onitsha, Nigeria: Tabansi Press.

———. 1954. *People of the City*. London: Dakers.

———. 1961. *Jagua Nana*. London: Hutchinson and Co.

———. 1962. *Murder at the Yaba Roundabout*. Lagos, Nigeria: Tortoise Series Books.

———. 1963. *Beautiful Feathers*. London: Hutchinson and Co.

———. 1966. *Iska*. London: Hutchinson and Co.

———. 1975. *Samankwe and the Highway Robbers*. London: Evans Brothers.

———. 1976. *Survive the Peace*. London: Heinemann Educational.

———. 1980. *Divided We Stand*. Enugu, Nigeria: Fourth Dimension Publishers.

Ike, Vincent Chukwuemeka. 1965. *Toads for Supper*. London: Collins, Fontana Books.

———. 1970. *The Naked Gods*. London: Collins, Fontana Books.

————. 1980. *Expo '77*. London: Collins, Fontana Books.

————. 1985. *The Bottled Leopard*. London: Andre Deutsch.

————. 1990. *Our Children Are Coming*. London: Andre Deutsch.

————. 1991. *The Search*. London: Andre Deutsch.

Iyayi, Festus. 1979. *Violence*. London: Longman.

————. 1982. *The Contract*. Harlow, England: Longman.

————. 1986. *Heroes*. Harlow, England. Longman.

Munonye, John. 1966. *The Only Son*. London: Heinemann.

————. 1969. *Obi*. London: Heinemann.

————. 1971. *Oil Man of Obanje*. London: Heinemann.

————. 1973. *A Wreath for the Maidens*. London: Heinemann.

————. 1974. *A Dancer of Fortune*. London: Heinemann.

————. 1978. *Bridge to a Wedding*. London: Heinemann.

Ngate, Jonathan. 1988. *Francophone African Fiction: Reading a Literary Tradition*. Trenton, N.J.: Africa World Press.

Nwapa, Flora. 1966. *Efuru*. London: Heinemann.

————. 1969. *Idu*. London: Heinemann.

————. 1981. *One Is Enough*. Enugu, Nigeria: Flora Wapa Co.

————. 1986. *Women Are Different*. Ibadan, Nigeria: Tana Press.

————. 1992. *Never Again*. New York: Africa World Press.

Okara, Gabriel. 1964. *The Voice*. London: Andre Deutsch.

Okri, Ben. 1980. *Flowers and Shadows*. London: Longman Drumbeat.

————. 1981. *The Landscapes Within*. Burnt Mill, England: Longman.

————. 1991. *The Famished Road*. London: Jonathon Cape.

————. 1993. *Songs of Enchantment*. London: Jonathon Cape.

Omotoso, Kole. 1972. *The Combat*. London: Heinemann.

————. 1974. *Fella's Choice*. Benin City, Nigeria: Ethiope.

————. 1974. *The Sacrafice*. Ibadan, Nigeria: Onibonoje.

————. 1976. *The Scales*. Ibadan, Nigeria: Onibonoje.

————. 1988. *Just Before Dawn*. Ibadan, Nigeria: Spectrum Books.

Saro-Wiwa, Kenule B. 1985. *Songs in a Time of War*. Port Harcourt, Nigeria: Saros International Publishers.

————. 1985. *Sozaboy: A Novel in Rotten English*. Port Harcourt, Nigeria: Saros International Publishers.

————. 1986. *A Forest of Flowers: Short Stories*. Port Harcourt, Nigeria: Saros International Publishers.

————. 1987. *Basi and Company: A Modern African Folktale*. Port Harcourt, Nigeria: Saros International Publishers.

————. 1988. *Prisoner of Jebs*. Port Harcourt, Nigeria: Saros International Publishers.

————. 1989. *Adaku and Other Stories*. Port Harcourt, Nigeria: Saros International Publishers.

————. 1989. *On a Darkling Plain: An Account of the Nigerian Civil War*. Port Harcourt, Nigeria: Saros International Publishers.

Tutola, Amos. 1952. *The Palm-Wine Drinkard and His Dead Palm-Wine Tapster in the Dead's Town*. London: Faber and Faber.

————. 1954. *My Life in the Bush of Ghosts*. London: Faber and Faber.

————. 1955. *Simba and the Satyr of the Dark Jungle*. London: Faber and Faber.

————. 1958. *The Brave African Huntress*. London: Faber and Faber.

————. 1962. *Feather Woman of the Jungle*. London: Faber and Faber.

————. 1967. *Ajayi and His Inherited Poverty*. London: Faber and Faber.

————. 1981. *The Witch-Herbalist of the Remote Town*. London: Faber and Faber.

————. 1987. *Pauper, Brawler, and Slanderer*. London: Faber and Faber.

Chapter 1
Chinua Achebe: Things Fall Apart (1958), No Longer at Ease (1960), Arrow of God (1963), A Man of the People (1966), and Anthills of the Savannah (1987)

Chinua Achebe has been the dominant figure in African writing since the publication of his first novel, *Things Fall Apart,* in 1958. Achebe has been honored throughout the world by governments, universities, and literary bodies for the writing that followed his first publication: four more novels, two volumes of short stories, a book of poetry, and other publications of cultural and literary criticism. He is a major interpreter of Nigerian society and culture and, by extension, that of other African communities.

Though Achebe was raised in a strict Christian home, he was also attracted to traditional Igbo culture. As he explored Igbo traditions, he reflected more on his European inheritance through the example of the lives of non-Christian relatives and other villagers. Eventually he became determined to reconstruct traditional Igbo life as it was lived before the advent of colonialism and then as it changed through European intervention. In his view African life for a number of related reasons was purposefully misrepresented by Europeans, as they established colonial rule. Achebe was moved to write in order to set straight the Nigerian experience of British imperial-colonialism. His reading of *Mister Johnson,* a much-respected treatment of Nigerian life by Joyce Cary, a former district officer in the British colonial service, prompted him to write his first novel. Cary's novel was much celebrated overseas as an accurate rendering of Nigerian life. For Achebe, who encountered the novel when at the University College, Ibadan, it was entirely fallacious. He thus decided to re-create his past in a novel for the purpose of enlightening his people about the inherent value of their culture and for the purpose of retrieving the dignity of these people, a dignity that had been all but lost during the years of colonial rule. He therefore determined to consider what was valuable in the precolonial past and what could be salvaged from that life and made useful in the present. Achebe begins his inquiry with *Things Fall Apart.*

Things Fall Apart is the first classic African novel. Published in 1958 and reprinted many times in various editions, translated into some thirty languages with sales estimated in excess of four million copies, it is as widely read as any book in the Anglophone world. Achebe's other novels, *No Longer at Ease* (1960), *Arrow of God* (1964), *A Man of the People* (1966), and *Anthills of the Savannah* (1987) are equally respected. Achebe's novels form a continuum over one hundred years of Igbo (and latterly) Nigerian history, dating from the period before the European colonial enterprise to the postindependence period. In *Things Fall Apart,* Europe has not arrived at the village of Umuofia, the novel's principal setting. When the novel ends, colonial rule has been established and the character of the community—its values, freedoms, and social and political organization—has been substantially and irrevocably altered.

The process continues in *Arrow of God.* The novel moves the historical examination forward to the point where colonial rule has been firmly established. The lives of the villagers of Umuaro have been circumscribed by European intervention but Achebe also shows how Igbo resiliency is able to accommodate itself to massive change. The novel tells the story of Ezeulu, chief priest of the god Ulu, the most powerful member of the community. It is a meditation on the nature and uses of power and on the responsibility of the person who possesses that power. Ezeulu becomes engaged in a struggle with the people of his village and the officers of the British political service. He is forced to reconcile, with tragic consequences, the conflicting impulses in his own nature—his wish to serve the protecting deity of the people of Umuaro and retain his sway over their religious observances, and his desire to gain greater personal power by pushing his authority to its limits. He fails, and ultimately out of this failure, his personal tragedy arises.

No Longer at Ease is set in the immediate preindependence years in Nigeria. The novel presents through its hero, Obi Okonkwo, a tragic story of the modern African state and speculates on the problems that will face the country as it prepares for independence. The novel balances an examination of Nigerian "modernity"—the political, social, and economic implications of the accommodation to colonial rule—with an awareness of the price Nigerians have paid for their "modernity."

A Man of the People examines questions of power and leadership in the emergent nation-state. The government of the country Kangan (a country that resembles Nigeria) is nominally in the hands of the people, but there is no responsible leadership, merely avaricious self-interest. Whereas Achebe's novels set in the past show how society achieved a balance between collective conventions and personal ambition and how that balance had provided social order, *A Man of the People* shows how a society that places little value on religious beliefs is susceptible to unrestrained acquisitiveness and unchecked political corruption. The novel ends with military intervention seen ironically as offering the only possible redemption for a society in which traditional and imported constitutional methods are both ineffective.

Anthills of the Savannah, set in a country that, like the Kangan of *A Man of the People,* strongly resembles Nigeria (and other postindependence African countries), dramatizes the legacy of colonialism and the uses and abuses that are made of it. It reveals the extent to which any political hope placed in the hands of the military is misplaced. Like its predecessors, this novel is an examination of power and the responsibility of those who possess it. A novel about political leadership, it is also an implied commentary on the role of the writer in society. Stories serve the purpose of displaying what has been lost to a society through historical interventions and evaluating what gains societies and their leaders have made, or imagine they have made.

Things Fall Apart (1958)

Achebe's inquiry into a hundred years of Igbo and Nigerian history begins with *Things Fall Apart.* The novel tells the story of Okonkwo's life and career in the village of Umuofio. His father is Unoka, a wastrel, known "in all the clan for the weakness of his matchet and his hoe" (4) but who, nonetheless, is a likable character, possessing admirable qualities if not those most admired and supported by the clan. Okonkwo is determined through hard work to achieve the highest titles in the clan. He embodies those qualities highly valued among his people: great energy and stamina and a strong sense of purpose, communal cooperativeness, and personal worth.

Okonkwo's fame is established when his story begins: "Okonkwo was well known throughout the nine villages and even beyond. His fame rested on solid personal achievements" (3). As a young man, he had thrown Amalinze, the Cat, "the great wrestler who for seven years was unbeaten from Umuofia to Mbaino" (3). Okonkwo thus brought "honor to his village." Since that time, "his fame had grown like a bush fire in harmattan." He has gained wealth and wives and has produced children; in addition, he is a member of the highest council of the clan. Okonkwo's rise to a position of wealth and authority is in part accounted for by the strength of his will and his body. These strengths have been tested early in his life, and Okonkwo has had more to overcome than most men of his age group. Burdened by an improvident father and, because of one very bad planting season, early failure as a farmer, Okonkwo does not yield to despair as a lesser man might: "It always surprised him that he did not sink under the load of despair. He knew he had been a fierce fighter, but that year had been enough to break the heart of a lion." But because he survived those challenges, he knew he could "survive anything." He ascribes his success to his inflexible will in a life the narrator describes as "dominated by fear, fear of failure and weakness . . . and so Okonkwo's whole life was ruled by one passion—to hate everything that his father had loved."

Unoka, Okonkwo's father, was "poor and his wife and children had barely enough to eat. He was "lazy and improvident, a 'debtor'" (3–4) and a "coward who could not stand the sight of blood" (5). Okonkwo's fear of being like his father is an ambiguous legacy. One the one hand it drives him to strive for success beyond that of his peers. On the other hand, it deprives him of the qualities his father valued: "one of those things was gentleness and another was idleness" (10). It is failing to possess the gentleness of his father that brings about, in part at least, Okonkwo's ultimate tragedy.

Another factor accounts for the course Okonkwo's life follows. According to the beliefs of the clan, Okonkwo's success is attributed to his *chi* or personal god, since a man's success or failure is attributed to how his *chi* responds to his conduct. The concept of the *chi* embodies an essential tenet of Igbo cosmology; this belief is summed up in the aphorism: "Wherever Something stands, there also Something Else will stand." Nothing is static, life is redolent with contradictions. The concept of the *chi* encompasses this duality. Thus the *chi* is the dominating ambiguous force in the life of an individual, but that individual life is circumscribed by communal ancestors, gods, and magic. All these forces operate in Umuofia and inform Okonkwo's life.

Okonkwo's story is set against the daily life in Umuofia. The novel shows community members in dynamic relationships with the seasons: they are subject to periods of intense labor, planting, and harvesting, followed by periods of leisure; and they are subject to the vagaries of the climate. The community is governed by rules of religion and politics, which are constantly discussed, debated, and amended, as circumstances dictate. It is a democratic society where titles are taken or given on merit and can be taken away should circumstances demand. The stability of the society is maintained through the tension that exists between communality and individuality. Individual enterprise is recognized and rewarded. But a strong religious principal keeps individualism in check. Achebe has said that "Igbo society has always been materialistic. This may sound strange because Igbo life had at the same time a strong spiritual dimension—controlled by other gods, ancestors, personal spirits or 'chi' and magic" (Achebe "The Role of the Writer" 179).

The materialism of Igbo society translates into an emphasis on male activities in the novel such as the acquisition of wealth and wives, the production of children, courage in war, and industry in the time of work. These activities inform the surface interest of the novel and the events of the first part of the book. Loosely connected scenes describe the daily round of life in Umuofia, all of which is circumscribed by what is or is not acceptable to

"Ani, the Earth Goddess and source of all fertility, . . . the ultimate judge of morality and conduct" in the clan (26). In other words, a powerful female principle pervades the whole society of Umuofia and sits in judgment of events in this community.

This is the society readers see in the first and longest part of the novel, a homogeneous society, not without problems, both personal and societal, but which operates on religious and political beliefs supported by custom. This section of the book is set in Umuofia before the coming of Europeans and it is here that Achebe demonstrates his concern that "the past needs to be recreated not only for the enlightenment of our detractors but even more for our own education. Because . . . the past, with all its imperfections, never lacked dignity. . . . This is where the writer's integrity comes in. Will he be strong enough to overcome the temptation to select only those facts which flatter him?" (Achebe "The Role of the Writer" 158).

Part one has 13 chapters and displays the Umuofian agricultural year: the communal events that characterize the religious year; the games, festivals, and celebrations; the relations between individuals and families within the clan. It is in this part of the book that Ikemefuna, a hostage from a neighboring clan, arrives in the village and is taken into Okonkwo's household. Ikemefuna becomes as a son to Okonkwo and friend to Okonkwo's son, Nwoye, in whom Okonkwo sees all the signs of the temperament and personality of his grandfather, Unoka. Eventually, the goddess declares that Ikemefuna must be killed. Okonkwo, knowing he should not commit the religious offense of participating in the sacrifice, but fearing he will be thought weak, kills Ikemefuna.

This is one of three offenses Okonkwo commits "against the earth." The first is when, in a fit of temper, he beats his wife for her fecklessness during a week of peace. The third is when he accidentally kills the son of a kinsman whose funeral observances Okonkwo attends. For this offense, Okonkwo is banished from the clan for seven years to the clan of his mother.

Part two of the novel describes Okonkwo's life in Mbanta, his mother's village. Here he tries to begin life anew and to prepare himself for his return to Umuofia. It is in this section of the novel that the critical social and religious conflict takes place. Christian missionaries arrive, followed by the British political administration and traders in palm oil. The former establish a church and at first attract the "worthless" members of the clan. But, gradually, men of prominence join the ranks of converts. This religious conversion, together with the establishment of a political judicial system administered by Europeans and the introduction of a cash-based trading economy, cause things to change irreversibly. The new Christian religion has sufficient appeal to undermine traditional Igbo religion. At the same time, because of the new value placed on palm oil and palm kernels, the acquisitive nature of the society is enhanced and the traditional balance between religion and materialism is disastrously upset. Ultimately the problem lies in language. As Okonkwo's friend, Obierika, says: "Does the white man under-stand our customs about land? How can he when he does not even speak our tongue? . . . Now he has won our brothers, and our clan can no longer act as one. He has put a knife on the things that held us together and we have fallen apart" (124).

Another example of the process Obierika describes is found in the second section of the novel in which Okonkwo's son, Nwoye, defects to Christianity: "It was not the mad logic of the Trinity that captivated him. It was the poetry of the new religion, something felt in the marrow. . . . He felt a relief within as the hymn poured into his parched soul" (104). Thus the disruptive processes of colonial intervention work at both the materialistic and the spiritual level.

Part three of the novel, proceeding from Okonkwo's return to Umuofia, brings the story swiftly to a close. Okonkwo's return is less satisfactory than he had hoped despite his plans to return to his former position in the clan. Things have changed, more so even than in Mbanta. The climax of the story is reached when a python—the embodiment of a sacred spirit—is killed by a Christian convert. Reprisal is taken by the villagers who burn the Christian church. The district officer calls Okonkwo and other elders together on the pretext of dis-cussing the animosity between the two factions. But he behaves treacherously by arresting them, placing them in irons, and putting them in jail. Okonkwo determines after this event that there is nothing left to do but fight. He kills a government messenger and, when he sees that he stands alone, hangs himself. Thus, he earns for himself a form of abominated death, what he had sought all his life to avoid—a dishonorable burial like the one given to his father.

The final paragraph reveals a historical irony of a different kind. The dan-gling body of Okonkwo is merely an "undignified detail" so far as the dis-trict officer is concerned. He plans to write a book called *The Pacification of the Primitive Tribes of the Lower Niger*. In his book the story of Okonkwo may make an interesting detail.

In *Things Fall Apart*, Achebe gives a fictionalized and dramatized account of colonial history by writing back against a European perspective. An African perspective is securely placed. And in the larger pattern, the histori-cal process is seen as inevitable. Much has been lost to the Igbo communi-ties depicted. To a considerable extent, things have fallen apart. But the center does hold, and embedded in the story is a recognition of Igbo resiliency.

No Longer at Ease (1960)

Achebe's second novel, *No Longer at Ease* (1960), depicts the uncertain-ties that beset Nigeria as independence from colonial rule approaches. The problems facing Nigeria, especially young Nigerians, are revealed in the experiences of Obi Okonkwo, on trial for unspecified offenses as the novel opens. A persistent question is asked in the courtroom (where he stands accused), at his workplace, and by his friends: "Why did he do it?" What Obi did is gradually revealed in the body of the novel in the form of an extended flashback.

The novel depicts Nigeria undergoing rapid change as independence approaches. The time of the novel is the late 1950s and the action of the book alternates between Lagos, the capital city, and Obi's home village of Umuofia. The ambiguities, pitfalls, and temptations in the rapidly evolving society are revealed in Obi's experiences and the fate that overtakes him despite his efforts to make a satisfactory life for himself. Obi's personal story becomes a metaphor for his generation of young Nigerians. What happens to Obi could, Achebe implies, happen to others of his generation, and so the novel, in one sense, is both a warning and a prophecy. The novel is also a complex structure of ambiguities and ironies.

Obi is the grandson of Okonkwo and the son of Nwoye, Okonkwo's son, who defected to the Christians and is now known as Isaac, a catechist in the missionary church. Obi is the first person in his village to achieve an overseas education. His education has been largely paid for by the Umuofia Progressive Union (UPU). The union is composed of Umuofia villagers who band together in Lagos for mutual support. The union expects Obi to repay his debt to them both literally and more obliquely through the influence he will have in a government job. Obi has studied English in London, much to the disappointment of the union members who wanted him to study law. But they console themselves that Obi will meet his obligations when he is appointed to an influential position as secretary to the government's Scholarship Board.

Obi begins his work with high principles, including a determination to avoid the corruption that he sees in the political and administrative situations around him. But heavy demands, typical of those made on people in Obi's position, eventually overwhelm him. He earns a good salary, much better than the average Nigerian. But it is not enough to cover his financial commitments. He is expected to live up to a standard befitting a highly educated employee of government. This means he rents an expensive flat on prestigious Ikoyi Island (formerly the exclusive preserve of colonial administrators). He buys an expensive car for which he has high operating costs— petrol, insurance, and servicing. He is expected to make regular payments to reduce his debt to the UPU, to send money to his parents, and to pay for the education of his younger siblings.

Obi's life is further complicated by his relationship with Clara. She is an "osu," an outcast in the eyes of traditional Igbo society because she is the descendent of cult slaves. The UPU disapproves of Obi's relationship with Clara, and Obi's parents reject it, which weighs heavily on Obi's personal morality. His father, although a devout Christian, reconciles his new religion with traditional beliefs by citing passages from the Bible where, as he shows, a man can be a devout Christian while at the same time a leper and, therefore, an outcast. Isaac's argument shows the extent to which Igbo sensibility is able to accommodate itself to change, to absorb and domesticate foreign notions. Okonkwo failed to do this in *Things Fall Apart,* whereas his friend, Obierika, more thoughtful, more intellectual than Okonkwo, understands that accommodation and compromise are not only necessary for survival but also inevitable. Obi is not won over by his father's careful argument. But when his mother says, quite simply, that if Obi marries Clara she will kill herself, Obi's moral resolve collapses—he sees Clara through a nasty divorce and abandons her; he accepts bribes and is eventually caught and charged with a criminal offense.

This is where the novel begins: with Obi in court facing the charges brought against him. The novel is an examination of the causes and consequences of Obi's actions, those of a fully realized individual character in the novel who may also be taken as typical of generation of young, educated Nigerians.

The novel, as has been noted, is set in the period immediately before Nigeria achieved independence from British colonial rule. This was a period of high optimism in the country and one might have expected Achebe to present in Obi a character whose beliefs and actions would reflect that optimism. And to some extent Obi does: in his discussions with friends the possibilities and pitfalls of the impending transfer of political power are considered. But Achebe's concern is not to celebrate in a simplistic way the exuberance over independence. His concern is to examine, implicitly, by direct statement and through dialogue, his society at the most critical point in its modern existence; to present the contending forces that will be at play; and to identify the temptations implicit in a self-governing state that has so many traditional political and cultural constituencies to reconcile in formulating postindependence policies. *No Longer at Ease* is, then, a story about accommodation—to politics, to materialism, to bribery—that can result in moral confusion. Society looks for new ways to effect a balance between traditional and modern values, and between religious and secular values. A process initiated in *Things Fall Apart* where materialism progressively overwhelms religious checks and balances develops here to the point where moral compromise is found everywhere and depicted in a variety of ways.

Obi's personal story reflects and embodies the ambiguities, uncertainties, and contradictions in society as a whole. Achebe makes plain that he sees Obi's story as a modern tragedy. The title of the novel, taken from T. S. Eliot's poem, "The Journey of the Magi," reflects the state of mind Obi finds himself in when he returns from England. And words from W. H. Auden that Obi cites in an interview for his government job make plain how Achebe wants us to see Obi and his fate. Auden's claim that "real tragedy takes place in a corner, in an untidy spot. . . . The rest of the world is unaware of it" (Auden "Musee des Beaux"). Eliot's phrase suggests Obi's deracinated state, as well as that of others who, to some degree, experience the same confusion of values as they try to accommodate themselves to a material urban culture where traditional values have been superseded by a new and not fully reconciled modern dispensation.

Even though Achebe understands Obi's contradictory situation, he blames him for not resolving his personal problems. Obi is not an admirable character. After his return from London he adopts a remote intellectual attitude from which he judges society. He draws on his training in western literature to define phenomena he observes around him. Obi calls the fragmented and contradictory Nigeria he returns to an "Augean stable." Even in contemplating the kind of leadership that might best serve Nigerians—one that believed in educating the masses, or one practiced by an enlightened dictator, a man of vision—Obi abandons such speculation, saying to himself that democracy cannot exist in the midst of so much corruption and ignorance. In this respect, the novel not only defines a current situation in the period just before independence, it offers an uncanny prophecy of the direction society would continue to follow, culminating in a series of military coups and greater acts of corruption in Nigeria.

Achebe's novels exist on a variety of ironic levels and in this novel the irony is achieved from the narrative form he adopts. Obi is on trial as the novel begins. At its close, he is found guilty of the charges brought against him and he is convicted of taking bribes. His descent into corruption begins with his mother's death and with the recognition that, despite all his previous moralizing, "there was nothing in him to challenge . . . honestly" the moral dilemmas in his life, a life he comes ultimately to define as "sheer humbug" (124).

Obi makes himself a victim. But Achebe asks us to consider the pressures brought to bear on him, and, further, to consider what ways out of his dilemma were available to him. Beyond the personal story of Obi the novel is about accommodation to change. It is about choice and how to make personal and public choices. It is about modernity and the cost to Nigerians, to individuals, and to society in general of achieving modernity. Obi's progress runs parallel to, and thus reflects, the confusion of values of a society once dominated by colonial rule as it moves swiftly—perhaps too swiftly—toward self-determination.

Arrow of God (1964)

Achebe returns to the past with his third novel, *Arrow of God* (1964). It is probably the most compelling depiction of the colonial period in Nigerian history. The world Achebe presents is like that of Okonkwo's in *Things Fall Apart* but more comprehensively rendered. The complexities of daily domestic life—its social, political, commercial, and religious arenas—are fully rendered. Two issues dominate the life of Umuaro—the proscriptions of the colonial administration, now fully established, and the tension between two religious factions.

At the center of the novel is the tragic story of Ezeulu, the chief priest of Ulu and the spiritual and political leader of his people. The novel, set in the context of colonial interference in custom and tradition, is an inquiry into the nature and uses of power as well as the personality and responsibility of the person who wields it. Ezeulu enters into a power struggle both with his own people and the British Political Service. Sensitive to the sources of his power and the reasons he was given it, Ezeulu meditates on how to serve his own people while accommodating the British and reconciling contending forces in his own nature—how to use his powers disinterestedly on behalf of the community and yet enhance his personal power in order to stave off elements in his community who seek to wrest his power from him. Ezeulu's tragedy arises out of his failure to reconcile these contending elements.

The novel is poised at that point in Ezeulu's life when he must resolve this dilemma between public service and personal ambition. Ezeulu is jailed at the British administrative headquarters because he has refused to accept a position in the colonial administration as a warrant chief. He is seen by Winterbottom, the district officer, as a firm candidate because he, Ezeulu, has acted to avoid internal tribal conflict in a dispute over land rights. His judgment has coincided with Winterbottom's and because the British seek to govern their subject peoples through a system of so-called indirect rule, they look to support those members of the local community who share their values and support their judgments. Ezeulu rejects the offer, seeing it as arrogant and thoughtless.

During his period imprisonment, two full moons pass and two sacred yams remain uneaten. The eating of the yams is the event that determines the rhythm of the seasons and announces the harvest. Despite the warm welcome accorded to him on his return to his village, Ezeulu determines to eat the uneaten yams at succeeding new moons. Thus the harvest is delayed. New yams rot in the ground and thus the life of the villagers is threatened by a famine. Ezeulu's dilemma is that he cannot respond to the needs of his people for food while at the same time honoring the demands of his god, Ulu. In defending the principles of his religion and supporting his god, Ezeulu makes the wrong choice. Faced by peril, the villagers desert Ulu and his priest and accept the offer of succor by the Christian community.

Ezeulu is regarded as half-man, half-god—on ceremonial occasions he covers half his body with white chalk to suggest this duality. Achebe illustrates the Igbo belief that people make the gods they worship. Achebe introduces Ezeulu's ambiguous position at the outset, as the priest muses on the nature and limits of his power, wondering if it real and asking himself what would happen if he failed to announce religious festivals, the feast of the Pumpkin Leaves or the New Yam feast.

Ezeulu's consideration of his powers becomes more than abstract speculation. He recognizes that the presence of white authority in his community will alter and reshape it. The white man has power and Ezeulu is determined to understand its nature so that he can turn it to his own uses. For this reason he sends one of his four sons, Oduche, to the Christian Mission School. His concern is for the clan but his motives are both misconstrued and used by his arch rivals, Chief Nwaka and Ezidemili, a rival priest of the god Idemili, to undermine Ezeulu's authority.

But Ezeulu's motives are not entirely disinterested. For while he seeks to understand and accommodate the power of the new, imposed regime in order to understand and convert it to the uses of his clan, he has personal motives as well. His ambiguous actions are revealed in his refusal to proclaim the harvest until the two ceremonial yams are eaten. He thus honors his god and the god's enjoinders. But a submotive is to increase his hold over his people. His personal motives, and his bitterness over the way he was treated by his people when he was in jail—only one came to visit him—supercede his judgment about the changing nature of the political climate. He finds out when the crisis of famine threatens the community that the will of the clan was greater than the will of the god. Pragmatics prevail. As the saying has it, if a god misbehaves he will be shown the wood he is made of.

Ezeulu is told by his people that they will take responsibility for breaking religious custom by harvesting their crops. Necessity prevails. The paradox in Ezeulu's actions is that he can be fully flexible in accommodating himself to the will of the white government, but wholly inflexible (and not typical of Igbo attitudes and actions in general) in adjusting to the realities of the villagers' need.

Another irony arising from events in the novel is that in turning to the Christians who offer support to the starving villagers, the rivalry between Ulu and Izidemili becomes obsolete. These events alter Ezeulu's reputation in the clan. He suffers great confusion of belief: he asks himself again and again what he has done wrong. His meditations supply no answers. And in this heightened state of confusion and anxiety, he is dealt a blow that destroys him. His son, Obika, although ill with fever, runs a funeral race on behalf of a dead clansman, determined to retrieve something of his father's reputation. On learning of Obika's death, Ezeulu's mind snaps and he left to live out his life in "the haughty splendor of a demented high priest" (286–87).

Ezeulu's tragedy results from his rationalization of his responsibility, the nature of his power, and his decision on a doomed course of action. He is the author of his own destiny: no external force is ultimately responsible. But the British authority has been an agent in his destiny. Ezeulu fails because he acts in a way that will bring about his community's destruction through starvation. Personal motives become entangled with public, political, and religious motives. Through Ezeulu's destruction the Igbo aphorism that "no man however great can win a judgment against the clan" is proven (287).

A Man of the People (1966)

Achebe's fourth novel is *A Man of the People* (1966). Whereas in *Arrow of God* Achebe was concerned with how power operates at the village level, in the fourth novel he mounts his inquiry on a national stage. *A Man of the People* is set in the immediate postcolonial period in an African country that resembles Nigeria but can stand for a number of African countries where events similar to those depicted in the novel have come about. The governance of the country is nominally in the hands of the people and it is the quality and integrity of the governors of the country—the elected members of government—that interest Achebe. He is concerned with questions of leadership. And whereas the village had a collective voice that eventually drove Ezeulu from power in *Arrow of God,* the nation, composed of many villages, has no collective voice.

In a village a man is known for what he was because he was known over a period of many years. In the conglomerate of a national assembly there was no way of knowing the quality of a man and his actions because he comes from a village distant from the house in which he sits in authority.

A Man of the People is about Chief Nanga and his colleagues in government and their rivals from other political parties who determine the affairs of the nation. It is a government informed by deceit, duplicity, and greed. Whereas in the novels Achebe sets in the past a balance was struck between collective religious observances and individual monetary pursuits, in the contemporary society of the fourth novel there is no evidence of religious beliefs that might keep the acquisitive side of society in balance. The result is unrestrained personal and political corruption. There are no restraints and Achebe evokes an atmosphere where it is every man for himself in acquiring as large a piece of the national financial cake as possible and by whatever means produce the best results.

Odili Samalu tells the story. When the reader meets him, he is a cynical and disillusioned school teacher, a university graduate who had once placed his faith in other university graduates, who were public minded in their determination to create a unified nation that is economically viable and politically stable. But high-minded, disinterested, well-educated political leaders have been discredited by the likes of Chief Nanga, thus paving the way to extend their personal fortunes at the expense of the taxpaying public.

The novel is told retrospectively by Odili and Achebe's purposes are revealed in the relations between Nanga and Odili, their various political activities, their period of friendship, and eventually their political confrontations. These latter culminate at a time of a national economic scandal and crisis, a rigged election, and finally a military intervention. Running parallel to the public themes, the novel explores the personal as well as public motives that inform the actions of the principal characters.

The strength of the book's argument—that mere anarchy has replaced the laws of the village—stems from the growing relationship between Odili and Nanga. Nanga is an engaging and credible character, like most politicians, and that is what makes his apostasy so real and terrifying. Achebe leaves the novel open-ended: an impasse is reached and intervention by the military is plainly not a viable solution to the problems of leadership in government that the book addresses.

The novel is about more than public political life in the postindependence African state. It is also about Odili's introspection and examination of his own motives. On graduating from the university, Odili sought membership in the privileged class. And when he becomes involved in contesting the seat Nanga holds in the national election campaign, he sees that in buying a car with party funds and using party funds to hire body guards to protect him, he is in danger of compromising his idealism even though he is acting out of necessity in terms of running his campaign. He recognizes as well that in pursuing Edna, a mistress of Nanga, initially out of motives of revenge, he is in fact in love with her. Ultimately Odili comes to the conclusion that though he knows he cannot win the election from Nanga (indeed he is badly beaten by Nanga's thugs and is in the hospital on election day), he knows that it was "nonetheless necessary to fight and expose him as much as possible" (108). Odili achieves his aim. Nanga and his corrupt colleagues are thrown out of government, not by the electorate, but by the army. Something, however temporary, has been achieved.

A Man of the People is a prophetic novel. It was published in January of 1966, coinciding almost exactly with the first military takeover in Nigeria.

Anthills of the Savannah (1987)

Achebe confirmed his place as the leading African novelist with the publication of *Anthills of the Savannah* in 1987. The novel is set in the fictional West African country of Kangan, a country that resembles Nigeria (and many other African countries), and it takes up the inquiry that Achebe initiated with *A Man of the People* (1966). *Anthills of the Savannah* ends with a military coup—as was the case with *A Man of the People*—giving one the sense that history goes on repeating itself, a measure of how far the country is from solving its political problems. Achebe examines the consequences of military, as opposed to civilian, rule. Military leadership, as revealed here, is little better than the civilian rule it replaced. In fact it is worse: political chaos has been replaced by a dictatorship; cynical self-interest has been replaced by megalomania. Kangan is ruled by a military governor and a cabinet of civilian ministers, a regime that can take no credit for its accomplishments. As one of the characters muses: "The prime failing of this government . . . is the failure of our rulers to establish vital links with the poor and dispossessed of this country, with the bruised heart that throbs painfully at the core of the nation's being" (141).

Anthills of the Savannah, with a multiplicity of viewpoints, is contemporary in setting yet makes reference to the relevance of historical tradition. The novel tells the story of Sam, His Excellency and would-be President for Life; Ikem Osodi, poet and editor of the *National Gazette;* Chris Oriko, minister of information in the cabinet of Sam's government; and Beatrice, an honors graduate from the university, a poet and short-story writer and avatar of Idemili, the embodiment of tradition and custom. Sam/HE (His Excellency), Ikem, and Chris are boyhood friends, their friendship dating back 25 years. Ikem and Chris have been instrumental in helping Sam to power. Achebe characterizes Sam's career thus: "From school to Sandhurst; then first African Second Lieutenant in the Army; ADC to the Governor; Royal Equerry during the Queen's visit; Colonel at the time of the coup; General and His Excellency; then Head of State after" (53). But this friendship dissolves when Sam/HE becomes distrustful of Ikem and Chris. Sam begins well enough, in the eyes of his two friends. Ikem says: "I believe that a budding dictator might choose models far worse than the English gentleman of leisure. . . . The English have for all practical purposes, ceased to menace the world. . . . The real danger is from that fat, adolescent and delinquent millionaire, America, and from all those virulent, misshapen freaks like Amin and Bokassa sired on Africa by Europe" (23). Chris writes a "detailed diary of what's happening day to day" and defends the fact that, at first, he remains in Sam's cabinet by saying: "I wouldn't be writing this if I didn't hang around to observe it all" (23). At first his writing is private, and his attitude is cautious. He advises Ikem to adopt a similar stance and to publish distorted, superficial, and therefore dishonest accounts of the political issues and events in the *Gazette*. But Ikem, even while recognizing the possible futility of his crusading editorials, feels a moral imperative to continue to publish them. For Ikem, his job is "not to marshal facts" but to marshal passion—"Passion is our only hope and strength," he says (160).

Sam/HE's behavior toward his friends becomes punitive when he heeds the advice given him by the head of another African country, President-for-Life, Ngongo: "Your greatest risk is your boyhood friends, those who grew up with you in your village. Keep them at arm's length and you will live long" (23). Ikem is accused of plotting to overthrow the government when he makes a snide remark about Sam's intention to have his face minted on the Kangan currency: "My view is that any serving President foolish enough to lay his head on a coin should know he is inciting people to take it off; the head I mean" (162). Ikem is arrested in the dead of night and murdered by his captors. Chris, who to this point has sought a mediating role, reveals the causes of Ikem's murder and is forced into hiding. When fleeing the city, Chris tries to stop a soldier from raping a young woman and is shot and killed by the soldier. Ironically, he dies as the news of Sam's overthrow is announced to the nation.

For Achebe, the trouble with Kangan (read: Nigeria and other states in similar disarray) is its leadership. Admitting that external factors have a bearing on the problems of the nation, he has Ikem say: "to blame all these things on imperialism and international capitalism as our modish radicals want us to do is, in my view, sheer cant and humbug" (159). Nor is the leadership problem to be solved by a "democratic dictatorship of the proletariat," because no two groups have been more derelict than workers and students in their commitment to public and civil causes (159). Ikem's solution is this: "We can only hope to rearrange some details in the periphery of human personality. Any disturbance of its core is an irresponsible invitation to disaster. . . . It is the same with society. You reform it around what it is, its core or reality; not around an intellectual abstraction" (160).

The writer's role is central in effecting this solution. There are persistent references to the liberating but simultaneously threatening role of "story" and "storyteller" in the book: "the story owns and directs us . . . the story is everlasting"; "storytellers are a threat. They threaten all the champions of control, they frighten usurpers of the right-to-freedom of the human spirit—in state, in church or mosque, in party congresses, in the university or wherever"; "every artist contains multitudes and expresses the ultimate enmity between art and orthodoxy"; "Writers don't give prescriptions—they give headaches" (160). Chris, Ikem, and Beatrice are writers but it is Beatrice who ultimately proves the most effective of the three. Beatrice is the central character in the novel, Achebe's most powerful female character. She is closely linked to Sam/HE. Chris, Ikem, and Beatrice tell the story of their involvement in—and in the cases of Ikem and Chris, their sacrifices to—contemporary history. With great difficulty, Beatrice pieces together the story of the "unbelievable violences we went through." Through her association with the legendary Idemili, the daughter of the Almighty who was sent to earth to temper man's power, Beatrice is a link with the past and a protector of its values and concerns. Achebe tells us that Beatrice did not know these legends and traditions of her people because they played but little part in her upbringing. But she is intuitively aware of her dual mythic identity, eventually undergoing a transformation when the goddess possesses her for divine purposes. Beatrice's power as Idemili's avatar is revealed when Sam/HE invites, or rather, commands her to attend a dinner at his presidential retreat. Among the guests—"the new-power brokers around his Excellency"—is a special guest, Lou Crandfield, an American journalist who presumes, after several drinks, to tell the president how to run his country. Beatrice assumes the role of avenging goddess and determines not only to remind HE of his power but also to prevent him from abusing it.

In recounting the parable of Idemili's coming to earth—in which she took the form of a pillar of water that fused "earth and heaven at the navel of the dark lake" (81)—Achebe equates HE with "a certain man handsome beyond compare but in randiness as unbridled as the odorous he-goat" (93). The man so angers Idemili by flouting her injunctions that she sends her royal python to bar his way to his village. The man, proving himself unworthy of possessing power, soon dies. Achebe presents these myths of the ancestors as being sustained and having power in the present. The scene that leads to Achebe telling the parable is the last meeting between Beatrice and Ikem. He arrives at her apartment soaking wet: "It was literally like barging into a pillar of rain, you know" (93). Ikem has brought with him a prose poem which he reads to Beatrice. Their conversation then turns to the rights and lives of women in their society and extends further to a discussion of the means and impediments to achieving freedom. Through Ikem, Achebe conveys his beliefs about the complex and often paradoxical elements that shape human destinies. Ikem, like Beatrice, is identified with Idemili, the avenger of humanity's misuse of power. Chris, too, recognizes the mythic dimension of Beatrice's character and her connection with Idemili:

Chris saw the quiet demure damsel whose still waters nonetheless could conceal deep overpowering eddies of passion that always almost sucked him into fatal depths. Perhaps Ikem alone came close to sensing the village priestess who will prophesy when her divinity rides her abandoning if need be her soup-pot on the fire, but returning again when the god departs to the domesticity of the kitchen. . . . He knew it better than Beatrice herself. (105)

Beatrice senses her identity as well with "Chielo in the novel [*Things Fall Apart*] the priestess and prophetess of the Hills and the Caves" (104). She knows, as well, the legend of Mother Idoto and Idemili who was sent to "wrap around Power's rude waist a loincloth of peace and modesty" (80). When that power is abused by Sam, Beatrice assumes the avenger's role and in seducing him, reminds him of his responsibility.

The novel ends at an impasse. According to Beatrice's account, the regime that replaces Sam's is no better than his. History once more repeats itself. But the novel ends on a hopeful note as Ikem's ideals live on through the voice of Emmanuel, a defected student leader who was with Chris when he died: "It wasn't Ikem the man who changed me. I hardly knew him. It was the ideas he set down on paper. One idea in particular: that we may accept a limitation on our actions but never, under any circumstances, must we accept a restriction on our thinking" (223). Ikem's child, born after his death to his girlfriend, Elewa, is named Amaechina which means "may the path never close": this, too, is sign of hope at the end of the novel.

Anthills of the Savannah completes a sequence of novels that reveal the changes wrought in Nigeria during the twentieth century. Achebe is concerned, in the midst of rapidly changing social and political realities, to examine the beliefs and actions, and the consequences of these actions, in ways that will both inform and possibly prompt readers—citizens—to action and to hold in check those motives that can so easily and disastrously affect human lives. Achebe, in a wholly different way than his Chief Nanga, *is* a Man of the People.

ADDITIONAL READINGS

Achebe, Chinua. 1958. *Things Fall Apart*. London: Heinemann.

———. 1960. *No Longer at Ease*. London: Heinemann.

———. 1964. *Arrow of God*. London: Heinemann.

———. 1964, June. "The Role of the Writer in a New Nation." *Nigeria Magazine* 81.

———. 1966. *A Man of the People*. London: Heinemann.

———. 1975. *Morning Yet on Creation Day*. London: Heinemann.

———. 1987. *Anthills of the Savannah*. London: Heinemann.

Avden, W. H. 1976, 1991. "Musee des Beaux Ants" in Collected Poems, ed. W. Mendelson. N.Y.: Vintage Books.

Booker, M. Keith. 1998. *The African Novel in English: An Introduction*. Portsmouth, N.H.: Heinemann; Oxford: James Currey.

Cary, Joyce. 1939. *Mister Johnson*. London: Michael Joseph.

Ezenwa-Ohaeto. 1997. *Chinua Achebe: A Biography*. Bloomington: Indiana University Press; Oxford: James Currey.

Gikandi, Simon. 1991. *Reading Chinua Achebe: Language and Ideology in Fiction*. Portsmouth, N.H.; and London: Heinemann.

Innes, C. L. 1990. *Chinua Achebe*. Cambridge: Cambridge University Press.

Killam, G. D. 1977. *The Writings of Chinua Achebe*. London: Heinemann.

Chapter 2
Buchi Emecheta: The Bride Price *(1976) and* The Joys of Motherhood *(1979)*

Buchi Emecheta is, with Nadine Gordimer, Africa's best-known woman writer. Since 1967 she has published a dozen novels, two childrens' books, and works of teenage fiction. Buchi Emecheta was born in Yaba, Lagos—then Nigeria's capital city, the seat of colonial government—in 1944 at the close of World War II. Her parents were Igbos from the village of Ibuza and Emecheta spent long periods in her parents' village, learning about Igbo religious beliefs and cultural values. Her divided life gave her an early understanding of the complexities of traditional village life as well as the values practiced in the pan-Nigerian city of Lagos that, while predominantly a Yoruba city, attracted members from most of Nigeria's cultural communities. Moreover, she early became aware that the societies in which she was growing up were dominated by male proscriptions and values, a fact that would inform all of her writing in later years.

Emecheta decided at a young age to get an education that would support her determination to become a writer. She fulfilled her dreams, but not before overcoming arduous conditions that would have broken a less resolute person. She left school at age 16 to marry a husband chosen for her according to the traditions of her people. With two small children, she left Nigeria with her husband, who went to London to continue his studies. In London, the couple encountered racial prejudice and lived a borderline and impoverished life. It fell to Emecheta to provide for her growing family (there were soon five children) while her husband prepared for examinations that he never passed. Emecheta found employment as a librarian and as a community worker while at the same time continuing her studies. She eventually gained a degree in sociology. Her marriage broke down when she was 22 years old. But she prevailed over the worst of conditions to earn a living and care for her children.

At this time, she began her writing career. In 1972, *The New Statesman* magazine published stories that would eventually become part of her first novel, *In the Ditch* (1972). *In the Ditch* is an autobiographical novel that describes the experiences of Adah, a persona for Emecheta herself. Adah, like Emecheta, marries early in Nigeria, travels to London with her husband, bears five children, and sees her marriage break down. We follow her life as she copes with her unsuccessful marriage, near poverty, and racial abuse, and as she struggles to provide for and raise her children while at the same time getting an education and becoming a writer. Emecheta's second novel, *Second-Class Citizen,* was published in 1974. It continues the story of Adah by moving back in time to describe her childhood and her growing up in Nigeria. Thwarted in her desire to get an education (women with education were generally seen as useless in their roles in traditional societies), Adah, like Emecheta, travels to London and overcomes the hardships described in *In the Ditch,* especially the hard road to winning acceptance as a writer. (The two books were published in a single volume entitled *Adah's Story* in 1983.)

Emecheta's third novel, *The Bride Price* (1976), is the first of her historical novels. The novel is set in colonial Nigeria in the early 1950s and tells the story of Aku-nna. In the novel, Emecheta contrasts traditional Igbo village life with the developing urban and modern culture of Lagos. Emecheta uses the experiences of Aku-nna to comment implicitly on the oppressive life of women in Nigerian society.

In *The Slave Girl* (1977), Emecheta moves even further back in time. The year is 1910 and the setting is again Ibuza. Ogbanje Ojebeta's happy life is abruptly ended when her parents die and, at age seven, she is sold into slavery (for eight pounds) by her brother. Her life in slavery in the household of Ma Palagada is the subject of an ambiguous critique by Emecheta. She is critical of the practice of slavery. At the same time, she shows that Ogbanje Ojebeta lives in relative comfort and safety as a slave. Moreover, Ogbanje Ojebeta is able to gain some education. But her fortunes are reversed a second time when Ma Palagada dies and Ogbanje is returned to her village where she experiences a more subtle and pernicious form of bondage—the bondage of custom, which sees women as wholly subservient to men. This fact of her life is secured when Ogbanje marries an educated man who repays the bride price to Ma Palagada's son. In his household, she finds herself in another version of servitude. The novel ends with Ogbanje accepting her inferior status, her spirit broken.

The Joys of Motherhood (1979) is probably Emecheta's best-known book. In this novel, Emecheta draws together the complex of themes that have interested her to this point in her career: the opposition between traditional and modern values in Nigeria in the period surrounding World War II; the adversarial relations between men and women; and the place of education, especially in the lives of children.

In 1983, Emecheta published *The Double Yoke,* a straightforward story that dramatizes the difficulties experienced by Eta Cambia (the only male hero in Emecheta's work) and No, his girlfriend, as each seeks entry into a university. Eta Cambia wins a scholarship and No, in an excess of joy at his success, gives herself to him. At first, Eta Cambia had been proud to think that his future bride would be a university graduate, but when he finds that she is pregnant, in a fit of anger, rooted in notions of traditional male dominance, he now accuses No as having the loose morals of a prostitute. No, as well as experiencing Eta Cambia's rejection, encounters discrimination and sexual harassment at the university. She finally succumbs to the sexual advances of her professor. But she turns the tables on him: she threatens to expose him if she is not awarded a first-class degree. Eventually, Eta Cambia and No are reconciled. The novel makes a telling comment on the practices of a modern Nigerian university.

Destination Biafra (1982) is a novel that examines a multiplicity of issues that informed the Nigeria-Biafra war of the late 1960s and early 1970s. Emecheta is impartial here in treating an event that nearly destroyed Nigeria. Through the adventures of her heroine, Debbie Ogedemgbe, Emecheta provides a kind of overview of the conflict: the political and cultural reasons for the war, seen from both the federal and the Biafran positions, the role of the French and the British in determining the progress of the war, the suffering of the ordinary people caught up in the crossfire of the conflict, and the endless suffering of the soldiers themselves. Debbie moves more or less unimpeded through the battle lines of the two "nations" and, through her experiences, Emecheta is able to offer a complex and shrewd evaluation of the causes and prosecution of the war. There is, as well, a good deal of comment on the sexual politics of the time, seen through Debbie's encounters with many different men in a wide variety of situations.

The Rape of Shavi (1983) marks a complete departure from the novels that have come before it. *The Rape of Shavi* is a futuristic novel, a fantasy, and an allegory. The time is future time; the place, the idyllic African country of Shavi, as yet untouched by contact with any other culture. The scene shifts into present time and real locales when a group of Englishmen, escaping a threatened nuclear war in Europe, crash-land a homemade airplane in Shavi. The idyllic, just, courteous, and accommodating culture of Shavi soon falls apart under the more powerful European imperial/colonial ills of greed, sexual pressure, and rape. A Shavian prince is taken to England when the Englishmen eventually return. There he espouses European values and returns to Shavi with guns, wages war on his neighbors, and introduces fear and suffering where once there was peace and harmony. The novel is a fairly obvious allegory on European/African relations, rehearsing, in short form, the history of the European imperial-colonial venture in Africa.

Gwendolyn (1989), republished in 1990 as *The Family*, is a realistic novel set in Jamaica and London, and this time the characters are West Indian rather than African. The novel, which opens in Jamaica, is the story of Gwendolyn Brilliantine, whose parents have gone to London, leaving her in the care of her grandmother. At age nine she is raped by her Uncle Johnny. The people of her village do not believe that the rape took place and make her life in Jamaica miserable. When she eventually goes to London, things do not improve. She is raped again, this time by her father. Paradoxically, this brings her mother's wrath down upon her and she nearly goes mad. Even when the father commits suicide out of guilt over his desperate deed, Gwendolyn is not reconciled with her mother. In the end, however, Gwendolyn makes a satisfactory life with a white boyfriend. Emecheta insists here that people of color living in England lack sufficient education and understanding of English culture to overcome the overwhelming racial prejudice they experience.

Another variation on a familiar theme in Emecheta's "London" books is found in *Kehinde* (1994). There seems to be a selective autobiographical element in the novel. It tells the story of Kehinde, a Nigerian, who has lived for many years in London with her Nigerian husband, Albert. Life is difficult for Albert and he eventually returns to Nigeria.

Kehinde remains for a time in London. When she eventually joins Albert in Lagos, she finds he has taken a second wife. Kehinde accepts this fact: more importantly, she finds that she can no longer tolerate Nigeria. She returns to London, works at various jobs and eventually, like Emecheta, is awarded a degree in sociology.

The Bride Price (1976)

The Bride Price (1976) is Emecheta's first historical novel and the first set in Nigeria. The time is just after the close of World War II. The novel opens in Lagos and moves to the town of Ibuza, in the then Eastern Region of Nigeria. Ibuza is a town made up of six villages and is near to major market centers—Asaba on the western banks of the Niger River, and Onitsha on the eastern banks of the river. The story moves through these various locales as it tells of the life of Aku-nna who is born in Lagos and lives there for 13 years with her mother, her brother Nna-nndo, and her father Ezekiel Odia. Various family members and friends shape Aku-nna's life. Her father has fought with British forces in Burma. He now works for the railway, but suffers from injuries sustained in the malarial-infested swamps of Burma. These eventually become septic and untreatable, and he dies, leaving Aku-nna and her brother orphaned in Lagos.

Ma Blackie, Aku-nna's mother, who has returned to her village, comes to Lagos to retrieve her children. She takes them to Ibuza where the rest of the novel is situated as it follows Aku-nna's continuing difficulties in adjusting to life there. Aku-nna's life had been shaped by Lagos, a multiethnic and multicultural capital city, where certain traditional customs are retained but are in the process of being modified because of contending cultural, religious, and economic factors. Life in Ibuza is the opposite of life in Lagos. It is dominated by traditional customs and beliefs. Christianity has made substantial inroads into the community. There is a school run by the Church Missionary Society and a church. Igbo adaptability is evident in the ways in which new beliefs and values are incorporated into the fabric of Ibuza life. But in times of stress and crisis, traditional values prevail.

That this is so coincides with Emecheta's purpose in writing the story of Aku-nna's life. Aku-nna remains an alien in her own culture. Her alienation begins when her mother marries her husband's brother, Aku-nna's uncle. Her desire to continue her education, begun in Lagos, is frowned upon—what good is education for a woman in a male-dominated community where women perform all domestic functions? Aku-nna is allowed to continue her education, however, because it is judged this will increase her bride price. She is courted by many eligible young men of Ibuza. But she falls in love with Chike, an educated man and a school teacher. Their love is forbidden and ultimately becomes tragic because Chike is an *osu,* a descendant of slaves. It is also suggested that Aku-nna is *obanje,* a person doomed to a cycle of birth, life, early death, and rebirth.

Reacting with great hostility to Aku-nna's love for Chike, one of her suitors kidnaps her, a method condoned by Ibuza society in the taking of a bride. Aku-nna escapes the situation by telling the would-be husband, Okoboshi, that she has already had sexual relations with Chike and thus she is tainted. Aku-nna and Chike elope, leave the community and travel to Ughelli, the site of the first discovery of oil in Nigeria, where Chike finds work.

But their flouting of tradition has heavy consequences. Ma Blackie is cast out of her husband's house, even though he has been offered a substantial sum of money as a bride price by Chike's father. Aku-nna's happiness with Chike is compromised by her inability to accept the rejection of her family and her village. She dies giving birth to a daughter. The curse upon her (that anyone who defies convention and its goddess avatar will die in childbirth) is fulfilled. The newborn daughter is named Joy, an ironic note of hope sounded in the tragic conclusion to Aku-nna's story.

Emecheta integrates a number of concerns and themes in the novel. Her descriptions and dramatizations of traditions and beliefs imbedded in Igbo culture are the familiar fare of a number of works by her peers—Chinua Achebe, Elechi Amadi, T. M. Aluko, and Flora Nwapa. The final paragraphs of the novel raise a number of questions about Emecheta's purposes in writing the book. Is her stance neutral in merely displaying the force of beliefs at work in Igbo society in the period of the novel? Does Emecheta see value in and support the traditional beliefs as they are worked out in the novel? Or does she display them for the purpose of exposing their deleterious effect on Nigerian society, especially on its women?

The Bride Price is, as the title implies and as the action of the novel reveals, about the circumstances of women in African society. Emecheta's examination of their experiences is focused on Aku-nna and the almost unending struggle she has in reconciling her early experiences of Lagos culture with the more formalized and rigid proscriptions of Ibuza. In a broader sense, the novel reflects how Nigerian society may be changing rapidly as traditions are challenged by new imperatives such as the adoption of western ways into extant cultures. This adoption is implied in many ways: by Nigeria's involvement, perhaps unwilling but unavoidable, in World War II; the muted references to the independence movement gaining momentum at the time of the novel. ("Zik," Dr. Nmandi Azikiwe, one of the architects of the movement, is mentioned in the novel); a burgeoning cash economy with oil replacing agricultural products (ground nuts and palm oil) as its base; and by the quest by young Nigerians for western-based education exemplified in Aku-nna's success in competitive examinations and Chike's position as a teacher in a Christian, thus western, school, and with a place waiting for him in the university.

But these influences are subsumed by tenets of a caste system that dominates the affairs of all of the principal characters. This is the focus of Emecheta's inquiry. And this is presented from the implicit point of view of Aku-naa. She presses for personal freedom and autonomy and she achieves this to the extent that she gains some education, elopes with Chike, and bears their child. She questions conventions that encroach on her happiness and her sense of fulfillment: male domination, bride prices, denial of education for women, traditional religious beliefs. But question convention as she does, she cannot overcome the psychological imperatives of these conventions. In the end, she is overwhelmed by conventions that are fully substantiated as the novel closes.

Where does the author stand? What is her position regarding the events she portrays? The novel closes on an impasse; conservative forces retain their strength and continuity, and we are left to wonder why.

The Joys of Motherhood (1979)

Set in Nigeria in the 1930s and moving forward to the time of independence from colonial rule, a time of enormous political and economic change, *The Joys of Motherhood* tells the story of Nnu Ego. She is born in the village of Ibuza. Her father, Nwakocha Agbadi, is a local chief. Nnu Ego is a beautiful young woman and her father arranges a customary marriage for her with Amatokwu, one of her many suitors, from the neighboring village of

Umo-Iso. The marriage fails when no children are produced, and after a time living in Amatokwu's household with a second wife who does bear children, Nnu Ego returns to her father's home. Agbadi arranges a second marriage for Nnu Ego, this time to Nwaife Owulum, who works as a domestic servant for the Meers family in Lagos. Nnu Ego travels to Lagos to begin her second marriage. Nwaife is not a pleasant man. Truculent and at times, brutal, he makes excessive sexual demands on Nnu Ego. With his employers, the Meers, his is excessively obsequious. Nnu Ego opens a street stand and sells cigarettes to help with family finances. She gives birth to a boy who brings her great happiness. But the boy dies suddenly and Nnu Ego, in complete despair, attempts suicide. (This attempt is the opening scene of the novel, one that sets the tone for the rest of the novel). She recovers and, after a time, gives birth to a second son, Oshia.

When World War II approaches, Nwaife loses his job with the Meers, who return to England. After a period of unemployment during which the family exists on Nnu Ego's meager earnings from the street trade, Nwaife finds work as a seaman and leaves Lagos. A third son, Adim, is born shortly after Nwaife leaves home. When he returns to Lagos he learns that his elder brother has died. According to custom, Nwaife becomes responsible for his brother's wife and her family. Adaku is the second wife and she moves into Nwaife's household. Nnu Ego and Adaku do not get on together and the tension in the family is not helped by Nwaife's slim earnings from his job with the railway. Calamity follows calamity. Nnu Ego gives birth to twin girls. Adaku gives birth to a son who dies. Nwaife is conscripted into the British army when World War II breaks out and leaves Nnu Ego and Adaku to provide for themselves and their families. Adaku becomes first a street seller of foodstuffs and fruits and then a prostitute. With the proceeds she gains from selling her body, Adaku is able to open a successful and legitimate business.

Nnu Ego survives through her ingenuity until Nwaife returns from war. He makes her pregnant again, and again she gives birth to twin girls. Nwaife takes yet another wife, Okpo. Shortly thereafter, Nwaife attacks a man who is tormenting his daughter and is sent to prison. Nnu Ego, Okpo, and their children return to Ibuza. Nwaife, on his release from prison, travels to Ibuza where he lives with Okpo.

Nnu Ego's main interest in life has been to see that her two sons are well educated. In due course, they travel to the United States and Canada, there to continue their educations, to marry North American women, and to lose touch almost completely with their mother. This loss, together with her rejection by Nwaife, causes Nnu Ego to despair of finding happiness. She dies a lonely death by the side of a road. Her estranged sons return to Nigeria to attend her funeral and to erect a shrine in her honor.

The relatively straightforward narrative pattern of the book belies a complex structure of encounters and ironies. Emecheta raises and examines a number of propositions about the position of women in Nigerian society in the period of the book's action. And she places her examination in a series of related oppositions: between village and urban life and therefore between tradition and modernity; between male and female positions within both traditional and modern settings; between family and community; and between members within families that are based on polygamy. What we see in this historical novel is a series of irreconcilable opposites. The pattern of the book, the thematic issues inherent in it, are familiar subject matter in African literature. Despite being set in the period of World War II, the novel has a current relevance because, while conditions may have changed, they are replaced by relationships that produce the same results as those seen in *The Joys of Motherhood*.

Emecheta's main concern is with domestic relations and, more precisely, with the position of women in both traditional society, as represented by the village, and with traditional values as these are carried into complex city life and, in some respects, modified there. She is concerned, within this context, with relationships between husbands and wives and, equally importantly, with relations between wives and wives. Traditional society is patriarchal in this novel, and male proscriptions dominate the lives of women. Emecheta acknowledges that in the traditional context women are mere chattels and that their principal role is to attend to the needs of their men and to produce children, especially male children. But Emecheta's depiction is not one-sided. She gives us a number of strong women who do not accede weakly to conditions that threaten them. Nnu Ego, once her happy childhood is over, faces conditions and is forced into circumstances that bring almost no happiness. Her father is often brutal in his treatment of her. Her first husband abandons her. Nwaife, threatened by the humiliation he feels as a white man's servant—cleaning, polishing, doing family laundry—takes out his frustrations on Nnu Ego.

The patriarchal society also and inevitably values male children over female. Nnu Ego's sons early discern their special position in the family and in society. Daughters are valuable only in terms of the bride price they may eventually command. Nnu Ego sees that money earned from her daughters' marriages can go toward paying for her sons' education. The sons, in turn, accept as given the sacrifices their mother makes for them.

The most engaging questions in the novel concern the extent to which Nnu Ego's life is a success or a failure, or ambiguous, in terms of traditional sanctions regarding motherhood and the relative value of children according to sex. On the one hand, Nnu Ego is caring for all her children, but in accepting that male children are more valuable, she lives out a limitation of the society, as revealed and embodied in the neglected death Nnu Ego achieves. On the other hand, her sorrow at their abnegation is balanced by the recognition that she has succeeded in doing what she set out to—ensure that their education is complete. She experiences great suffering when she recognizes the extent of their abandonment in marrying white women. Colonialism is the agent of their transformation. Those successful in gaining a western education can leave behind—as Oshia and Adim do—traditional values, paying only lip service to them. They have escaped for better or for worse the proscriptions that have bound their mother and made her unhappy.

The Joys of Motherhood is a pivotal novel in the African literary canon. It evokes a period of transition in Nigeria, bridging as it does the colonial period that comes under heavy scrutiny as a result of Nigeria's participation in World War II and the resultant contact with other so-called subject races who have come to realize a kind of parity with their white masters. Participation in World War II hastened the move toward independence. The political liberation of Nigerians, however, is no guarantee of the liberation of individual Nigerians, as Emecheta shows quite clearly. She presents a powerful picture of the intersecting clashes between cultures, between tradition and modernity, and between genders. She presents the responses of families and cultures to new ideas working powerfully and relentlessly, particularly in the lives of women. Nnu Ego's story is one aspect of this alteration of values. Adaka responds differently than Nnu Ego and makes a different kind of life for herself. We see little of her, but Emecheta lets us know that there are possible alternative responses open to women in families dominated by men. The novel presents problems of the most serious kind in the lives of Nigerian women of Nnu Ego's generation. She does not proscribe solutions to these problems and, in that sense, the novel is open-ended.

Taken together, Emecheta's novels present a wide evocation of the lives of Nigerian women and, while they were not written in a sequential chronology, they can be arranged by readers in that pattern. Like Achebe's novels, these works form a continuum of Nigerian social history.

ADDITIONAL READINGS

Bazin, Nancy Topping. 1986. "Feminist Perspectives in African Fiction: Bessie Head and Buchi Emecheta." *Black Scholar* 17 (2): 34–40.
Emecheta, Buchi. 1974. *Second-Class Citizen*. London: Alison and Busby.
———. 1976. *The Bride Price*. London: Alison and Busby.
———. 1977. *The Slave Girl*. London: Alison and Busby.
———. 1979. *The Joys of Motherhood*. London: Alison and Busby.
———. 1982. *Destination Biafra*. London: Alison and Busby.
———. 1983. *Adah's Story*. London: Alison and Busby.
———. 1983. *The Double Yoke*. London: Ogwugwu Afor.
———. 1983. *The Rape of Shavi*. London: Ogwugwu Afor.
———. 1989. *Gwendolyn*. Oxford, England: Heinemann.
———. 1994. *In the Ditch*. London: Barrie and Jenkins.

———. 1994. *Kehinde*. Oxford, England: Heinemann.

Fishburn, Katherine. 1995. *Reading Buchi Emecheta: Cross-Cultural Conversations*. Westport, Conn.: Greenwood Press.

Umeh, Marie, ed. 1995. *Emerging Perspectives on Buchi Emecheta*. Trenton, N.J.: Africa World Press.

Chapter 3
Ayi Kwei Armah: The Beautyful Ones Are Not Yet Born *(1968)*

Ayi Kwei Armah's *The Beautyful Ones Are Not Yet Born* is, after Chinua Achebe's *Things Fall Apart,* probably the best-known and most widely read and discussed of any West African, or even African, novel. Published in 1968, the novel quickly generated a wide-ranging controversy and assumed the status of a classic African novel by the end of the 1980s.

Kwei Armah was born in 1939 in the port city of Takoradi in Ghana (what was at that time still the British colony of the Gold Coast). He attended Achimota College in Accra, probably the most highly respected secondary school in the country. He worked briefly for Radio Ghana, and then continued his education in the United States, first at Groton College in Massachusetts and then at Harvard University. He majored in social and political studies (having begun with the study of literature). His growing political awareness was sharpened by events both in independent African countries that had recently achieved independence from colonial rule (Ghana was the first such colony to achieve political autonomy in 1957) and in the burgeoning black activism in the United States.

Armah gained his B.A. degree in sociology from Harvard University and his M.F.A. from Columbia University. After completing his studies in the United States, he worked in Algiers in 1963 as a translator for *Revolution Africaine*. He then returned to Ghana to work as a broadcaster for Ghana Television, and, later, as an English teacher at Navrongo secondary school in 1966. He moved to Paris and from 1967 to 1968 worked as an editor for *Jeune Afrique*. He taught at the University of Massachusetts in 1970 and later that year moved to Tanzania where he taught for four years at the College of National Education at Chang'ombe. This was followed by a brief period in Lesotho and an appointment at the University of Wisconsin in 1979. Since then, Armah has made his base in Dakar in Senegal.

Armah has published six novels and several semiautobiographical articles. The first three novels record his progressive pessimism and disillusionment with postcolonial African society. Of these, the best known is *The Beautyful Ones Are Not Yet Born* (1968). *Fragments* (1970) and *Why Are We So Blessed* (1972) pursue the theme of personal disillusionment in the context of the early postindependence period in African countries.

Armah's interest shifts to the history of Ghana in three novels that follow: *The Healers* (1978), *Two Thousand Seasons* (1973), and *Osiris Rising: A Novel of Africa, Past, Present and Future* (1995). These latter three novels evoke African (Ghanaian) societies in the precolonial and early colonial period, offer comment on what was the nature of the social arrangements of the countries depicted, noting in particular what was good in them that could be retained, and what conditions shaped them as the European quest for wealth and power supplanted traditional values.

Armah, like his contemporaries in the first wave of African writers, writers whose sensibilities and concerns were shaped by the imminence of independence from colonial control, is concerned with a number of related themes: with political, social, economic, and cultural issues; with the political potential of his country as it is shaped by internal conflicts, and by continuing foreign political and especially, economic, pressures.

As a writer and intellectual Armah explores the question (and his writing offers implicit answers) about how art can serve society, how it can assist in effecting change for the betterment of society and the individual within society. More specifically, it asks the question: how can an educated elite contribute to the general well-being of society?

The Beautyful Ones Are Not Yet Born records Armah's disillusionment with the postcolonial experience of Ghana as the optimism bred of independence was wasted by the Nkrumah regime. Kwame Nkrumah led the British colony of the Gold Coast to independence in 1957, the first African country to gain autonomy from the British Crown. Renamed Ghana, the country, practicing Nkrumah's policy of nonaligned development along socialist principles, began well enough; indeed Ghana was the envy of other former colonial states. The situation quickly changed, however, and Nkrumah declared Ghana a one-party state, thus silencing political opposition. Nkrumah declared himself leader for life and gave himself the title "Osagyefo," "The Redeemer." Ghana, ironically, was to lead the way into a display of postindependence corruption that could not be estimated at the time. Achebe in *No Longer at Ease* and Wole Soyinka in *A Dance of the Forests* gave fair warnings of the dangers that might inhere in the gaining of independence. But no one at the time predicted the situation that Armah deals with in his novel.

Nkrumah and his corrupt government were overthrown in a military coup d'etat in 1966. It is this period in Ghana's history, the final stages of Nkrumah's megalomaniac reign as "Osagyefo" and its atmosphere of political disillusion and disaffection, its unrestrained corruption, that Armah evokes in *The Beautyful Ones Are Not Yet Born.*

The Beautyful Ones Are Not Yet Born has a simple and straightforward plot. It tells the story of "the man," an unnamed railway clerk, and his relations with his wife and family, his fellow workers, and his few friends. The novel reveals through his actions, his inner thoughts, and his encounters with various people, his quest for understanding and for determining his place in a corrupt society. Under its simple surface, the novel is carefully plotted, describing and dramatizing complicated and connected issues.

There are three parts to the novel of more or less equal length. Part one describes a day in the life of the man and his encounters with various people—a bus driver, his fellow railway workers, a timber merchant who attempts to bribe him, and his wife, Oyo. These various encounters are described at length and in great detail. Everywhere he goes, the man encounters physical, moral, and spiritual corruption: the bus driver steals from the company he serves; his fellow workers seek illicit rewards in a society that implicitly condones bribery; the merchant offers a substantial bribe in order to move his timber; his wife condemns his refusal to share in the rewards of corrupt practices. The tone of the novel is set in the first few pages where we are told that "victorious filth prevails" (2) and where moral and social corruption are sustained by images of decay and filth—rotting refuse, excrement, nose droppings—by which Armah shores up his narrative. These images are consolidated in references to the Chichidodo, "a bird [that] hates excrement with all its soul. But [that] feeds on maggots and as you know the maggots grow best inside the lavatory" (45). The Chichidodo is clearly an image of the corrupt members of Ghanaian society and their practices.

Through all of his experiences during this one day, a day replicated in his life throughout the novel, the man muses on his own actions as these relate to the people he encounters. He questions the legitimacy of his determination to retain his personal integrity. He is scorned by his fellow workers, the timber merchant, Amanakwa, and, worst of all, by his wife for his refusal to accept the offered bribes. His moral position is summed up in his reluctance to put his name on the deed to the fraudulent purchase of a fishing boat by his relation, Koomson, an alleged socialist reformer who is, in fact, a corrupt member of government.

Part two of the novel traces the history of Nkrumah's progress from idealistic national leader to corrupt and disassociated megalomaniac and the man's connection with various characters who share in one way or another his disillusionment with the present situation. Teacher (the most prominent member of this small group), Manaan, and Kofi Billy all have shared in the optimism about the bright future implied in Nkrumah's ascendancy. All have been destroyed by his apostasy. Through their reflections, Ghana's post-colonial history is revealed, as well as the birth, growth, and death of the initial idealism of Nkrumah's regime. The Nkrumah years are symbolized in the novel by the contracted life span of the "manchild" who goes through a full cycle of birth, growth, and death in nine years, the period of Nkrumah's regime.

Part three describes events leading up to the military coup that over-throws the government and the reactions of the public to this event. A lengthy part of this section of the novel describes the escape of the corrupt minister, Koomson (aided by the man), by crawling through the excrement in the pit latrine at the man's home.

What is Armah's achievement in the novel? He has written a novel that places characters in a historical context in order to display the conditions in which people live, conditions in which a few prosper handsomely at the expense of those who create the wealth. Koomson is typical of the politicians who rob the people under the guise of fostering their needs. He and his colleagues are deposed by the coup d'etat. But what will replace them and their regime? The extent to which cynicism at the national level has become entrenched can be seen in this series of responses to the coup:

Now another group of bellies will be bursting with the country's riches. (185)

End bribery and corruption. Build socialism. Equality. Shit. A man just has to make up his mind that there was never going to be anything but despair, and there would be no way of escaping it, except one. (180–81)

New people would use the country's power to get rid of men and women who talked a language that did not flatter them. There would be nothing different in that. There would only be a continuation of the Ghanaian way of life. (190–91)

The future goodness may come eventually. But before then where were those things in the present which would prepare the way for it? (188)

Armah's analysis of the condition of Ghana (seen presciently as applying to other postcolonial, postindependence African countries) proceeds from the question "How long will Africa be cursed with its leaders?" The promise of incipient independence, the belief that "something good was being born . . . the beauty that was in the waking of the powerless. . . . " (100), quickly turns into a polarizing situation where "there were men dying from loss of hope, and others . . . finding gaudy ways to enjoy power" (94). "How could such a thing turn so completely into this other thing?" (100), Armah's characters asks in disbelief.

Koomson, his wife Estella, his children, and his peers in government and business epitomize the abuse of power. Their behavior and values are at once frivolous, gaudy, and, at the same time, wholly immoral and amoral. There is little satire in the novel. Armah's intentions are far more serious than the kind of rebuke that satire offers. But what satire there is is directed at Koomson, his family, and his peers. For example, Armah mocks the ostentatious display of wealth in their houses and dress, in their preferences for goods and mannerisms that are non-African—imported cars, drink, and fashion, and their adoption of double-barreled names—Millis-Hayford, Plange-Bannerman, Attoh-White, Kuntu-Blankson.

Koomson and his kind will use whatever means are necessary to achieve and protect their position. Koomson's style of living is represented by "The Gleam," the dream and celebration of riches epitomized by the brightly lit Atlantic Caprice hotel with its suggestion both of the Atlantic slave trade (and the current bondage of the masses) and the utter frivolity and vacuousness of the lives the rich live. The insidious nature of The Gleam is revealed in the hopes and dreams of those, who, like the man's wife Oyo, aspire to this corrupt status.

The man stands alone between these two opposing groups. Teacher, for all his education and intellectual brilliance, has abandoned society and lives alone, naked, in his cave. Manaan goes mad at the end of the novel. The young Nkrumah inspired both Teacher and Manaan by his populist message:

He was good when he had to speak to us, and liked to be with us. When that ended everything was gone. It must be power. He is not the only one whom power has lost. It happened to those around him. . . . But how could this have grown rotten with such obscene haste? (103)

Even the man is forced into constant speculation on why he holds the moral position he does. He is a good man, but he is not an everyman, a representative person. He keeps his integrity intact in a world rank with corruption. Yet time and again he experiences self-doubt about the reasons for not engaging in the corrupt practices around him, about denying his family the simple comforts he could provide by choosing a different way. He muses on what his own life would have been like had he continued his education at the university instead of giving that up for life with Oyo. But his integrity prevails, and, in the end he wins the respect of his wife who, before the coup and the disgrace of Koomson, castigated the man for not providing for her and her family in the way Koomson had for his wife, Estella.

Koomson is the benchmark against which the man tests his own sensibility. As ambiguous as his responses are at times, he sees himself as fundamentally opposed to what Koomson stands for. Koomson had once been a man of the people, a railway worker and docker, a member of that class of colonial society from which Nkrumah drew his initial support. But Koomson, seeing the main chance, betrays his class and his fellow workers. His alienation becomes complete. In Armah's view, Koomson and his class, as rulers, are worse than their former white rulers. And they are worse, too, than those Ghanaians who hoped and expected to gain power when independence was achieved, a group of middle-aged Africans who had curried favor with the British as the transfer of political power approached. Armah's satiric treatment of this group verges on caricature:

They were lawyers before, something growing greasy on the troubles of people who worked the land, but now were out to be their saviours. Their brothers and their friends were merchants eating what was left in the teeth of the white men with their companies. . . . There is something so terrible in watching a black man trying at all points to be the dark ghost of a European. . . . How could they understand that even those who have not been anywhere know that the black man who has spent his life fleeing from himself into whiteness has no power if the white master gives him none? We knew then, as we know now, that the only real power that a black man can have will come from black people. The old lawyers and their rallies gave us one good thing to make our days less heavy, something we could laugh at. (95–97)

Nkrumah prevails against these men and leads Ghana to independence—and into the cycle of despair the novel describes. An irony here is that in seeking to bring into being a Ghana different from the colony controlled by overseas political and economic power, Nrkumah falls victim to the postcolonial fact that he, too, has no power except that conceded by the white man. The motives and means of international finance capitalism would destroy Nkrumah and his dream. Real Politik is different and more powerful than political idealism. Ramah, another in the man's small circle of disaffected friends, spends no time in the novel presenting the circumstances that conspired to destroy Nkrumah. He poses a series of questions to which no answers are provided. And this is a weakness in the novel, powerful as it is in describing the first seven years of Ghana's independence. Because of this, Armah's vision is seen as merely pessimistic. Firm as he is in creating the conditions in which the Ghanaian people live, whatever their social status, and whatever the implications of the coup d'etat as these will affect them, Armah posits, if anything, a bleak and repetitive future. As the novel closes, the man sees a police officer accepting a bribe from a lorry driver, a bribe the lorry driver expects to pay. Any recommendations for change of the system are made only by implication. For the most part, Armah describes what is rotten rather than proposes, by implication, what might be.

Despite the fact that the bitterness, anger, and pessimism at times almost reach despair, this is a deeply concerned book that defines with precision and castigates remorselessly political hypocrisy, opportunism, and corruption, as well as the illegitimate quest for and abuses of power. Armah describes an unequal society. Underneath the intense surface portrayal of a society gone hopelessly wrong, there is an idealism that provokes what for Armah is an honest accounting, one to be pondered as a protest on behalf of humanity. *The Beautyful Ones Are Not Yet Born* describes a pattern of betrayal that is repeated over and over again in African political life in works by Achebe, Soyinka, and Ngugi wa Thiong'o—to name only but the most prominent writers. However bitter and cynical the work may appear—and these charges are often made and sustained—Armah is a writer who cares and whose vision is ultimately idealistic.

ADDITIONAL READINGS

Achebe, Chinua. 1958. *Things Fall Apart*. London: Heinemann.

———. 1960. *No Longer at Ease*. London: Heinemann.

Armah, Ayi Kwei. 1968. *The Beautyful Ones Are Not Yet Born*. London: Heinemann.

———. 1970. *Fragments*. Boston: Houghton Mifflin.

———. 1972. *Why Are We So Blessed?* New York: Doubleday.

———. 1973. *The Healers*. Nairobi, Kenya: East African Publishing.

———. 1973. *Two Thousand Seasons*. Nairobi, Kenya: East African Publishing.

———. 1995. *Osiris Rising: A Novel of Africa, Past, Present and Future*. Popenquine, Senegal: Per Ankh.

Booker, M. Keith. 1998. *The African Novel in English: An Introduction*. Portsmouth, N.H.: Heinemann; Oxford: James Currey.

Fraser, Robert. 1980. *The Novels of Ayi Kwei Armah: A Study in Polemical Fiction*. London: Heinemann.

Lazarus, Neil. 1990. *Resistance in Postcolonial African Fiction*. New Haven, Conn.: Yale University Press.

Soyinka, Wole. 1963. *A Dance of the Forests*. Oxford: Oxford University Press.

Wright, Derek, ed. 1992. *Critical Perspectives on Ayi Kwei Armah*. Washington, D.C.: Three Continents Press.

Chapter 4
Miriama Ba:
So Long a Letter (1981)

Miriama Ba's *So Long a Letter* is as fine a book as has come out of Africa, unsurpassed in economy and allusiveness of expression by any other book except perhaps Chinua Achebe's *Things Fall Apart*. In fewer than 100 pages, Miriama Ba's *Letter* encompasses those issues and advocacies that concern other African writers. The brevity and intensity of her writing, the adumbration of allusions, the aphoristic nature of expression is the work of a keen, compassionate, and fully honest intelligence. An intensity of human life comes off the page in passages of narrative, dialogue, and reminiscences. Miriama Ba elaborates the epistolary genre to convey the drama of human emotions in the way a novelist would do, taking the reader through the fullness of her heroine's, life.

Miriama Ba disclaims the notion that personal experience has shaped the content of her *Letter*. Yet there is much to suggest that this is not strictly so. She was born in Dakar, Senegal, in 1929, a member of a prominent Senegalese family. Her father was Senegal's first minster of health when Senegal, under the leadership of Leopold Sedar Senghor, became independent from France in 1956. She was educated in Dakar and attended the Ecole Normal Teachers College, from which she was graduated with high honors in 1943. She became a primary school teacher and later an inspector of schools. She married a parliamentarian, and together, they had nine children before the marriage ended. She became an activist for women's rights. *So Long a Letter* (published in 1979 as *Une Si Longue Lettre*) won the first Noma Award for Publishing in Africa at the 1980 Frankfurt Book Fair. The

English translation of the book by Modupe Bode-Thomas was published in 1981. Miriama Ba died after a long illness in 1981. Her second novel, *Le Chant Ecarlate,* was published after her death in the same year. The English version was published in 1986 as *The Scarlet Song.*

Ramatoulaye is the heroine of *So Long a Letter.* The book takes the form of a letter to Aissatou, her childhood friend, now living in America; it is written at the time of Ramatoulaye's husband's death. The book is a recollection and reflection on her life, her marriage, the lives of her nine children, her relationships with family and other members of her community, and her emotional and psychological states of mind. She shares her innermost thoughts with Aissatou, who will soon visit Dakar. The book is written as a letter, but is made to encompass elements characteristic of the novella—narrative, description, monologue, and dialogue.

The setting of the book is Dakar at a time of rapid transition from colonial rule to independent status. Custom and tradition contend with modern, imported values. Customary religions and cultural values vie with Islamic proscriptions and Christian teachings, particularly with respect to marriage and sexual relations. Characters in the novella compete with each other for domination through three generations. Miriama Ba explores all of these intermingling connections in a book so dense with meaning, through statement and implication, that it almost defies dissection.

The time span encompassed by the letter is from Ramatoulaye's youth through 30 years of marriage to Modou (seen by Ramatoulaye's mother as "too perfect to be honest" [37]), the birth of 12 children, her desertion by Modou, his later death, and her efforts to fashion an independent life for herself and her family in the aftermath of his death.

Aissatou's life follows a path almost parallel to Ramatlouaye's. She, too, has married a professional man and had children with him. Mwado Ba, the husband, has, like Modou, deserted Aissatou for a younger woman. Taking second wives is condoned according to Islamic custom. These husbands subscribe to the words of Allah that "there is nothing one can do when Allah the Almighty puts two people side by side" (36). Equally, there is nothing one can do when Allah does the opposite. One principal concern of the *Letter* is to show how Islamic customs operate with respect to polygamous marriages and the responses of wives and women to the patriarchal authority that condones and supports these customs. Aissatou refuses to remain in a polygamous marriage, repudiates Mwado Ba, trains as an interpreter, and makes a new life for herself in the Senegalese Embassy in the United States.

Ramatoulaye remains married to Modou when he takes a second wife, a school friend of his daughter. But she withstands custom in her private life even while publicly honoring it at the time of Modou's funeral where custom requires that Modou's brother can expect to take Ramatoulaye in marriage. Ramatoulaye recognizes that she and Aissatou are "first pioneers of the promotion of African women" (14) in resisting male dominance.

Ramatoulaye resists the defense of Modou's desertion, that being that his actions are sanctified by Islam. She repudiates custom by refusing to marry Modou's brother. She further rejects the offer of marriage by an earlier suitor, Daoudu Dieng, because he will expect her to obey him in ways that are no longer acceptable to her. Ba, through Ramatoulaye's and Assaitou's actions, presents a case for the emancipation of women that was both original and bold for its time.

Ramatoulaye says to Aissatou in her letter that the issues of female emancipation they address in their actions, actions designed to lift them out of "the bag of tradition, superstition and custom" (15), are coincident with those of women across West Africa from Dahomey [*sic*: Benin] to Guinea who were "true sisters, destined for the same mission of emancipation" (15). She says, as well, that during their early schooling, they have been given initial inspiration and support in their quest by an enlightened and sympathetic French headmistress. In an essential way, *So Long a Letter* is a tribute to the teaching profession and the liberating effect of learning.

Opposed to the liberating effects of teaching, especially teaching by women, are both Islamic law and tradition. What Ramatoulaye contends with is the insistence on the part of its advocates that customary practices be maintained—that women and wives be treated as inferior to men and husbands, and that native law and custom are immutable. Devotees of Islam hold the same inflexible beliefs. Ramatoulaye and Aissatou challenge these beliefs and eventually prevail against them. And Miriama Ba illustrates the variation in these customary practices in current society through the experiences of other, and younger, women—Binetou, Modou's young second wife; young Nabou, Mwado's second wife; and Jacqueline, a Christian from the Ivory Coast who has married Samba Diach, a doctor friend of Modou's and a Muslim. The freedom in the lives of these young women is circumscribed by the bondage of custom. Binetou becomes Modou's chattel and his victim. Having ostracized Ramatoulaye and their children, Modou removes Binetou from school not only to circumvent the harmful effects of an education similar in influence to that received by Ramatoulaye and Aissatou, but also to maintain complete control over her. He also paid her 50,000 francs "as if it were a salary," (56) assigning to her a mere commercial value. In honoring custom, Modou stifles Binetou's life, rendering it useless. Islamic customs dictate Modou's treatment of Binetou. Similarly, tradition and custom account for the way in which Mwado's marriage to young Nabou evolves. Mwadi had married Aissatou against his mother's wishes. But when he decides to marry a second and younger wife, he appears to yield to his mother's insistence that he honor tradition to mask his purely personal desire to have a younger woman. Tante Nabou, the mother, has inherited a tradition which predates the period of colonization. She is heir to the glorious name of the Sine Drouf. She is an aristocrat and matriarch who holds in slight regard, if not outright contempt, lesser members of the community, the griots, even though they retain and pass on the oral history of the family and clan, and goldsmiths from which tradition Aissatou springs, Aissatou being considered "a woman who burns up everything in her path like a fire in a forge" (42). Tante Nabou uses tradition and hierarchy as a way of masking her own selfish desires. Young Nabou is allowed a limited education: she trains for and becomes a midwife, but all the while Tante Nabou maintains control over her with the observation that a woman does not need too much education—just enough, in this case, to bring some money into Tante Nabou's household. But Tante Nabou fears that young Nabou, like Aissatou before her, will gain enough education to cultivate a similar force of intellect and spirit.

The third victim of the dualities or pluralities of custom and belief is Jacqueline. A Christian from the Ivory Coast, Jacqueline marries against her parents' wishes. Samba Diack brings her to Senegal where she feels the pressure of Islamic conduct and is dismissed by her husband's family. Moreover, her marriage is a bad one: her husband is promiscuous and gradually abandons his wife and children. The pressure is too great, and Jacqueline endures a physical and spiritual collapse. She complains of swelling in her body and is subjected to an endless regime of medication and psychiatric care. Eventually she is reanimated when she is assured by the head of the hospital's neurology department that her problems are not physical but that of "mental alienation" (45). His recommendation is that she confront the source of her despair. Ba questions the attitudes and behavior of people in a society who can show such cruelty and indifference to a family member. She also questions the sometimes all too facile relevance of western medicine and its use of chemical treatments for complex personal problems. It is a measure of Ba's comprehensive delineation of her society that she can bring under close scrutiny all aspects of the cultural determinants that restrict women.

Ba offers two further instances of male-female relations to evoke the certainties, as well as the contradictions and ambiguities, of her world. These have to do with two of Ramatoulaye's daughters, Daba and Aissatou. Daba, the eldest of Ramatoulaye's children, is the classmate of Binetou. She scorns her friend and father and insists that her mother divorce Modou. Enlightened and ambitious like her mother, Daba gains a university degree, becomes engaged to marry a worthy man and, no slave to convention, creates for herself a world shaped only by her independent assessments and judgments.

Aissatou, named for her mother's best friend, becomes pregnant by Ibrahima Sell. At first, Ramatoulaye is angry—a residue of custom condemning premarital sex informs her response. She is also concerned that her daughter will be expelled from school when her pregnancy is made public knowledge. But when she learns that Ibrahima is a good man and will stand by her daughter, her anger dissipates and her fears are allayed. Aissatou and

Ibrahima prevail with the support of their parents. They are modern young people who understand and adapt to the swiftly changing world of modern Africa.

Chapter 27 offers a summing up of the experiences dramatized in the novel. Ramatoulaye is the agent of Ba's conclusions, conclusions that are an affirmation of her current life, a joyous affirmation of the gains made by women through education and individual courage, while recognizing that women are still "muzzled . . . by religion and unjust legislation" (88). Ba affirms, nevertheless, "the inevitable necessary complementarity of man and woman" (89), for this can prompt love, however imperfect, and will, in turn, account for the "success of family" (89) upon which the "success of a nation" inevitably depends. Ba's faith in the power of love is undeviating throughout the book. She recognizes that "life is an eternal compromise" (72) and that, through accepting this, one can move forward.

Interestingly, the agent of the continuity of human experience resides in "the power of books" (32), the repository of "Thought, History, Science, Life . . . the sole instrument of interrelationships and of culture . . . books knit generations together in the same continuing effort that leads to progress" (32).

So Long a Letter exemplifies Ba's claims for the power of the book, for what that power represents, and how that power can be moved from page to person.

ADDITIONAL READINGS

Achebe, Chinua. 1958. *Things Fall Apart*. London: Heinemann.

Ba, Miriama. 1980. *So Long a Letter*. London: Heinemann.

———. 1986. *The Scarlet Song*. Translated by Dorothy S. Blair. New York: Longman.

Cham, Mybe B. 1987. "Contemporary Society and the Female Imagination: A Study of the Novels of Miriama Ba." *African Literature Today* 15: 89–101.

Davies, Carol Boyce. 1986. "Motherhood in the Works of Male and Female Igbo Writers: Achebe, Emecheta, Nwapa and Nzekwu." In *Ngambika: Studies of Women in African Literature*, ed. Carole Boyce Davies and Anne Adams Grave, 241–246. Trenton, N.J.: Africa World Press.

Makward, Edris. 1987. "Marriage, Tradition and Woman's Pursuit of Happiness in the Novels of Miriama Ba." In *Ngambika: Studies of Women in African Literature*, ed. Carole Boyce Davies and Anne Adams Grave, 271–281. Trenton, N.J.: Africa World Press.

Chapter 5
Sembene Ousmane: God's Bits of Wood *(1962)*

Sembene Ousmane has had a distinguished career as both a novelist and a filmmaker. His best-known work of fiction is *God's Bits of Wood,* translated from the French *Les Bouts de Bois de Dieu* (1960) and published in English in 1962. His work in film dates from 1963. Thus, his two artistic activities run roughly concurrently. Unlike most of his writer peers, Sembene Ousmane had almost no formal education. He was born on January 1, 1923, in the fishing village of Ziguinichor in the southern province of Casamance in Senegal, at the time a colony of France. He had early training in the Muslim religion from an uncle who was a Koranic scholar. At age 12 he traveled to Dakar, the capital city of Senegal, and had a two-year period in French schools. He left formal education behind at age 14 and apprenticed as a mason. From that time forward, he worked in various occupations and trades—as a bricklayer, plumber, mechanic, fisherman, and dock worker. He continued his studies of the religion of Islam and also became involved with trade union activities. He fought in World War II in Europe and Africa as a member of the French Colonial military. He left the army in 1946. He was closely involved in the Dakar-Niger railway strike of 1947–48. He has lived for periods of time in both Senegal and Europe, mostly in France.

Ousmane draws on all his varied experience in his work as writer and filmmaker. His first novel, *Le Docker Noir,* was published in 1956 (and was published in English only in 1987 as *The Black Docker*). In this novel, Ousmane draws on his experiences of working on the docks of Marseilles to display the inequities between black and white stevedores. The novel is not generally highly regarded. It is, in a sense, an apprentice work where the many story lines and subplots are not brought into a coherent whole. But it does display an embryonic talent and addresses many of the issues that are fully shaped in Ousmane's masterpiece, *God's Bits of Wood*, where Ousmane displays an unflinching and undeviating concern with a number of intersecting public and personal issues—relations between whites and blacks, colonizers and colonized, rich and poor, youth and age, powerful and powerless.

Ousmane treats issues of race in his novels but only insofar as this informs the class struggle. He is concerned especially with the wide disparity between rich and poor, exploiter and exploited, considerations that overlap race.

Unlike most of his peers in the first generation of African writers, Ousmane is not much concerned with the legacy of the past. Some attention is paid to the accumulated wisdom of the elderly characters in the novel, but only as this is serviceable in the present. Ousmane's concern is with conditions—economic, political, social, and cultural—in the present and how these may be altered to improve the present, lead to a better future, and, especially, to rectify the wide disparity in the quality of lives of those whose labor for little reward creates wealth, privilege, and power for the few. His central position is Marxist and his analysis of conditions in Senegal (which he sees as needing massive change) develops along Marxist/Leninist lines.

Ousmane writes in French for the same reason Chinua Achebe writes in English. By using the language of the colonizer he can reach across local linguistic barriers to ensure that his writing, with its implied recommendations for social change, reaches the widest possible audience. The extent to which his audience is literate is, as *God's Bits of Wood* reveals, problematic; indeed, numerous references are made to the linguistic gulf that separates the French colonizers and colonized Africans. But interpreters and translators literate in French and the various African languages in the country close the gap to the extent that the broadest issues are made plain enough.

The setting of *God's Bits of Wood* is Senegal. The location of the novel moves between Dakar on the Atlantic Ocean coast in the west and Bamako in the east. At the center of the novel is the strike that halted traffic on the Dakar-Niger railway from October 9, 1947, to March 19, 1948. African workers were looking to achieve the same conditions of service as in an earlier strike in 1938. Their efforts were unsuccessful and the strike was brutally suppressed. The purpose of the current strike was to overthrow enormous inequities between Europeans and Africans working for the railway company, specifically to gain equality in salaries, to gain regular salary increases, family allowances, old age pensions, and acceptable housing.

The novel is often described as a prose epic, and "epic" here is a term used loosely to describe the heroic struggle of an oppressed people against what seem on the surface to be insurmountable odds. Ranged against the strikers are the forces of the French government—police, soldiers, the law. There are strike breakers and, worse still, apostate African religious leaders and businessmen who grow rich in their support of the colonial regime. Opposing the colonial government and its support of the railway company are a large number of supporters of the strike—railway workers, their families, and a wide range of characters in communities who suffer greatly for aligning themselves with the strikers.

Ousmane describes in detail the lives of many of these characters and the complexities of their relationships. He evokes the near-squalid conditions in which these people live in Dakar and Theis, the centers of the strike, and remains firmly on their side. After all, their cause had been his when he had participated in the strike. Drawing on his personal experience and matching his intellectual commitment as a Marxist to his command of the novel form, Ousmane dramatizes the sources of the strike and the difficulty of sustaining solidarity among the strikers and their families over a long period. Ousmane understands and conveys the variety, complexity, and intensity of the physical, emotional, and psychological demands the strike makes on his people. Eleven of 21 divisions in the novel are given to individual characters whose lives bear witness to the heavy cost of sustaining the strike.

The novel also portrays the determination of the French to maintain control of their colony. One finds here in the actions and speeches of various French characters the familiar racial assumptions about white versus black, superior versus inferior based on color and intellectual ability. Ousmane brings these white actions into focus in order to discount them. The Africans who work for the railway show that they have mastered the imported western technology that is altering their lives. And in mastering it, as Ousmane shows, they create for the owners of the railway wealth that they, the workers, do not share. The strike achieves in the end what the workers want: the government and the company are made to realize that they depend entirely on African workers to operate the railway, which will take their crops and the yield of their mines to markets beyond Africa.

The strikers achieve their goals but experience great personal hardship thereby. As the strike stretches out, food and water become scarce and starvation threatens; the distribution of what food there is is controlled by the French and the cost is prohibitive; rats and vultures become food stuff; people forage in refuse dumps for putrid scraps. Against this background of increasing stress and increasing violence, a detailed and balanced picture of human responses and courage is presented. The strength of the novel rests in large part on Ousmane's ability to keep in balance the public and personal experiences dramatized in the book.

Ousmane establishes the central issue in the opening pages of the novel through the musings of Niakoro, an aged woman of the community. A strike is being planned. Contrary to established custom, the opinions and advice of her age group have not been sought, even though she knows, from having seen the consequences of the earlier strike (what she describes as a "savage memory" [187]), that people of her age are likely to suffer the most when feelings are intensified and punitive actions are taken by the French. Niakoro is the first of the characters we meet, all of whom contribute to the strike.

The most prominent of these characters are Bakayoko, Doudou, and Lahib. These three men are the founders of the union and the organizers of the strike. Doudou is secretary-general, the leader who negotiates with the French authorities who, when they see the seriousness and solidarity of the workers, attempt at first to negotiate partial agreements. Lahib is the acknowledged intellectual leader of the triumvirate who easily engages in the dialectic with French authorities and transposes the intellectual foundation of the strike into terms used by Bakayoko in public meetings with his comrades.

Bakayoko is a charismatic leader. He travels the length of the railway line inspiring, supporting, and sustaining the strikers in achieving their goals. He is presented as an almost mythic figure, an epic hero, always appearing when negotiations with the French are at an impasse, always rallying his comrades when their spirits flag and when despair and capitulation are a possibility. His impassioned speeches at Keita and Dakar override French authority and eventually cause the collapse of their position and their agreeing to all of the strikers' demands.

Prominent among the French opposition are DeJean and M. Edouard. At first these men scorn the strike: they rely on the precedent that an earlier strike had been broken and that history will repeat itself given their legal and military authority. They enter into negotiations believing that their interests will prevail. But when union solidarity prevails, they attempt to win their cause with bribes to buy off union leaders. When bribes are offered, Doudou knows that the strikers will win. The strike seriously affects the economy of the country, and as profits begin to disappear, the French capitulate.

Matching in importance the role of the union leaders of the strike are a number of women whose actions, experience, and courage support and sustain the strike. The women suffer most greatly, but through their ingenuity and steadfastness, they overcome shortages of food and water to support each other and care for the men and children. They provide the ultimate support by organizing a painful yet triumphant march from Theis to Dakar. The march is prompted by the gratuitous insult offered them by the French who say that because they are members of a polygamous society sanctioned by Islam, they are not entitled to full family allowances as demanded by the strikers. They are called whores and concubines by the French, insults they will not endure. Their triumphant march, ending in a rally in Dakar attended by the governor of the colony, the mayor, and the deputy, places the final seal of success on the strike.

The strike proceeds in an atmosphere of escalating threat and violence. Colonial authorities, convinced in the way of all colonizing powers that they have brought civilizing elements to a people formerly bereft of them, insist on the rectitude of their actions while feeling, as the strike proceeds, scorned by the people they think they have helped, their altruism a shallow mask for the exploitative purposes of their administration. As they resort to greater and greater violence—women and children are killed, people are tortured in prison—it becomes clear that they fear a greater consequence than the strike. Reference is made to the creation of separate communities and states in the Congo and in South Africa to contain insurgents. But under all this is the real fear that to lose the strike is to eventually lose the colony, to see in the strike a prophecy of a successful independence movement. The French simply refuse to accept the fact that history is passing them by. *God's Bits of Wood* was published in the year of Senegal's independence from France.

Ousmane's novel is more than a backward glance celebrating the sacrifices and triumph of the strike and the multitude that supported it. It is that, of course. But it is a testament to the will of the people who seize the opportunity to right enormous wrongs. Ousmane is uncompromisingly on the side of the poor and exploited. His account of motive and action is balanced. The strength of the novel is in presenting the French position with full understanding so that the success of the strike is shown as the greater achievement.

Ousmane has gone on to publish more fiction and to make films about the postcolonial situation in Senegal. He, like many other African writers, most notably Achebe and Ngugi wa Thiong'o, sees in the actions of independent governments a betrayal of the people who brought them to power. *God's Bits of Wood* remains relevant in the present and demonstrates that the will of a people, motivated by the quest for justice, will prevail.

ADDITIONAL READINGS

Blair, Dorothy S. 1976. *African Literature in French: A History of Creative Writing in French from West and Equatorial Africa.* Cambridge: Cambridge University Press.

Irele, Abiola. 1981. *The African Experience in Literature and Ideology.* Exeter, N.H., and London: Heinemann.

Jones, James A. 2000. "Fact and Fiction in *Gods Bits of Wood.*" *Research in African Literature* 31 (2): 117–31.

Ousmanne, Sembene. 1962. *God's Bits of Wood.* Translated by Francis Price. Garden City, N.Y.: Doubleday.

———. 1987. *The Black Docker.* Translated by Ron Schwartz. London: Heinemann.

PART II
A SELECTED HISTORY OF
EAST AFRICAN LITERATURE

Literature in English in East Africa has its origins in the same processes as in West Africa. In the nineteenth century, adventurers, explorers, geographers, and agents of the imperial powers—Germany and England—and missionaries—John Speke, Richard Burton, H. M. Stanley, Sir Harry Johnston, David Livingstone—charted what are now Uganda, Kenya, and Tanzania and confirmed the regions' suitability for imperial expansion. Annexation of East African territories was confirmed in 1885 by the Treaty of Berlin; and colonization confirmed in Uganda in 1893, Kenya in 1895, and Zambia in 1924. Tanganyika, a colony of Germany until the close of World War I, became a mandated territory of the League of Nations in 1919 and subsequently a United Nations trust territory in 1946, continually administered during that time by the British. Uganda gained its independence in 1962, Kenya in 1963, and Zambia and Tanzania (Tanganyika joined in a political partnership with Zanzibar) in 1964.

The pattern of annexation and governance parallels that of West Africa with the essential differences being that while there was almost no settler population in West Africa, the colonial and postcolonial history of East Africa, especially Kenya, was shaped by a settler population, which annexed African lands and eventually brought about the struggle for independence, popularly called the Mau Mau Rebellion.

Kenya was the focus of the most urgent colonization. Large tracts of land were annexed from Kenyan communities and paid for with a pittance. Coffee, tea, and pyrethrum plantations produced crops that were taken from the rich farmlands of the interior and transported by rail to Mombassa on the Kenyan coast and shipped overseas. Labor was exploited and poorly paid as communities were driven from their ancestral lands.

Resistance, often in the form of guerilla war, was mounted by Kenyans from the 1890s forward. The lives and exploits of the leaders of these movements—Koilatel, Arap, Waiyaki, Harry Thuku, and Jomo Kenyatta—are recounted in the novels of Ngugi wa Thiong'o, supremely in *Petals of Blood*.

Kenyan militant resistance to the British (who controlled the colony legally and forcefully until 1963) reached its height in the Emergency, the so-called Mau Mau Rebellion, which lasted from 1952 to 1956. This independence movement was treated with the harshest measures by the British. Concentration camps were established and thousands of Kenyans were imprisoned without charge. Torture was a commonplace. Many prisoners were hanged without trial. Ultimately the Emergency was put down and its leaders put to death. Ngugi evokes these conditions in *Weep Not, Child; A Grain of Wheat; Petals of Blood;* and *Matagari*.

But by this time the winds of change were blowing through Africa. In 1964, Jomo Kenyatta, reputed to be the leader of the revolutionary forces, emerged as the first president of an independent Kenya. Kenyatta repudiated the forest fighters who forced the country's independence. His powerful denial is a source of Ngugi's scorn in the series of novels he published in the postindependence period.

The English language has had an uncertain position in East Africa, largely owing to Swahili being adopted as the official language in Kenya and Tanzania, as well as being a powerful presence in Uganda. Because Swahili is in formal competition with English, and because of the shared teaching of languages in primary and secondary schools and the relatively small departments of English Language and Literature at the University of East Africa (which divided into its constituent colleges to achieve independent university status in 1970 in Nairobi, Kampala, and Dar es Salaam), literary activity in English languished in East Africa compared to that of West Africa.

What English language training there was was dictated by governmental and commercial needs and so English was taught for practical purposes and not for artistic purposes. As well, English was used in the Christian churches to prepare parishioners, as Taban Lo Liyong wryly observes, "at recruiting candidates for a Christian Heaven and eliminating others for a Christian Hell . . . " (10). His countryman, Leonard Okola, noting the quick rise of literary production in West Africa, suggested in 1967 that literary production in East Africa will begin when the problems and emotions associated with the gaining and using of independence have settled down. What Okola suggested has come to pass: there is now a substantial body of writing in English. The debate about the uses of English as opposed to African languages continues and some writers, most notably Ngugi, have turned to their own languages for purposes of literary expression.

Ngugi wa Thiong'o (first known as James Ngugi) initiated the modern tradition in writing from East Africa (Kenya, Uganda, and Tanzania) with the publication in 1964 of his first novel, *Weep Not, Child*. He remains East Africa's best-known novelist, although the writing of M. G. Vassanji has now taken a place of prominence in writing about that part of the world, which represents the countries of East Africa and its myriad sensibilities.

From the publication of Ngugi's first novel in 1964, 44 writers—novelists, poets, and playwrights—have seen their work into print, not large numbers when compared with writers from the West Coast of the continent, but given the disparity in populations and the presence of Swahili, as has been noted, the body of writing in English is now relatively substantial.

Ngugi's second novel, *The River Between*, was published in 1965, the same year that Barbara Kimenye published *Kasalanda*, followed in 1966 by *Kasalanda Revisited*. These are collections of short fictions that describe the variety of life in a Ugandan village under the sway of colonial rule. Kimenye evokes the subtle tensions in the village, particularly the tension between traditional conservatism and the radicalism introduced by the colonial—that is, western—presence. The stories, displaying the complexity and variety of village life, suggest a hope for stability and gradualism in an environment that slowly and, viewed historically, inevitably gave way to disruption and political and social chaos. The stories in the two volumes are interesting now for their presentation of gentler times. Barbara Kimenye also published ten books for young readers, five of which describe the life of Moses, a young boy growing up in Kenya.

After Ngugi, the most prominent writer from East Africa is the Ugandan writer and scholar, Okot pBitek. Okot pBitek draws his inspiration from his Oculi culture in Uganda. In 1966 he published *Song of Lawino*. Okot (he is generally known by his first name) developed a new and unique form of literary expression. *Song of Lawino* tells the story of a disaffected wife, Lawino, as she watches her husband, Ocol, make himself ridiculous by adopting the most superficial of western values to shape his life. Through Lawino, Okot offers shrewd, often humorous comment on the influences, revealed through the behavior of Ocol, of Christianity, education, and commercial activities. *Song of Lawino* incorporates songs of praise and celebration, dirges, and laments, which Okot combines to offer both direct and indirect comment on the tranquility and honesty of the village set against the corrupting influences of the modern (western) city, including the corrupting consequences of the pursuit of money. In other words, Okot portrays the conflicting forces in Acoli (read African) society that are the results of colonization.

Song of Lawino is Lawino's lament and, as such, is one-sided in the scorn it heaps on Ocol. Ocol is given his chance for rebuttal in *Song of Ocol* (1970). But Ocol, a member of the western-oriented academic community, makes the best use of his position by describing the benefits of western education and, superceding that, the inevitability of the historical forces in which all Ugandans are caught up. He advises that people make the best uses of what is given, there being no chance to reverse the flow of history. Ocol's *Song* is not an outright affirmation of the uses of western things— particularly education, commerce, and religion. Rather, because it is juxtaposed with Lawino's lament, we should read it as a questioning, a plea to consider the forces at work in society and to derive the best that can be attained from these influences.

Okot also published two more "songs": *Song of a Prisoner,* an examination of the unrealized hopes implicit in "Uhuru," the Swahili word for "freedom" or "independence" and *Song of Malaya,* a story of the implications and complications arising out of the rapid urbanization that took place in the postindependence period. Okot is especially concerned to present the opinion regarding sexual relations, the traditional conviction being that sexual activity should be aimed at the perpetuation of the family and the clan and the more modern opinion being that which sanctions casual sex. *Song of Malaya* looks seriously at how the latter attitude may increase prostitution, with its disintegrative and debilitating personal and social effects. Indeed the "malaya" of the song's title means "prostitution."

Okot is a serious social critic whose writing and teaching career was devoted to drawing from his own culture those values and practices that could enhance the quality of life of his people and, by implication, the peoples of East Africa. Okot, therefore, published a number of formal academic studies, all of which demonstrate in various ways his perceptions of the fundamental opposition between African and non-African (mostly European) rights and freedoms, both societal and individual.

Grace Ogot was a contemporary of Okot and published her first novel in the same year as *Song of Lawino.* East African's first woman novelist, she has published two novels, *The Promised Land* (1966) and *The Island of Tears* (1980); two collections of short stories, *Land without Thunder* (1968) and *The Other Woman* (1976); a novella, *The Graduate* (1980), and a rendering of a myth drawn from her Luo background, *Miaha* (1983).

The Promised Land tells the story of a young farmer and his wife who migrate to Tanzania and get caught up in a network of tribal animosities that compromise their lives. Ogot castigates the rampant materialism of the times, which is seen as responsible for the greed and jealousy that infects the village where the young couple locate. As well, Ogot presents what can be seen as an ideal—perhaps idealized—portrait of the wife, a woman who obeys her husband, who shares his commitment to his family and his community, and who attempts to avoid the acquisitiveness she sees around them.

Ogot's short stories draw on both urban and rural experiences where the author describes and dramatizes the tensions between the two types of communities. Like her East African author peers, Ogot mourns the loss of rural values as vested in the village while recognizing that she must confront the inevitable fact of progressive urbanization. Ogot's style is often flat and her characters wooden. But the writing is redeemed, to some extent, by the levels of irony she employs.

Samuel Kahiga published *Potent Ash* (1968), a collection of short stories, with his brother, the novelist Leonard Kibera. The stories, which focus for the most part on the Kenya Emergency and the war of independence, deal with the causes of the various social conflicts in contemporary Kenya and the lives of individuals circumscribed by these conflicts, while at the same time showing the individual's helplessness in resolving the conflicts.

Kahiga published two novels, *The Girl from Abroad* (1974) and *When the Stars Are Scattered* (1979), which describe various difficulties in love relationships that have their origins in generational differences, educational disparity, or religious differences. Kahiga is sensitive and neutral in exploring the personal lives of his characters. He published *Flight to Juba* in 1979, a collection of short stories about young people growing up in Kenya.

Peter Palangyo in known for only one novel, *Dying in the Sun* (1968), and was for a long time Tanzania's only published novelist. The hero of the novel is Ntanya, and he, like so many other heroes and heroines of African writing, experiences the pull between western values and those of his village. Ntanya is called back to his village when his father dies. It is his duty to attend to the mourning and funeral duties. The father, however, was a brutish man, much despised by his fellow villagers and feared by his son. He was responsible for his wife's death, and for this alone Ntanya hates him. Nevertheless Ntanya honors custom. His return to his pastoral early years gives him the opportunity to reflect on the contrasts between the life he lives as an educated man away from his village and the values he sees in rural life as promoting and sustaining peace, tranquility, and love. The novel records Ntanya's introspective journey. As such it is at odds with most of the writing coming out of East Africa in its time, avoiding entirely the large social issues arising in the aftermath of colonialism.

Okello Oculi is another in the list of writers—Ngugi, Okot, Lo Liyong, and Kibera—whose works are concerned to dramatize the disparities between tradition and modernity, village and city life, particularly the values associated with each pairing as these may promote happiness and health as opposed to alienation and despair.

In his first published work, *Orphan* (1968), Oculi tells the story of an orphaned village boy whose life is compromised by the alienating affect of western values. The boy and the village are seen as representing Uganda and the tension in the book arises from the inability of the villagers to confront the alienating force and preserve much of what is valued in tradition. Oculi, like Okot, employs a variety of literary devices and styles—prose, poetry, song, proverbial materials, colloquial and stylized speech—to reveal the multitude in his literary landscape.

Oculi's next book, *Prostitute* (1968), which employs many of the same literary techniques, tells of the hard life of a prostitute in the squalid slums of the modern city. Oculi eschews western values and deplores the complacency that allows slums like those he depicts to grow. At times, Oculi's language is lyrical. For the most part, however, it is the hard language of social commentary. *Malak* (1977) was inspired by the horrors committed by Idi Amin and is a sustained protest against oppression, especially the kind that became more and more typical of military regimes in postindependence African states. Finally, *Kookalem* (1976) is the story of Kookalem, a village woman whose life is one of unremitting suffering. The tone is mordant but Oculi's compassion for his heroine, and for those whose circumstances are like hers, is unstinting.

Robert Serumaga published his only work of fiction, *Return to Shadows,* in 1969. It is a literary and cultural landmark in Uganda. The novel employs a complicated narrative framework (at times confusing because of the shifts in time and location the author employs) to encompass all those themes that became familiar in African literature—the struggle for the survival of democracy when beset by a series of military coups, the story of personal tragedies arising from police and military brutality, the shifting values of African society when custom and tradition contend with modernizing forces, and the greed arising from apostasy in the ruling classes, whether civilian or military. Joseph Musizi is the central character in a large cast of characters. He is educated overseas in London and is a lawyer and an economist. He is also a humanist, a man with the vision and training to foster a just society. But given the political climate and the avarice that inform the country, Musizi's vision is doomed. Serumaga presents a bleak yet honest picture of his Uganda. His novel is of historical as well as literary importance.

Gabriel Ruhumbika has published one novel in English, *Village in Uhuru* (1969), and two works in Swahili, abandoning English like Ngugi, his counterpart in Kenya. Political issues interest Ruhumbika and, in a novel of wide historical sweep, he raises such pressing issues affecting Tanzania as the conflict between traditional rulers and their councils and the intentions of the Tanganyika African National Union. The conflict in the book is vested in the tragic relationship between a traditional village headman and his son. The son advocates imposing modern methods of agriculture on a community existing at near poverty level. To achieve his aims the son sees that it might mean relocating an entire community. His plan is seen as lacking in compassion by the conservative villagers. The methods for reform displayed in the novel by Ruhumbika reflect Tanzania's advocacy of *Ujama*, African socialism. But Ruhumbika has not written a political tract, much as politics is the ground beat in the novel and though his skepticism over TANU policies shows through. In the final analysis *Village in Uhuru* is a compassionate book in dealing with human hopes and fears and relationships.

Leonard Kibera published *Potent Ash*, a short-story collection, with his brother, Samuel Kahiga, in 1968. He is best known for his one novel, *Voices in the Dark* (1970), arguably, after Ngugi's and Vassanji's fiction, the best novel written by a Kenyan. Like Ngugi in *Petals of Blood* and *Matagari*, Kibera condemns the betrayal of those who fought for Kenya's independence, a betrayal engineered by an emerging comprador bourgeoisie. The former freedom fighters are scorned, viewed as a national embarrassment, and consigned to the dung heaps of Nairobi. The bourgeoisie grows rich in their betrayal of the independence struggle by exploiting peasants and raping the country's resources. Kibera anticipates in his depiction of the collusion of church and state a theme more fully explored by Ngugi. Kibera's central character is Gerald Timundu, a playwright of modest success through whom Kibera explores the central role of the artist in pointing out the progressive dehumanization of society and, both by implication and direct statement, the need for justice. Kibera mixes anger and humor in conveying his concern for the dispossessed and disaffected.

Nuruddin Farah is, along with Ngugi, Lo Liyong, and pBitek, a major East African writer. He is the author of nine novels, all of which have attracted considerable critical attention, both because of the personal problems he deals with in his books and the innovative forms he derives to convey his stories.

From a Crooked Rib (1970) is set in Italian Somaliland and tells the story of Ebla and her various marriages and near-marriages. Ebla's society regards women as mere possessions, fit only to serve the needs of men. Farah's story shows how Ebla survives and retains her independence.

A Naked Needle (1976) deals with problems faced by a man, Koschin, a Somali teacher, and an Englishwoman, Nancy. Their marriage runs parallel to that of another couple in a mixed marriage in an ever-heightening revolutionary atmosphere in Mogadishu. Koschin chooses to ignore the worsening political situation, which allows Farah to interpolate into his domestic text satirical sketches of the new power-mongers.

In *Sweet and Sour Milk* (1979), Farah writes a crime thriller, creating a fictional world full of spies, brutal security officers, and informers in a totalitarian state. He exposes the dichotomy between traditional and modern beliefs and practices. Hoyaan is the central character in the novel and the book focuses on his search for his missing brother, Soyaan. His search leads him through the labyrinths of state political reality. His brother's disappearance is deliberately cloaked in ambiguity and Hoyaan remains frustrated at the novel's close. Obviously Hoyaan is a kind of everyman in a totalitarian state.

In *Sardines* (1981), Farah again deals with the plight of women in a state where the traditional practices make women passive and subservient. Medina, the book's heroine, abandons her weak husband, Sameter, and his domineering mother to make her own way in the world. In Farah's view, as implied in the novel, traditional oppression of women is analogous to state oppression of the general citizenry.

Close Sesame (1983) offers an alternative view of Somali society to that presented in *Sweet and Sour Milk* and *Sardines*. The three novels are meant in fact to be taken together as a trilogy under the title *Variations on the Theme of African Dictatorship*. The book tells the story of Deerye, a hero of the struggle for independence, who is forced to abandon his peaceful life in old age and die in a futile attempt to save his son, who is killed in a plot to overthrow an increasingly oppressive dictatorial regime.

Farah's sixth novel, *Maps* (1986), deals with issues, both personal and public, associated with the Ogaden War of 1977. Farah adopts a mythical and allegorical framework, which conveys through his hero, Askar, a man born of a Somali father and Ogadenese mother, the indeterminacy and futility of war.

Gifts (1992) is a love story that unfolds against the background of a country in a state of civil war. The title is ironic as the novel deals with the nature of the donorship offered to poor countries by international aid grant agencies. Farah suggests that the gift of aid is like the gift of love (thus the admixture in the plot of the public and private themes): it breeds debts and dependencies. It is, therefore, an ambiguous gift.

Secrets (1998) again uses the background of war engendered by long-standing tribal hatreds to show the confused and sometimes dangerous judgments made by people in a war. Against this background is the story of Kalaman, the child born of the rape of his mother by rival tribesmen. The central figure, however, is Sholoongo, a mysterious women who possesses the secret understanding of the lives of the people in Kalaman's life. But the secret is ultimately not revealed.

Charles Mangua published *Son of Woman* in 1971. The hero of the book is Dodge Kinunyu, a denizen of modern Nairobi, whose purpose in life seems to be only to enjoy the manifold pleasures the city has to offer to those who have the cash to sustain them. Dodge goes from adventure to adventure always dodging, as his name implies, any bitter consequences of his actions. Dodge appears in Mangua's second novel, *A Tail in the Mouth* (1972), where he continues his adventures and remains a vehicle for Mangua to exploit his hero's adventures for popular acclaim.

Mangua is the first in a series of writers who use popular fiction to cater to the tastes and expectations of their readers. Such fiction, like the movies, is always a shrewd guide to popular tastes and values. Adventure stories and crime thrillers fall in to this category of writing. Their historical significance lies in showing what popular values obtained in their time of writing. But because they cater to what *is* they tend not offer any sort of enlightenment. A measure of the demand for this kind of writing is that Mangua, an officer with the African Development Bank, sold ten thousand copies of his first novel in six months and fifteen thousand copies of the second book in only two months.

Other writers associated with Mangua are John Karoki, Stephen Ngubia, Geoffrey Kalimugogo, Yosuf K. Dawood, Meji Mwangi, and, the most successful of all, David Maillu. These writers deal with familiar—often stereotypical—characters in familiar, mostly urban settings, pursuing easy sex, easy money, and fleeting fame. There is usually a sensational element in the writing.

Superficial as these writers' works may be, lacking in psychological complexity as are their characters, they do depict the social mores of a real world. In their own way, they are as invaluable to students of cultural studies as are the more serious writers of their communities.

Austin Bukenya has a more serious intention in his novel, *The People's Bachelor* (1972). The novel is set on the campus of the East African University College of Dar es Salaam where Bukenya was a student. The novel is probably a *roman a clef* and like all campus novels provides a satiric comment on campus life. So, here we have the sexually insatiable white professor of the department and the coy African woman student suggesting she will trade sex for academic favors. The principal of the college, it is revealed, actually had earned the title of "Dr." that he uses. Beneath the teasing satire and ribald humor, Bukenya has the serious purposes of exposing failed opportunities in an institution that is meant to foster leaders of the nation at the time of independence. Like all satire, Bukenya's novel is selective in choosing his targets and exaggerates their behavior for the purposes of making the telling point.

One of only two East African Asian writers (the other being M. G. Vassanji), Peter Nazareth first became involved in literary pursuits when at Makerere University College in Uganda, where he edited the students' literary magazine, *Penpoint*. He wrote plays, which were broadcast on the BBC Africa Service, and published in *East Africa: A Makerere Anthology*, edited by David Cook, in 1965. His novel, *In a Brown Mantle* (1972), forecasts the military coup d'etat of Idi Amin and the expulsion of the Asians that followed. Nazareth's second novel, *The General Is Up* (1991), deals with the terrifying cruelties of Amin's reign.

Nazareth is a serious and concerned writer and a much-respected literary critic who argues for the central place of literature studies in the community. He has also done much to draw attention to the writing of his peer authors in East Africa, continuing this quest from his base in the United States where he teaches.

Meja Mwangi is a rare exception in East African writing: he is a popular writer who deals with serious social issues. He is a social realist. His manner of presentation aims at bridging the gap between serious writing, which aims at increasing an awareness of human potential, and popular fiction, which confirms what is already known but which, from Mwangi's perspective, needs reform.

Mwangi's novels span the Emergency period in Kenya, by which Kenya eventually won its independence from Britain, through to the immediate postindependence period to the present. His novels dealing with the Emergency are *Carcass for Hounds* (1974) and *Taste of Death* (1975). These novels forcefully convey the suffering of the freedom fighters and that of those who are their opponents, and especially those who, for various reasons, were nonaligned in the struggle. These are novels of action, and as such characterization is slight almost to the point of stereotype. But the period the novels describe was one that called for psychological introspection on the part of the participants engaged in war. In simple terms, Mwangi shows his people caught up in serving social and political causes that they but vaguely understand. However, the author knows—and history has confirmed—that the outcome of the struggle affects the fate of the nation.

The same characteristics of form and characterization and the same treatment of subject matter informs the novels that followed. *Kill Me Quick* (1973), *Going Down River Road* (1976), *The Cockroach Dance* (1979), and *Weapon of Hunger* (1989) deal in various ways with the homeless, hungry majority who live in hopeless states in Nairobi slums; ignored by the leaders of the state, they often turn to crime in order to survive.

Mwangi turns away from implicit social commentary in *The Bushtrackers* (1979), a crime thriller about poaching in East African game reserves. *Bread of Sorrow* (1987) is also written in the crime thriller mode and tells the story of a good, naive man who turns to a life of crime in order to survive. Some of the psychological insights Mwangi offers into the criminal mind, especially as these affect personal relationships, place the novel in the familiar genre of the psychological thriller.

The Return of Shaka (1989) invokes the spirit of the legendary Zulu leader in a tale of armed resistance set in then contemporary South Africa. *Weapon of Hunger* is a story about the activities of relief agencies in a time of drought and famine. His central character is a rock 'n' roll artist turned philanthropist. The serious examination of the ways in which relief efforts are compromised gives the book, despite certain melodramatic elements, a serious intent.

And Mwangi adopts once again a serious tone, providing psychological insight lacking in his earlier books, in *Striving for the Wind* (1990). In the book, Mwandi provides a fictional analysis, implicit in the action of his characters, about the capabilities of humans, individually and collectively, to rise above and to reform conditions that inhibit their lives and render them all but helpless. For the most part, despite occasions when he lapses, as it were, into purely popular writing, Mwangi is a serious writer, a relentless advocate for the poor and for the amelioration of the sordid circumstances in which so many Kenyans are made to live.

Rebecca Njau is only the second woman writer in the East African canon. The "pool" of the title of her only novel, *Ripples in the Pool* (1975), is symbolic of the life force of traditional Kikuyu belief, a statement about the value of traditions that have been forgotten or neglected by a young generation who prefers the excitement and enticements of things modern. Njau mixes reality and fantasy as she treats a variety of themes familiar in modern African writing; as well as the attraction of the new as opposed to values inherent in tradition, she deals with questions about the alienation of the land and the dispossession of the peasantry, the corrupt city and its corrupting influences on a young generation. The novel centers on the life of Selina, a village woman forced into prostitution, and her quest to retrieve her lost innocence. She turns to the village of her husband, Gaciru, and with the assistance of a friend, Kariga, attempts to lay to rest a curse placed on her forefathers. The novel ends in tragedy as young lovers, symbolic of hope for the future, are killed by Selina. The meaning of the book is ambiguous—the reader is not certain what the pool and its influence stands for; the death of the young couple seems at odds with Selina's initial purposes in returning to her village. Her response may be atavistic.

Njau has written plays—she was Kenya's first woman playwright—short stories, a collection of folktales, and a book whose title tells its obvious intent: *Kenyan Women Heroes and Their Mystical Power* (1984).

Abdulrazak Gurnah has published five novels beginning with *Memory of Departure* (1987). Set in an unnamed coastal town in East Africa, it tells the story of a population's concerns at the time of independence and how these shape the life of a young man in making a decision to eventually leave his community. The novel is told in the first person, and thus some autobiographical experiences may be transmuted into the text.

The same may be said about Gurnah's second novel, *Pilgrim's Way* (1988). It is the story of Daud, a Muslim born in Tanzania, and his attempts to come to terms with life in the provincial English town where he goes to study. There is much wit in Daud's confronting the philistine culture he finds in Britain, especially in the imaginary letters he writes. Determination is mixed with nostalgia as Daud tries to prevail over his difficulties.

The same concerns inform *Dottie* (1990) where, against a background of racial tensions, questions of belonging and thus the finding of personal identity are mused on by the eponymous heroine.

Gurnah's fourth novel, *Paradise* (1994), was shortlisted for the 1994 Booker Prize. Gurnah writes a much deeper and in some respects darker novel than his earlier works, drawing on storytelling, religions, and myths from both African and European literary traditions to tell the story of Yusuf, a boy who travels with his uncle Aziz, a merchant, on dangerous trading missions into the interior of the country. Yusuf prevails over difficulties that sorely test him and comes of age, achieving a full rite of passage.

In his latest novel, *Admiring Silences* (1996), Gurnah tells of the marriage of a Zanzibari man and English woman. He writes nostalgic and romantic stories of the Africa he remembers, an Africa totally at odds with the Africa he finds on return to his country.

All Gurnah's novels deal with questing figures, searching for an identity that will provide security and peace in their troubled lives.

M. G. Vassanji has established himself through his publication of six novels and a collection of short stories as a major African writer. His subject matter is the Asian experience of being born and living in East African countries—Kenya and Tanganyika/Tanzania—or reflecting on this legacy when living abroad. Vassanji is the finest authentic voice of Asian Africans and adds to East African literature in particular and African literature in general a dimension that only a writer of consummate power can provide.

The Gunny Sack (1989) tells the story of East Africa over four generations of Indians. The story begins in 1885 when Dhanji Govindji arrives at the village of Matamu in the Kilwa region of present-day Tanzania. Dhanji has traveled from Junapur in northwest India, with breaks in Muscat and Zanzibar. In Matamu, Dhnaji founds a family with the help of the local Mukhi. The history of the family is told by his great grandson, the heir of Dhanji and an African slave mother. The book's narrator is Huseni, who has taken the name of his African grandfather, Salim Juma. He is inspired to tell the story of his family when he discovers the gunny sack, the most prized possession of his grandaunt, Ji Bai. The gunny sack is the repository of family history, a Pandora's box of memories and mementos and operates as the organizing metaphor of the novel. The memorabilia that Salim takes from The gunny sack refresh his memories of the oral history of the family and cause him to dig further into the causes and effects of events associated with the the gunny sack's contents.

Vassanji's novel is the first to give a fully representative fictional accounting of the Indian/Asian association with East Africa. His account begins in the imaginary town of Matamu, dramatizing a variety of historical realities: German colonization and encroachment, after the Treaty of Berlin in 1884, on the indigenous population, Asian and African alike; the abortive Maji Maji Rebellion; the process of the movement toward independence of the East African colonies of Britain and Germany; the rise of TANU, the Tanganyika National Union; the dominating presence of Julius K. Nyerere and the Ujamaa period; the political pact with Zanzibar, which saw the creation of Tanzania; and the final alienation of the Asian community first through Idi Amin's appropriation of Asian possessions in Uganda, continuing with its spillover effect in Tanzania.

These are the historical points in time that frame the narrative. The novel records the ascension of the family though vision, hard work, and enterprise to a position of wealth and influence. They nevertheless have to live with shame because of Dhanji's theft of communal wealth. Dhanji has been driven to find his African son. The family reputation is ultimately restored through Gulam's death in a car accident: Gulam becomes a missionary martyr, which saves the family name, thereby opening the door to their later prosperity.

Vassanji provides a genealogical table of the families whose stories he tells. Some 30 people are mentioned, dating from Dhanji's liaison with Bibi

Taratibu, the African slave woman. Another 30 members of family arise from his marriage to Fatima, the daughter of a Zanzibari widow. Part of Vassanji's purpose is doubtless to show through his tracing of the history of Asian presence and enterprise in East Africa that the Asian community is in every essential way African. The history of the heirs of Dhanji, evoked through the mementos of the gunny sack, is a recognition of and tribute to the ancestors whose stories must be told. The lives of the various members of the family are revealed in intimate detail. Yet there is a quality of objectivity, a distance between the author and his people. And there is, too, the sense that in some respects the Asian community still views the land as alien. Placed by the British in entrepreneurial roles in East Africa, Asians were made to pay a heavy price in the postcolonial period, having to witness and, in some cases, participate in the earthshaking events that overtook their communities. The narrator, for instance, spends a period of time in the army. But overall, the Asian community maintains a distance from the hard political times in which the countries are embroiled. As Salim notes, his political activities were those of an observer: he was not part of the hard-core activists. And he notes that political insurgents are gathered up at one point in the narrative, there is only one Asian among them. The book advocates just such a disinterested stance, implying the author's conviction that an attempt to remake a country through the excesses of student activity is merely an "exercise run wild."

The narrative concludes with the Asian exodus from the homeland. The author equates "destiny" and "irony" as joint components of Asian experience and history as the gunny sack reveals it. The book concludes with the statement that "to have dreamed was enough." Salim says that redemption may lie in a dream and a faith in the future. We must, he says, "pick up the pieces of our wounded selves . . . because from our wounded selves flowers still grow" (276).

The Book of Secrets (1994) amplifies Vassanji's perception of East African history. The book spans almost a century and evokes the diverse communities of East Africa, the conflict between colonizing forces and the effects of colonial rule as East Africans work toward achieving independence. The novel is about a diary that Pius Fernandes, a retired Goan teacher living in Dar es Salaam, finds in 1988. The diary, written in 1913, belongs to Alfred Corbin, once an English colonial officer in East Africa. Its discovery helps to reveal events that lead Pius to consider his Asian community's history in East Africa, the colonial tensions in which the community was caught up, and his own sense of failure. The narrative alternates between excerpts from the Corbin diary, Pius's reflection on them, and his investigation into the events the diary describes. Interwoven with these are excerpts from the notebook Pius keeps.

Through the diary, Pius learns of the Shansi community of Kikono, a town on the border between Kenya and Tanganyika, where live the kind of Europeans who administered colonial law in the town (and by implication the country) and his own links with Kikono. The meaning of some of the events in his life becomes clear to Pius, particularly his ambiguous connections with Rita, who does not respond to his love and who has been intimately linked to Kikono. The diary also raises issues that remain out of Pius's reach.

The book's evocation of colonial and postcolonial history, both public and personal, is more intimate than that of *The Gunny Sack*. While Vassanji's panorama of East Africa is widened in *The Book of Secrets*, it is extended even further by an almost epic treatment in *The In-Between World of Vikram Lall* (2003). The novel begins at the time of Kenya's independence and, as with Vassanji's earlier novels, moves backward and forward in time. Against the events of the time (the Emergency period in which Africans challenged in a guerilla war the rights of British colonial rule, moved toward independence, and evolved under national rule), the novel traces the lives of three principal characters: Vic, the eponymous hero of the title, his sister Deepa, and Bill and Annie, British children and their African friend, Njoroge. The story is told retrospectively by Vic, now living in exile from Kenya in a small Ontario town, who says he's "been numbered one of Africa's most corrupt men," no small claim in a continent characterized in the postindependence era as a series of national "kleptocracies."

In Vassanji's world, Kenya is a land of violent upheaval, characterized by conflicting ideologies, uncertain loyalties, and easy and accommodating morality. Kenya's corrupt public morality in the immediate postindependence period affects the main characters in various ways. Njoroge remains an idealist, incapable of abandoning his youthful dreams of a burgeoning independent Kenya. Nor can he abandon his love for Deepa. Corruption, repression, and violence swiftly overtake the country in the 1960s and 1970s and Vic becomes embroiled in them. The novel dramatizes the worsening atmosphere of these years by entering the hearts and minds of Vic and Deepa and Njoroge and accounting for their choices and their fate. Vassanji engages his materials more comprehensively than in the earlier two books and at the same time more fully displays the lives and thoughts of the central, and representative, characters. The retrospective telling is what accounts for the convincing world he re-creates in the novel. Not even Ngugi, still the major voice among East African writers, shows more forcefully how public and personal histories intersect in the face of historical determinants.

ADDITIONAL READINGS

Booker, M. Keith. 1998. *The African Novel in English: An Introduction.* Portsmouth, N.H.: Heinemann; Oxford: James Currey.

Bukenya, Austin. 1972. *The People's Bachelor.* Nairobi, Kenya: East African Publishing House.

Cohen, David William. 1994. *The Combing of History*. Chicago: University of Chicago Press.

Farah, Nuruddin. 1970. *From a Crooked Rib*. London: Heinemann.

———. 1976. *A Naked Needle*. London: Heinemann.

———. 1979. *Sweet and Sour Milk*. London: Alison and Busby.

———. 1981. *Sardines*. London: Alison and Busby.

———. 1983. *Close Sesame*. London: Alison and Busby.

———. 1986. *Maps*. London: Pan.

———. 1992. *Gifts*. London: Pan.

———. 1998. *Secrets*. New York: Arcade Publishing.

Gurnah, Abdulrazak. 1987. *Memory of Departure*. London: Cape.

———. 1988. *Pilgrim's Way*. London: Cape.

———. 1990. *Dottie*. London: Cape.

———. 1994. *Paradise*. London: Hamish Hamilton.

———. 1996. *Admiring Silences*. London: Hamish Hamilton.

Kahiga, Samuel, with Leonard Kibera. 1968. *Potent Ash*. Nairobi, Kenya: East African Publishing House.

———. 1974. *The Girl from Abroad*. London: Heinemann.

———. 1979. *Flight to Juba*. Nairobi. Longhorn Publishers.

———. 1979. *When the Stars Are Scattered*. Nairobi, Kenya: East African Publishing House.

Kibera, Leonard. 1970. *Voices in the Dark*. Nairobi, Kenya: East African Publishing House.

Killam, G. D. 1984. *The Writing of East and Central Africa*. London: Heinemann.

Kimenye, Barbara. 1965. *Kasalanda*. London: Oxford University Press.

———. 1966. *Kasalanda Revisited*. London: Oxford University Press.

Mangua, Charles. 1971. *Son of a Woman*. Nairobi, Kenya: East African Publishing House.

———. 1979. 1972. *A Tail in the Mouth*. Nairobi: East African Publishing House.

Mwangi, Meja. 1973. *Kill Me Quick*. Nairobi, Kenya: Heinemann Educational.

———. 1974. *Carcass for Hounds*. Nairobi, Kenya: Heinemann.

———. 1975. *Taste of Death*. Nairobi, Kenya: East African Publishing House.

———. 1976. *Going Down River Road*. Nairobi, Kenya: Heinemann.

———. 1979. *The Bushtrackers*. Nairobi, Kenya: Longman.

———. 1979. *The Cockroach Dance*. Nairobi, Kenya: Longman.

———. 1987. *Bread of Sorrow*. Nairobi, Kenya: Longman.

———. 1989. *The Return of Shaka*. Neirobi, Kenya: Longman.

———. 1989. *Weapon of Hunger*. Nairobi, Kenya: Longman.

———. 1990. *Striving for the Wind*. Nairobi, Kenya: Heinemann.

Nazareth, Peter. 1972. *In a Brown Mantle*. Nairobi, Kenya: East African Publishing House.

———. 1991. *The General Is Up*. Toronto: TSAR Books.

Ngugi wa Thiong'o. 1964. *Weep Not, Child*. London: Heinemann.

———. 1965. *The River Between*. London: Heinemann.

———. 1967. *A Grain of Wheat*. London: Heinemann.

———. 1977. *Petals of Blood*. London: Heinemann.

———. 1981. *Detained: A Writer's Prison Diary*. London: Heinemann.

————. 1986. *Matagari*. Nairobi, Kenya: Heinemann.

Njau, Rebecca. 1975. *Ripples in the Pool*. Nairobi, Kenya: Transafrica.

————. 1984. *Kenyan Women Heroes and Their Mystical Power*. Nairobi, Kenya: East African Publishing Bureau.

Oculi, Okello. 1968. *Orphan*. Nairobi, Kenya: East African Publishing House.

————. 1968. *Prostitute*. Nairobi, Kenya: East African Publishing House.

————. 1976. *Kookolem*. Nairobi, Kenya: East African Publishing House.

————. 1977. *Malak*. Nairobi, Kenya: East African Publishing House.

Ogot, Grace. 1966. *The Promised Land*. Nairobi, Kenya: East African Publishing House.

————. 1983. *Miaha*. Nairobi. Heinemann Educational Books.

————. 1968. *Land without Thunder*. Nairobi, Kenya: East African Publishing House.

————. 1976. *The Other Woman*. Nairobi, Kenya: East African Educational Publishers.

————. 1980. *The Graduate*. Nairobi, Kenya: Uzima Press.

————. 1980. *The Island of Tears*. Nairobi, Kenya: Uzima Press.

Okot pBitek. 1966. *Song of Lawino*. Nairobi, Kenya: East African Literature Bureau.

————. 1970. *Song of Ocol*. Nairobi, Kenya: East African Publishing House.

————. 1971. *Two Songs: Song of a Prisoner, Song of Mal-aya*. Nairobi, Kenya: East African Publishing House.

Palangyo, Peter. 1968. *Dying in the Sun*. London: Heinemann Educational.

Ruhumbika, Gabriel. 1969. *Village in Uhuru*. London: Longman.

Serumaga, Robert. 1969. *Return to Shadows*. London: Heinemann Educational.

Taban Lo Liyung. 1965. "Can We Correct Literary Barrenness in East Africa?" *East African Journal* (December).

Vassanji, M. G. 1989. *The Gunny Sack*. Oxford: Heinemann International.

————. 1994. *The Book of Secrets*. Toronto: McClelland and Stewart.

————. 2003. *The In-Between World of Vikram Lall*. Toronto: Doubleday.

Chapter 6
Ngugi wa Thiong'o: A Grain of Wheat *(1967),* Petals of Blood *(1977), and* Matagari *(1989)*

Ngugi wa Thiong'o is East Africa's first and best-known writer. He has published some 13 works of fiction, including novels, short stories, plays, and literary, political, and cultural commentaries. He has lived in exile from his country, Kenya, since 1982. Yet he remains a major critic of and spokesperson for Kenya's political and cultural life.

Ngugi was born in Kamiriithu, near Limuru, Kenya, in 1938. He was christened "James" and as James Ngugi published his first writing. In 1970, he abandoned Christianity and with it the name "James." He took the name "Ngugi wa Thiong'o," by which he has been known since that time.

Ngugi had his early education in the Church of Scotland mission school and his secondary education at Alliance High School in Nairobi, the most renowned secondary school in Kenya. He then attended Makerere University College in Kampala, Uganda, where he studied English literature and language. Ngugi began his writing career when he was a student at Makerere College. His first published work appeared in *Penpoint,* the college's literary magazine. His first dramatic work was *The Black Hermit,* written for and performed as part of Uganda's independence celebrations by the Uganda National Theatre in November 1962. (The play was published in 1970 in a collection of short plays in the volume *This Time Tomorrow.* His short stories from this period were collected and published in 1975 in *Secret Lives.*)

He graduated in 1964 and, after a time working as a journalist and columnist from 1961 to 1964 for the *Sunday Post, Daily Nation,* and *Sunday Nation* in Nairobi, went to Leeds University in England where he worked on Caribbean literature as an M.A. project. He continued graduate studies at

Northwestern University in the United States before returning to Kenya, where he taught in the English Department in the University College of Nairobi. There he was, with his colleagues Henry Owuor-Anyumba and Taban Lo Liyong, responsible for formulating a proposal for the "Abolition of the English Department," the aim being, in Ngugi's words, "to establish the centrality of Africa in the Department." Ngugi's position proceeds from the belief that "Literature does not develop in a vacuum. It is given impetus, shape, direction and even area of concern by social, political and economic forces in a particular society. . . . There is no area of our lives which has not been affected by the social, political and expansionist needs of European capitalism . . . ." (*Homecoming,* 149–150). The aim of the realigned course of studies that followed from the acceptance and implementation of the "Abolition" proposal was to consider literary texts for their bearing on a developing postcolonial Kenyan society. The course of study developed by Ngugi and his colleagues was at the time the most innovative in Africa.

Ngugi's first novel is *Weep Not, Child* (1964); it is also the first novel published by an East African. It won the East Africa Literature Bureau prize for fiction. The novel is set in the period leading up to and during the first years of Kenya's independence war, popularly called at the time the Mau Mau Rebellion. It tells the story of how the Emergency affects the lives of the family of Ngotho as this is conveyed through the experiences of Ngotho's youngest con, Njoroge. A pupil at a Christian school when we first meet him, Njoroge believes he has been appointed to serve his people once independence has been won. Njoroge is inspired by his Christian convictions and by the speeches of Jomo Kenyatta, the leader of the independence struggle. But as the struggle proceeds, Njoroge's faith and beliefs are seriously challenged. He sees his father alienated from his hereditary land by the white farmer Howlands for whom he is forced to work as a serf. He is eventually accused of collaboration with the freedom fighters. Ngotho is tortured by Jacobo, a Kenyan collaborator with the whites. Jacobo in turn is killed by Boro, Njoroge's older brother. Boro also kills the white farmer, Howlands. Njoroge is jailed, tortured, threatened with castration, expelled from his European school, and forced to work as a clerk in an Indian shop. His dreams destroyed, Njoroge attempts suicide, saved only by his mother.

The River Between (1965) is Ngugi's second published novel (but the first one he wrote). It is a reworking of his play *The Black Hermit.* The novel dramatizes the conflict between religious groups that occupy opposing banks of the river Honia in the 1930s and 1940s. Kabonyi is the leader of the traditionalists, and Joshua the leader of the Christians. Waiyaki, the central figure in the novel, attempts to reconcile these two groups. He sees himself as the possible savior of his people as predicted by the sage Mugo wa Kibero, and thus at first tries to honor traditional beliefs while he is absorbing Christian practices during his attendance at the mission school. For his Christian beliefs, he is repudiated by the traditionalists; because of his association with the traditionalists, he is eventually expelled from the mission school.

Waiyaki then founds his own school with the help of his friends Kamau and Kinuthea. His life is further complicated by his love for Nyambura, one of the daughters of Joshua. Nyambura's sister, Muthoni, tries to reconcile traditional and Christian beliefs by undergoing the circumcision rite. But she dies when the wound becomes septic.

Waiyaki's situation worsens still further when Kabonyi founds the Kiama, an antigovernment and anti-Christian movement. Members of the Kiama accuse Waiyaki of treachery because of his love for Nyambura. Waiyaki affirms his love for Nyambura before the Kiama and both he and Nyambura are found guilty of the charges brought against them. They are led away. Although the novel's close is ambiguous, their deaths are hinted at.

In his first two novels, Ngugi introduces a number of related themes and treatments that become the subject matter of all of his subsequent writing—questions about the ownership of the land, the source of life for the Kenyan people as promised in the Gikuyu creation myth; the alienation of the people from the land as an effect of the British colonization of Kenya; the corrupting influence of Christianity; the uses and kinds of education, both traditional and modern; and the processes which can be used to return the country to its people.

With the publication of *Petals of Blood* (1977), Ngugi abandoned writing in English, seeing in its use a continuing manifestation of cultural imperialism, and turned to Gikuyu as his language of literary expression. Ngugi's mission was to use literature to prompt and promote social, political, and economic change. To do this effectively, he determined, it was necessary to reach the masses in their own language.

His first venture in Gikuyu was *Ngahika Ndeenda* (*I Will Marry When I Want*) in 1980. Written in collaboration with Ngugi wa Mirii, the play was produced at the Kamiriithu Cultural Centre but closed down by Kenyan authorities after several performances once they saw its effect on villagers whose attention was drawn to how they were being exploited by a monied class of Kenyans. The play tells the story of Kiguunda, a farmer and former freedom fighter, his wife, Wangeri, and their daughter, Gatoni, and how they are tricked into selling their land to Kioi, a wealthy businessman who has dealings with foreign investors. Kioi's son, John Mukuumi, is engaged to be married to Gatoni. To find money for a proper Christian wedding, Kiguunda mortgages his land. But when Gatoni is found to be pregnant by John Mukuumi, the wedding is called off, the bank forecloses on Kiguuna's loan, and he loses his farm. He and his family are left homeless. Christianity is seen as the agent of capitalist exploitation, and Ngugi is relentless in exposing the hypocrisy of westernized Kenyans.

Ngugi's second venture in the use of Gikuyu is *Caitaani mitharaba-ini* (*Devil on the Cross*, 1982). Ngugi presents variations on themes that persist in his writing: the alienation of the people from their land; the destruction of ordinary Kenyans as producers of wealth; and the collusion of church, state, and police in connection with overseas investors. Ngugi is not content simply to describe the plight of the people: he proposes a counterattack against their exploiters through the actions of four principal characters—Wariinga, Wangari, Muturi, and Gatuira. Wariinga—described by Ngugi as "my Wariinga"—is the hero of the novel. She acts on behalf of the people by executing a member of the oppressor class who represents the forces that exploit them, a man who almost ruined her life when she was a young and innocent girl. A parallel plot to the story of Wariinga and her comrades is made up of scenes devoted to the Devil's Feast, where various leaders of society attempt to excel each other in describing the means they will use to exploit and subdue the masses. Here, as in his other works, Ngugi sees Christianity as a hypocritical force that is invoked to justify criminal acts.

Ngugi is concerned with a wide range of related social and political issues, but his interests are consolidated in two principal areas: the causes for and prosecution of the independence struggle and the legacy of that struggle in modern times. *A Grain of Wheat* deals with the former, while *Petals of Blood* and *Matagari* deal supremely with the latter.

A Grain of Wheat (1967)

A Grain of Wheat is the classic novel of the independence struggle in Kenya. Here Ngugi has developed a complex narrative that moves back and forth between the past and the present, thereby encompassing the historical antecedents to the movement for independence that culminate in the insurgence described by the international press as the Mau Mau Rebellion, which eventually won for Kenya her independence. The temporal action of the novel is set in the four days leading up to Uhuru Day, Kenya's Independence Day, December 12, 1963. There are a large number of characters in the novel whose stories are told in relation to the independence struggle, but Ngugi is primarily concerned with the lives of four principal characters—Mugo, Mumbi, Gikonyo, and Karanja—none of whom has participated in the fighting but each of whom bears a weight of guilt because of his or her actions in the Emergency period. And their guilt is a result of their relationships with Kihika, their childhood friend and a famous freedom fighter who has been betrayed to the British by one of the villagers. Two of Kihika's comrades, General R and Lt. Koinadu, attend the Uhuru celebrations to discover and denounce Kihika's betrayer—whom they believe to be Karanja because he has joined the Home Guard in the struggle against his countrymen.

Ngugi gives us a view of a whole country involved in the independence war. The British colonial position is most carefully rendered in the character of John Thompson, a former soldier in the British army in World War II who, out of disaffection with postwar England, has come to make a new life for himself in Kenya. Like Howlands in *Weep Not, Child,* Thompson is utterly unaware of the African sensibility in regard to the traditional claim to ancestral land. He is committed to the notion of the benevolent paternalism, the "civilizing mission" of colonial practice. He sees the British Empire as expounding and implementing a "great moral idea" (54). His habit of mind proceeds from the exponents of empire whose works he has studied— Rudyard Kipling and Lord Lugard, one of the principal architects of colonial practice in Africa—and from the education he received at Oxford. Thompson plans to write a book entitled "Prospero in Africa," in which he will expound a great scheme of assimilation based on British colonial ideology. But Thompson is a false visionary: he cannot, does not, even consider an African point of view.

And so when the Emergency begins and intensifies, when an almost mythic hero of British resistance to the independence war, Colonel Robson, is killed by freedom fighters, Thompson's mental and spiritual controls disintegrate. In short time, he turns into a near monster, inflicting savage punishment on captors interned in the notorious Riga Camp. Thompson discovers that there is no moral base to his position. He lashes out, seeks scapegoats, and sanctions the execution of 11 prisoners.

The Emergency is the culminating point in the history of resistance by Africans against colonial practice. Ngugi lists the names of those Kenyans who martyred themselves over a period of more than sixty years for Kenya's independence from foreign domination. The list includes Waiyaki, Harry Thuku, Jomo Kenyatta, and, perhaps the best known of all, Dedan Kimathi. Their actions are recounted here both for historical reasons and, more specifically, to show their inspirational effect on Kihika.

Kihika is a leader in the messianic tradition, and he conceives a vision of national unity as powerful, but much more realistic than that of Thompson. Kihika has been brought up a Christian and he sees early the correspondences between Gikuyu and Christian creation myths. He sees how the Christian doctrine was used to seduce people from their traditional beliefs. The Bible becomes the source for the course of action required to win back the land and so Kihika turns the language of the Christians on themselves. The passages underlined in Kihika's Bible (used by Ngugi as mottoes in the novel)— Revelations 21:11, I Corinthians 15:36, and St. John 12:24—provide authenticity, legitimacy, and support to Kihika. These passages in Kihika's Bible are associated with the situation in Kenya through their emphasis on sacrifice, providing assurance of the legitimacy of the sacrifices made. For Kihika, sacrifice will prompt change and draw attention to the reasons for the sacrifice. The basic analogy is with the plight of the Israelites in Egypt.

The historical background of the novel is associated with Kihika, and Ngugi is at pains to make certain that the antecedents to the current struggle are understood. But Ngugi is equally interested in character, and in the moral choices that individuals make, as well as their reasons for making them. The novel is concerned equally with revealing the complexities of individual states of mind and the complexities of social and personal relationships as it is in providing the background against which the actions and thoughts of his characters are displayed.

The public and the personal themes intersect in the novel as Ngugi explores the various dimensions of betrayal and the consequent need for expiation and forgiveness. Ngugi places his characters in situations designed to test their moral strength. The struggle in Kenya, which intensifies human relations and places heavy emotional and psychological weight on individuals, is an appropriate locale for testing moral choice. Ngugi's examination of betrayal and, therefore, of moral conduct, is vested in the four principal characters in the novel into whose minds he takes us, minds resonant with ambiguities and contradictions.

All but Mugo come from the same village. Mugo is an outsider who comes to Thabai to escape his abused past, to live his life as a farmer, and to isolate himself from the community. He does not have the intimate association with Kihika that the others have. Mugo is the most complex of the four characters. He is also the catalyst in resolving the guilt that affects Gikonya, Mumbi, and Karanja. Brought up in squalid conditions by a drunken aunt, Mugo resolves early in his life to protect himself from society, and therefore reacts strongly to anything that threatens his isolation. Kihika threatens Mugo's resolve. And so Mugo betrays Kihika to Thompson. His reasons are complex: he does not want to be drawn into the independence struggle. Moreover, the struggle for land and the disruption it causes implies, for Mugo, a return to the destitute conditions of his childhood. And, equally important, despite his resolve not to connect with other humans, he is jealous of Kihika's success and fame. Mugo says, quite simply: "He came into my life . . . and pulled me into the stream. And so I killed him" (161). Ngugi humanizes Mugo by revealing a mind at the point of collapsing under the burden of guilt it bears. At the height of the Uhuru festivities, he refuses to let Karanja, the prime suspect in the killing of Kihika in the judgment of General R and Lt. Koinadu, take the blame for his crime. His overwrought conscience will not allow him to sacrifice a second victim.

Karanja, the most pitiable of the four characters, is juxtaposed with Kihika. The latter is the embodiment of the struggle to free Kenya. Karanja represents the colonized mind. He is convinced of the superiority of the white man. Because of this he joins the Home Guard. He is callous in his victimization of his own people and he is obsequious to white authority. Karanja is a pathetic figure. Others achieve release from their guilt: Karanja, it is implied, will carry his with him forever. It is an irony, as Ngugi's next several novels show, that characters like Karanja profit in the postcolonial Kenyan society while those who fought for freedom are spurned.

Like Karanja, Gikonya knows that he is not the kind of person to do heroic deeds. He nevertheless becomes involved in the Emergency. He is married to Mumbi and when he is sent to prison for alleged participation in the struggle, he goes willingly, sustained by his faith in her love for him. But his spirit breaks in prison and he experiences a mental breakdown. He renounces his oath and is set free. Like Mugo, he suffers the guilt of his betrayal. And he experiences a second betrayal. He returns to his village to find that Mumbi has had a child by Karanja, to whom she had given herself in a moment of joyful abandon on learning of Gikonyo's release from prison. Gikonyo's great joys in life were his love for Mumbi and his carpenter's craft. But now, just as the soil has become "dry and hollow" for Mugo, so for Gikonyo the wood with which he worked no longer "sent a thrill of wonder" through him. Eventually he overcomes the jealousy that possesses him and seeks reconciliation and a new life with Mumbi. As he has done with Mugo, Ngugi takes us into Gikonyo's reenactment and reassessment of his life in the four days leading up to the celebration. But unlike Mugo, Gikonyo knows that he cannot make a public confession of his treachery in repudiating his oath to serve the nationalist dream. Mugo, however, becomes the unwitting confessor to both Mumbi and Gikonyo. Each reveal their betrayal to Mugo and, as a result of their confessions, are able to come to terms with their limitations.

Mumbi's betrayal of Gikonyo to Karanja is an expression not of simple lust but an extension of the unrestrained joy she experiences on learning of Gikonyo's release from prison. She suffers too much for this. Karanja gloats over his triumph, not only over Mumbi but also over Gikonyo, his rival since boyhood for the affections of Mumbi. Gikonyo realizes almost too late the price she has paid. In the end, Gikonyo accepts her child and carves for her a wedding stool, the symbol of a new birth and a new beginning.

The complex pattern of guilt and its release is resolved on Uhuru Day, a day over which has hung a "disturbing sense of inevitable doom." On the personal level, problems in the lives of the principal characters have been resolved. At the public level, the novel, in tracing the motives and actions of the white colonists and the success of the independence struggle in wresting power from them, offers not an optimistic but rather a gloomy forecast for the future. There is already evidence that the revolution is being betrayed by Kenyans. General R suggests in a speech with which the novel closes that Kenyans in positions of influence in the new government are annexing the land for personal profit, in effect denying the generality of Kenyans the fruits of their struggle and suffering. Already, an unequal world of "haves" and "have nots" is being redefined. Ngugi, in the closing passages of *A Grain of Wheat,* anticipates the subject matter of *Petals of Blood. A Grain of Wheat* is Ngugi's tribute to the freedom fighters who won for Kenya her independence from colonial rule. It is equally a warning against the betrayal of the revolution.

Petals of Blood (1977)

For Ngugi, the revolution that won for Kenya her independence has been betrayed. His political writing makes clear his assessment and judgment as to why and how this is so. *Petals of Blood* dramatizes the processes of the betrayal and exposes the motives and actions of those who have inherited political and economic power from the deposed colonial regime. A growing class of Kenyan politicians and middle-class entrepreneurs, in conjunction with international financiers, conspire to exploit peasants and workers, the producers of the country's wealth, in ways worse than their former colonial masters. Ngugi is on the side of the dispossessed and exploited. And while he acknowledges that fiction cannot be the agent of change, "it can express and expose the conditions which destroy the hopes and aspirations of . . . [the] oppressed. In the end this is where the force of writing operates. It will prompt the action of those people, the true agents of change" (Shreu, 1977, 35).

Petals of Blood is in four parts— "Walking," "Towards Jerusalem," "To Be Born," and "Again . . . La Lutta Continuua." The story is told through various narrative strategies: by members of the town of Ilmorog, through the remembrances of the principal characters, and often by an omniscient narrator in the first-person plural. To widen and deepen the narrative and its rendering of the Kenyan situation, Ngugi employs a variety of time frames. The present-tense action of the novel takes place over 10 days. The stories of the lives of the main characters take place over 12 years. And Ngugi moves easily backward and forward in historical time from 1896 when the annexation of Kenya by Europeans began. Some periods re-create the prehistorical periods of Africa. To locate the Kenyan situation in a wider and global context, Ngugi equates the struggle for justice that is at the heart of his novel to other movements of a similar kind—those in Mozambique, Angola, Zimbabwe. Thus the names of leaders of such movements—Chaka, Toussaint, Samori, Nat Turner, Arap Manyei, Mondlane, Cabral, Kimathi, Nkrumah—are mentioned in various places in the text and have a powerful resonance. Ngugi acknowledges indirectly, in various passages, his debt to political thinkers who have influenced him—Marx and Fanon—and to apocalyptic poets who write in the tradition of which *Petals of Blood* becomes a part—Blake, Whitman, and Yeats, to name but three.

Ngugi derives the title for his novel from a 1965 poem, "The Swamp," by the St. Lucian poet Derek Walcott. Walcott's poem suggests there is a powerful and deadly force in nature that is a constant threat to humankind. Humankind may conceive a beatific vision of being in harmony with nature, but they must also be aware of the lurking danger at their feet. The phrase "petals of blood" applies to the bean flower that pupils discover on farms on school visits. It also applies to the plant from which *thenge'ta* is distilled and which becomes, when mass-produced and sold, a seductive opiate for the masses. "Petals of blood" also refers to the flames in fires that twice bring disaster to characters in the novel.

Ngugi brings together in *Petals of Blood* issues that have given him growing concern as his writing career moves forward. His central concern is to describe and dramatize the betrayal of the independence movement by those who are its authors and how this affects the masses of people; to display the nature and cost of the progressive "modernizing" of Kenya as this coincides with the emergence of a monied, exploitative middle class and as it relates to the alienation of Kenyans from the land; to consider the place of religion, both traditional and Christian, in emerging Kenya and how these intersect with the role of education. The thematic thrust of the novel is conveyed through Ngugi's examination of the actions of the novel's four principal characters—Munira, Wanja, Abdullah, and Karega—as their lives intersect and as they make different responses to a worsening situation in Kenya.

Petals of Blood takes the form of a detective novel. Three men, all prominent businessmen—Kimeria, Chui, and Mzigo—have been murdered in New Ilmorog, and Chief Inspector Godfrey of the Kenyan police force comes to New Ilmorog from Nairobi to conduct an inquiry into the crimes. Four suspects—Munira, Wanja, Abdullah, and Karega—are arrested. These four have been intimately linked in the past, often in ways they at first do not know, with the murdered men. They have been burned in a fire that destroys Wanja's brothel and seriously injures Wanja. Inspector Godfrey knows that each of the accused has a possible and different motive for murdering Kimeria, Chui, and Mzigo. As Godfrey's inquiry moves forward, the lives of the accused and their prior associations with the murdered men are gradually revealed.

Munira is the first suspect. The son of a wealthy, righteous Christian father, whose life spans 75 years, the period of modern Kenyan history, Munira, judged a failure by his family and his frigid and overly zealous Christian wife, leaves home and seeks solitude in Ilmorog, an out-of-the-way and derelict village. In Ilmorog, Munira has modest success as a school master. But his fear of connection and involvement with people compromises his teaching as does his lack of imagination when responding to such fundamental questions from his students as "'what is law? what is nature? . . .' he had never thought deeply about these things . . . ."

Abdullah, the second suspect, is the son of an African mother and an Indian father. Like Munira, he is also disaffected, but for different reasons. Abdullah was a freedom fighter and lost a leg in the fighting. He is denied the rewards of the independence he fought for and becomes a despised figure on the streets of Nairobi where he scratches out a living with a donkey cart, reclaiming saleable items from the rubbish heaps of the city. Betrayed by the growing middle class, Abdullah travels to Ilmorog with his donkey and an orphan boy, Joseph, whom he has saved from the gutters of the city. In Ilmorog, he runs a small shop and alternates between moods of surly silence and abrasive irony, most of which he directs at Munira and his school.

Wanja, the third suspect, comes to live in Ilmorog with her grandmother, Nyakinyua, on land that has traditionally belonged to her family. Wanja was born in Limuru, as were Munira and Abdullah. She had hoped for a joyous life despite the harsh treatment meted out by a money-grubbing father. But, as a schoolgirl, she is seduced by a wealthy married man who casually spurns her when she becomes pregnant. She destroys her newborn child, embittered by guilt and the knowledge that she can never have another child. For a time she works as a bar girl, a member, writes Ngugi, "of the most ruthlessly exploited category of women in Kenya" (Shreu, 1977, 35).

Wanja and Munira come together in Ilmorog with the hope that the prophecy of the sage, Mugo wa Mwathi, that she can have another child will be fulfilled. It is not. They soon drift apart: their liaison is joyless—she needs Munira only to test the potency of the prophecy; his need for her is purely carnal.

Karega is the fourth suspect, and through his connections with the other three characters, Ngugi exploits the coincidences that characterize the detective novel form. Karega is the younger brother of Nding'uri, a comrade of Abdullah in the forest fighting. Nding'uri was hanged, betrayed to the British authorities by a man from his own village. This man turns out to be Kimeria, who is also the seducer of Wanja. Karega learns about his brother's fate from Abdullah. And Karega has been the lover of Mukami, the younger sister of Munira. Mukami's father forbids the liaison because of Nding'uri's involvement in the freedom struggle. Mukami drowns herself. Munira, on learning of his sister's relationship with Karega, who has become a successful teacher in his school, turns against Karega, motivated both by his anger over Karega's fatal relationship with his sister and by his jealousy of the romantic relationship that has come about between Wanja and Karega.

Ilmorog remains a backwater where a severe drought threatens the lives of the villagers, and Karega, thus, organizes a march on Nairobi to confront their absentee member of parliament (M.P.), Nderi wa Rieri. Abdullah leads the march and shows his former powers of command. After an arduous journey the villagers confront the M.P. He, failing to understand their desperate condition, tells his constituents simply to go home and work hard. Their frustrations boil over and they chase the M.P. through the streets of Nairobi. Ironically, this draws national attention to their plight—the press takes up their cause and relief for the condition is promised.

In Nairobi, Karega comes in touch with a nameless lawyer who devotes his work to the amelioration of the suffering of the poor and needy. He becomes a mentor to Karega, who asks him for advice on how to achieve a similar goal. The lawyer gives Karega books on history, political science, and literature, all written by his countrymen and none of which help Karega. The lawyer points out that no learning is neutral: it is placed in the service of the ruling class as a means of justifying their conduct. Karega determines that only by organizing the exploited mass of people to take positive action will their conditions be changed.

The ironic success the villagers have in drawing attention to their plight promotes a larger and more devastating irony and brings about the ruin of Ilmorog, such as it is. Construction begins on a trans-Africa highway linking Nairobi to Ilmorog and beyond to the great cities of Africa. Ilmorog experiences a period of feverish growth and becomes, almost overnight, a modern city. A church, a police station, and banks are built. A cultural tourist center—Utamaduni—is created to attract tourists but, in reality, to serve as a front for the plundering of the country's natural and human resources. The real implications of modernization reveal themselves as peasants are seduced into taking bank loans to improve their farms; when they are unable to meet payments, they have their lands taken as the banks foreclose on the loans. For a time, Wanja and Abdullah prosper in business and see modest sales from selling *thenge'ta*. But the rights of production are taken from them by Kimeria, Chui, and Mzigo, who build a distillery to mass-produce the liquor that provides them with a fortune. Wanja, no longer willing to be exploited, becomes an exploiter, determined to prosper in the corrupt community. She opens a brothel. Munira becomes a drunk and then a reformed and charismatic Christian. Abdullah becomes a derelict on the streets of Ilmorog. Karega organizes workers to agitate for better conditions in the *thenge t'a* distillery.

The novel closes in melodramatic fashion. Wanja lures Kimeria to her brothel and stabs him to death. Her act is not discovered, however, because Munira sets fire to the building for the deluded reason that he is saving Karega from Wanja's evil influence. Abdullah had also planned to kill Kimeria for betraying Nding'uri. The crime solved, Inspector Godfrey returns to Nairobi secure in his belief that in supporting a "system of private property, private ownership of the means of production, exchange and distribution" he is acting in a way "synonymous with the natural order of things" (333).

For Ngugi, what happens to Ilmorog—its conversion from a worn-out village to a shining new city—is typical of what has happened in other cities in Kenya (Nairobi, Thika, Kisumu, Nakuru) and is symbolic of how finance capital works in displacing the people from the land and forcing them into debt, penury, or labor that barely provides a living.

It is these people Karega seeks to serve through his organizing activities. For Karega—and obviously for Ngugi—the redemptive struggle will continue from the present well into the future. The past is no use to the present struggle. Ngugi's rendering of history is consistent with his political beliefs and motives, tracing as it does—and as Marx described it—a move from feudal organization to bourgeois-capitalist and proletarian. At the close of *Petals of Blood*, class antagonism between the capitalist and the proletariat is polarized. Ngugi celebrates Africa's glorious past and its many heroes in numerous passages in the novel. But as he sees it—and has Karega enact it—contemplation of the past offers no shortcut to the problems of the present and the future. Karega finds hope in fostering solidarity among the peasants and workers, "the true producers of wealth . . . the wealth that feeds, clothes, houses everyone in society. They also produce all the wealth that goes out of the country." In the present, his hopes are circumscribed by the activities of the murdered men and by the activities of the M.P., Nderi wa Rieri, who organizes and controls a secret organization known as the KCO, "the most feared instrument of selective but coercive terror in the land," (174–86) an organization devoted to restraining by whatever means any group that threatens the corrupt ruling class of which Nderi wa Rieri is an epitome.

As the epigraph to the final section of the novel declares, "La Lutta Continuua" (The Struggle Continues). Ngugi has identified what for him are the most serious problems in his society. He describes a class struggle that in the time of the novel is at an impasse. The novel ends with the faint but firm sound of marching peasants and workers rallying to their cause. And it poses the implicit question: can the people do anything to reverse their position as helpless victims?

Matagari (1989)

Matagari (1989) is Ngugi's sixth novel, the second written in Gikuyu and then translated into English. The Gikuyu title of the novel is *Matagari wa Njiruungi* which, translated, means "the patriot who survived the bullets." In writing the novel, Ngugi draws on a number of literary styles and sources—realist fiction, Gikuyu conventions of storytelling, mythic characterization, and satiric exaggeration. The setting is postindependence Kenya where the hopes and expectations have been betrayed by an apostate class of Kenyans in, for Ngugi, criminal collaboration with foreign capitalists. Here, as in *Petals of Blood,* Ngugi continues his quest of exposing betrayal, corruption, collusion, and the denial of human rights to Kenyan citizens.

Matagari has three sections, whose titles suggest a symbolic relevance to the general purposes of the book. The sections are entitled "Wiping Your Tears Away," "Seeker of Truth and Justice," and "The Pure Resurrected." Matagari is the main character of the novel. There are three others who have major supporting roles. Guthera is a prostitute who has had a number of bitter and ironic reversals in her life before meeting Matagari. Joining him, she determines to devote her life to improving the lot of suffering people, especially women. Ngaruro wa Kitira is a factory worker who is inspired by Matagari to become a union leader and to mount a strike against the Anglo-American Leather and Plastic Company. Muriuki, the third of the secondary characters, lives in an abandoned car and survives by scavenging in a local rubbish heap. By the novel's close, he takes up where Matagari leaves off, the cry of "Victory shall be ours" from the massed peasants, workers, and students and other patriots following in his wake.

Matagari has been a freedom fighter who, after a period of time in the postindependence period emerges from the forest, puts on his belt of peace, and goes in search of his people—parents, wives, and children—so they can live together in the house that Matagari built. He has fought for the right to own his own house. The house is an allegorical assignment of the nation itself, a nation that Matagari built with his struggles in the forest. But he finds it has been stolen from him by the white settler, Williams, and his African toady, John Boy, and that the house is now owned by John Boy Junior—a collaborator with the whites as his father has was before him.

Matagari goes on a nationwide quest asking priests, students, teachers, merchants, and peasants where he can find truth and justice. They are difficult to find, the degree to which they have become corrupted signified in Matagari's confrontation with the Minister of Truth and Justice. Instead of truth and justice, he finds that children are forced through poverty to live in used car dumps, that union leaders are harassed by security forces in the pay of capitalist exploiters, that young women are forced into prostitution. These dispossessed are ranged against the wealthy few—whites who are overseas financiers and blacks who have grown rich through collusion with a remnant of the former white settler population.

Seeing all this, Matagari determines that "justice for the oppressed springs from the organized and armed power of the people" (138). He takes off his belt of peace signifying that he will once more take up the cause for which the independence struggle was undertaken. He recovers his weapons and determines to take back his house and, through this, his country. In the end, and while still involved in his quest, Matagari is swept away by a river in flood. His end is ambiguous—did he die; did he survive? Whatever the case, his inspirational leadership lives on.

The themes Ngugi incorporates in *Matagari* are repetitions and refinements of themes he has exploited in his earlier novels: the failure of western education to contribute to the creation of a balanced and just society and the apostasy of the Christian church in failing to alleviate the suffering of the poor. The Christian church is Ngugi's persistent target and he exploits the Christian precepts in various ironic and satiric ways. In an important way, Matagari reconstitutes the biblical roles of Moses and Jesus. He will lead his people and he will lay his life down for them. As a leader and a savior, he asks the suffering masses to come to him. But like the people of biblical times, the people do not recognize his message of peace, of truth and justice. They look, as was the case with the reception of Christ in the Bible, for a militant leader.

When Matagari is eventually arrested, he shares a jail cell with 10 detainees who are equated with the Apostles of Jesus. These are people who ought to work for truth and justice—a teacher, a student, and a union leader prominent among them. They have tried to fulfill these roles in various ways by challenging entrenched authority. They have failed because they have been arrested. They have recanted. But they reverse their current positions because of Matagari's legendary and magical powers. The biblical analogies are plainly apparent—their gathering together with Matagari in jail is compared to the Last Supper. In case any reader—or listener—fails to follow Ngugi's intention (the book was widely read aloud to illiterate people in Kenya), Ngugi has Matagari speak the familiar words from the Bible: "This is my body, which I give to you. Do this unto one another until the Second Coming. He then took the cup, and after blessing it said: And this cup is the testament of the covenant we entered with one another with our blood. Do this until our kingdom comes, through the will of the people" (57). When Matagari and the others are mysteriously released from prison, their escape is compared to that of Paul in the Capernicum Prison. As Matagari leaves his fellow prisoners he says, "you will see me again in three days" (57).

Although the biblical analogies seem straightforward and readily apparent, there are ambiguities in Ngugi's use of biblical materials. He attacks a religion in which he had great faith at one time, a religion that has failed him. And while he repudiated Christianity as practiced in Kenya at the same time as he repudiated his Christian name, he nevertheless continues to see a potential in pure Christianity for good, for achieving what Christ intended. In exploiting the Christian materials in the way he does here, Ngugi finds a compelling and familiar framework for the message he wants to convey to the sufferers who are his main concern.

But if there is ambiguity in his use of Christian materials, there is no ambiguity in his exposure of the exploiting class in his country, especially the Kenyans represented by Settler Williams and John Boy Junior. These two are directors of three international banking institutions whose acronyms are A1C1, AC10, and BUI which, translated from the Gikuyu, mean "The Real Thieves." The Minster of Truth and Justice is treated equally scathingly. He describes himself as "An African Anglophone and Proud of It" (102). Surrounded by a cadre of sycophants—academics and ministers of the church protected by an armed guard—he proclaims a doctrine of "Parrotry." His simplistic and collusive admonishments to the people are published in the country's only newspaper, *The Daily Parrot*. Parrotry proclaims that the minister and his collaborators in their postcolonial liaisons are the creators of the current affluent state of the nation. Ngugi's satiric treatment of these characters and institutions is relentless. Satire works by exaggeration; its targets are selective and its purpose is to hold up to ridicule and scorn hypocrisy and duplicity. Readers and listeners will have no misgivings about his targets and the conclusions he draws about the proud and wealthy Kenyans.

Ngugi chose Gikuyu as the language for his book with the conviction that this is the best medium to alert a generality of people to the degree to which they have been betrayed and are being exploited. With *Matagari* his hope was that he would prompt the masses to the kind of action that would restore their dignity and win them their just share of the wealth they create. The extent to which he achieved this, at least in part, is found in his "Note to the English Edition:"

The novel was published in the Gikuyu-language original in Kenya in October 1986. By January 1987, intelligence reports had it that the peasants in Central Kenya were whispering and talking about a man called Matagari who was roaming the whole country making demands about truth and justice. There were orders for his immediate arrest, but police discovered that Matagari was only a fictional character in a book of the same name. In February 1987, the police raided all the bookshops and seized every copy of the novel. (viii)

Ngugi is a political writer in the fullest sense of the word. He uses his pen to assert that the disparity between rich and poor is accounted for by the entrenched and neocolonial Moi government in Kenya. He puts his faith in the generality of people. What is needed is what Matagari and *Matagari* proclaim: a leader who will lead the country to equality through the application of honesty, truth, and justice. And more powerfully than at the close of *Petals of Blood*, his present hope for the future is unshakable. He writes: "There is no night so dark that it does not end in dawn." His stance is militant: "Justice for the oppressed comes from a sharpened spear" (131). And a sharpened pen.

ADDITIONAL READINGS

Cook, David, and Michael Okenimpke. 1983. *Ngugi wa Thiong'o: An Exploration of His Writings*. London: Heinemann.

Killam, G. D. 1980. *An Introduction to the Writings of Ngugi*. London: Heinemann.

Ngugi wa Thiong'o. 1967. *A Grain of Wheat*. London: Heinemann.

———. 1972. *Homecoming*. London: Heinemann Educatinal Books.

———. 1977. *Petals of Blood*. London: Heinemann.

———. 1989. *Matagari*. London: Heinemann.

Shreu, Anita. 1977. "Interview with Ngugi wa Thiong'o." *Viva* (July): 35.

Sicherman, Carol M. 1990. *Ngugi wa Thiong'o: The Making of a Rebel, A Source Book in Kenyan Literature and Resistance*. London: Hans Zell.

Walcott, Derek. 1965. *The Castaway and Other Poems*. London: Cape.

PART III
A SELECTED HISTORY OF SOUTH-CENTRAL AFRICAN LITERATURE

When we speak of South-Central Africa we mean the present-day countries of Zambia, Zimbabwe, Malawi, Botswana, Swaziland, and Lesotho. The first two were, until the period of independence (1953–63), named Northern and Southern Rhodesia, while Malawi was named Nyasaland.

Literature from South Central Africa appears later on the scene than that from West and East Africa. There are many factors that make this so, but the most important one is population. There is a correlation between the population of a country and the number of writers (or members of any of the professional classes) that a country will produce. There are other complicating factors as well. While the English language had been used for a century or more before independence in these various countries was achieved (for exploration and missionary activity—the two, as in the case of David Livingstone, often went together—for commerce, and for land settlement treaties), the strength of indigenous languages combined with a refusal to yield to the implementation of English meant that writing in English was slow to appear. And since it has there has not been much of it.

The relatively late and scant appearance of writing in English from these countries is related as well to political issues and to censorship, in various guises, which imposed harsh penalties, usually in the form of prison sentences, on writers who did not conform. Jack Mapange, probably Malawi's best-known writer, and Felix Mnthali, a Malawian poet and, for a time, senior civil servant in the government of Hastings Banda, were jailed for their writing. Thus, for some time, writing in English in Malawi went underground. When it emerged, several writers achieved international recognition.

Prior to achieving political autonomy, Southern Rhodesia had a troubled colonial/settler history, troubles which continue to this day in modern-day Zimbabwe. Southern Rhodesia became self-governing in 1923 and remained an independent country until it formed the Central African Federation with Northern Rhodesia and Nyasaland in 1953. Opposition to white dominance began at this time and indigenous political parties were formed. These parties were very quickly banned and in light of this burgeoning movement toward self-determination on the part of the black population, the then prime minister of Southern Rhodesia, Ian Smith, proclaimed a Unilateral Declaration of Independence in 1965. Southern Rhodesia became the independent country Zimbabwe in 1980 after a period of sustained political struggle.

Writing in English from this part of Africa was slow to get going and slower to develop than in other parts of black Africa. There is now a body of fiction (and poetry and drama) which, although small by comparison with countries in West and East Africa, addresses itself to large contemporary problems. Of this body, Bessie Head is the major author, a writer who achieved international recognition before her early death. The other authors listed here, from various countries, are together forging a literary tradition of contemporary as well as historical relevance.

Blanket Boy's Moon by Atwell Sidwell (A. S.) Mopeli-Paulus, written in collaboration with Peter Lanham, was published in 1951. The novel was a popular success. It depicts the life of migrant workers in the townships of Johannesburg. Against this general background, the story traces the causes and prosecution of ritual murder in rural Lesotho. Mopeli-Paulus sets down information about Lesotho life and customs, about British administrative practices, and about the appalling conditions in which migrant mine workers found themselves in South Africa. This novel, along with Mopeli-Paulus's less successful second work, *Turn in the Dark* (written in collaboration with Miriam Basner and published in 1956), is the first in a long line of fictions that dramatize steadily darkening conditions.

David Rubadiri is the first South-Central writer to achieve international recognition. His novel and only work of fiction, *No Bride Price*, was published in 1967. Rubadiri was born in Nyasaland (now Malawi) but claims for his novel an East African setting. (He does not acknowledge the arbitrary boundaries imposed by colonial powers). The novel is the story of Lombe, his career as a civil servant, his rise to fame, and his fall in fortune. Lombe is circumscribed by corruption in a country moving from colonial dependency to self-determination. His career in public life is ruined by the false accusations made by his corrupt minister. Rubadiri introduces what was to become a familiar theme in postindependence African writing—the betrayal of a country by its political leaders. For Rubadiri, Lombe's personal story is an epitome of the progress of the country itself.

No Bride Price is also the first novel in English to show with sympathy the position of the Asian community in East Africa, particularly the ways in which they are exploited, humiliated, and repudiated by Africans. Rubadiri is also famous for his two much-anthologized poems, "Stanley Meets Mutesa" and "A Negro Labourer in Liverpool."

Aubrey Kachingwe, another Malawian, published *No Easy Task* in 1966. This novel deals with the multitude of people and problems associated with achieving independence from a colonial power. Kachingwe's setting is the imaginary African country of Kwacha, which he populates with politicians, prostitutes, night club owners, taxi drivers, and soldiers returning from overseas service.

The story is told by a journalist, the son of a Christian cleric. Through the journalist's records, Kachingwe deals with the temptations and ambiguities in the lives of people from all walks of life. What particularly engages his attention is the overwhelming presence of prostitution in the city. Kachingwe's novel bears many resemblances to *People of the City* and *Jaqua Nana,* by the Nigerian writer Cyprian Ekwensi and to the work of Ngugi wa Thiong'o and Meji Mwangi of Kenya in that the author is interested in the underbelly of society and how the poorer classes of people are exploited by those countrymen who are meant to help them.

A third novelist from Malawi is Legson Kayira. Kayira published *I Will Try* in 1965. The book is an autobiographical account of his journey from what was still Nyasaland to Khartoum, a journey of over 2,500 miles that took two years to complete. Kayira eventually made his way to the United States, where he studied at Washington State University and later to England where he studied at Cambridge.

Kayira has published four novels, which range from gentle portrayals of everyday life in the Malawian countryside to satiric and ironic examinations of various social issues to a darkening expose of political corruption.

Kayira's first novel is *The Looming Shadow* (1968). Set in Nyasaland (Malawi) in the colonial period, the novel tells of conservative elements in society that employ traditional witchcraft—which may involve murder—to resolve various problems in village life and conduct, and their rivalry with the Christian community. *Jingala* (1969), Kayira's second novel, is also set in a traditional village, far away from modern centers. The story fastens on the tension between Jingala (the eponymous hero of the title) and his son. The tension arises out of the son's desire to become a Roman Catholic priest and the father's opposition to his son's wish. But modern values, vested in the son's desires, encroach on the village and Jingala's eventual death is seen as symbolic of the death of the village and traditional conduct. The theme is a familiar one in writing from the continent and symptomatic of how pressing and sensitive the subject is in the minds of African writers.

Kayira moves the action of his third novel, *The Civil Servant* (1971), to the modern city. It tells the sad story of Chipewa, a head clerk in urban bureaucracy, and his illicit love affair with Isabella, whose husband has left Malawi to work in the mines in South Africa. The husband is killed in a mining accident and Isabella also dies, but not before she has given birth to a son. Chipewa is reunited with his wife from whom he has been estranged. The book closes with Chipewa proposing that he and his wife adopt Isabella's son. Clearly, there is a platitudinous element in the novel, but Kayira does address the serious problem of the migration of labor to the deadly mines of South Africa.

The Detainee (1974) exposes the corruption of a postindependence African government and thus falls into a pattern persistent in emergent African writing. The cynical political and economic manipulation, the betrayal of the high optimism of the period by political leaders in league with the military and the police, the use of thuggery, despotism, and censorship—all come under Kayira's omniscient authorial scrutiny. These topics are also exploited by Chinua Achebe, Ayi Kwei Armah, Wole Soyinka, and Ngugi wa Thiong'o. The novel finds its events and energy in the Malawi regime in of Dr. Hastings Banda, the country's first prime minister in the independence period.

Dominic Mulaisho published *The Tongue of the Dumb* in 1971. It is one of only a few novels in English by a Zambian writer. The novel dramatizes the clash between the traditional and the modern in an African village as this is shown through the deep antagonism between Lubinda and Mpona, the village chief who, while he shares his villager's anger over various colonial demands made on them—including an exorbitant poll tax and the imposition of compulsory western-style education—nevertheless acquiesces to the district commissioner's demands. For doing this he is attacked by Lubinda, who denounces Mpona as a witch. Mapona, however, is freed of the charge and Lubinda, now himself discredited, dies.

A parallel plot in the novel deals with the antagonism between two priests, Father Oliver and Father Gonzago. The former is a man of tolerance who believes that persuasion is the way to lead the villagers toward God. The latter is dogmatic and rigid in his beliefs about the christianizing mission. But when he has a horrific dream, he realizes that he has abrogated his oath through his behavior and that, in the end, Father Gonzago's way is the right way.

The Tongue of the Dumb is a big book and in its spaciousness Mulaisho is able to provide much evidence of the nature and influence of myths and rituals in a traditional society. And using this evidence, he is able to construct a plot that deals with the confrontation between conservative and radical positions but also with the contest between self-serving ambition and selfless service to the community.

Mulaisho's second novel, *The Smoke that Thunders* (1979), is an attempt to dramatize Zambia's struggle for independence in the context of the federation with the Rhodesias. It is a story about the struggle between colonialists and African nationalists. The setting is the British colony of Musi-o-Tunya near Victoria Falls. The setting, the story, the struggle—all are emblematic of people and events all over colonized Africa in the book's time period.

Dambudzo Marechera (1952–87) was the *enfant terrible* of Zimbabwean literature and, if we believe his own view of himself, of all African literature. He was, before his too-early death, a man of overwhelming public consciousness, believing that all ideologies and institutions connected with Africa—colonialism, postcolonialsim, education, literature, art, philosophy—must be submitted to public examination. His writing was a quest to find an appropriate form for his angry and uncompromising judgments.

House of Hunger (1978), Marechera's first published book, contains nine stories that describe the author's growing up years and the brutal treatment he received, the violence of the independence struggle, and the racist guerilla warfare against the background of Ian Smith's Unilateral Declaration of Independence from Britain. Marechera employs different narrative voices in telling his stories. *Black Sunlight* (1980) tells of a political cell, the Black Sunlight Group, that is gathered in the Devil's End Caves where they discuss various questions—such general questions as anarchy as a social procedure for effecting political and social reform, and such specific issues as the place of intellectuals and artists in a politically urgent world. At the heart of their concerns is the nature of African identity. *The Black Insider* (1990) is set in a time of war and deals with a group of intellectuals and artists who seek refuge in the faculty of arts building of a university discussing various questions related to their social status. Eventually the war overwhelms them and again the questions they pose raise issues without providing answers.

Marechera also published *Mindblast; or, The Definitive Buddy* in 1984. The volume contains three plays, a prose narrative, a selection of poems, and a diary. Taken together, they are an attack on postindependence Zimbabwean leadership, on rampant materialism, fiscal corruption, and racial and ethnic intolerance. For Marechera the current political condition differs little from the colonial regime it has replaced. *Cemetery of the Mind*, Marechera's poetry, was published posthumously in 1992.

Marechera's countryman, Shimmer Chinodya, has published three volumes of prose fiction as well as five books for children. Chinodya's first two publications, *Dew in the Morning* (1982) and *Farai's Girls* (1984), are stories of growing up in rural Zimbabwe. They reveal the idyllic life of the countryside and contrast that with the complexity and corruption of the city. Chinodya also includes speculation on the relationship between past and present and on the psychological implications of growing up in the midst of continuing traditional values. *Harvest of Thorns* (1989) is an altogether different book. It is about the struggle for Zimbabwean independence in the 1950s through the 1970s. At the center of the book is a hero who joins the guerilla movement that eventually assists in bringing about independence but who has, in the end, nothing to show for his participation in the struggle. His fate is like that of Ngugi's heroes in Kenya.

Chenjerai Hove has published four works of fiction—*Bones* (1988), *Shadows* (1991), *Shebeen Tales* (1994), and *Ancestors* (1996). Hove also recreates the struggle for independence in Zimbabwe. *Bones* tells the story of Marija, a typical farmworker through whose experiences we learn something of the struggle in rural areas. Her story is the more poignant because she loses her son in the independence struggle. Hove conveys his pride in the sacrifices of the independence fighters while drawing attention to the uncertain achievements of the postindependence years. These speculations and inquiries are taken up in the second novel, *Shadows.* His concern is with rural and urban people, with the responses of different generations in an emerging independent Zimbabwe. In *Shebeen Tales,* Hove is more direct in indicting the postcolonial government for its crass self-servingness and for ignoring the needs of the populace. *Ancestors,* cast in a magic-realistic style, tells of a woman without speech and who, forlorn and lonely, nevertheless conveys her voiceless state—the metaphor is obvious—to a man a century later, a man who might take into his concerns the plight of women like her.

Tsitsi Dangaremba trained as a medical doctor and clinical psychologist and these qualifications are evident in her writing. She has published a play, *She No Longer Weeps* (1987), and also works in film production. Her novel *Nervous Conditions* (1988), which achieved international acclaim, is set in the 1960s, when Zimbabwe was still colonial Rhodesia but independence was foreseeable. So the title of the novel refers both to the tensions in the country and the anxiety in the minds of its citizens. Tambu is the heroine of the novel. She has left the place of her rural upbringing and has become a schoolteacher, one of the few Africans to enter the world of the white establishment. She finds her loyalties pulled in two directions, to the colonial authorities who employ her and to successful colonized Africans whose privilege is greater than her own. In specific terms, she is subject to the authority of an uncle.

When her cousin, Nyasha Dangaremba, has a nervous breakdown, Tambu sees the repressive nature of colonial authority. Nyasha's breakdown, her anorexia and bulimia, stand as symptoms of the ills of this authority and are presented as a powerful indictment of her father's self-serving anglophilia. Tambu fares much better than her cousin. She returns to a colonial convent school the better to prepare herself for the business of the modernizing state, to act as a corrective to the repressive system that has shaped her nature and which she plans to assist in reforming. Tambu, as well as indicting a repressive social and personal colonialism, enters a strong plea for the creation of social organizations that will recognize the powerful contributions that women can make in the developing society.

PART IV
A SELECTED HISTORY OF SOUTH AFRICAN LITERATURE AND POLITICS

This section of the book deals with South African literature in English as well as its politics. It is important to understand that South Africa has 11 official languages, all of which have their own literatures and most of them in published forms. It also must be noted that even though the languages of the original peoples of South Africa, the Khoi and San, have died out, a recognition of the nature and worth of their cultures is often incorporated into the literatures in other South African languages. A further fact of the linguistic situation is that before the twentieth century, Dutch, French, German, and Malay Portuguese were spoken and written widely and their legacy carries into present times. Black writing in English comes from a special class and reflects the ideas and ideals of that class. In postapartheid South Africa, indigenous language literatures are gaining strength and interest.

SOUTH AFRICAN POLITICS

Racial discrimination with its consequent political and social implications has its origins in the first white annexation of the land, dating back to the establishment of a Dutch East India Company staging depot by Jan van Reibeck in 1652. The staging depot soon became a permanent colony. The importation of slaves from Dutch possessions in South East Asia resulted in the creation of a class of people of mixed ancestry—termed "colored"—from the intermingling of these slaves with Africans and Europeans. Racism also has origins in the late-eighteenth-century and early-nineteenth-century beliefs and practices of the Boer Calvinist farmers and their conviction of their superiority over the black races into whose territories they traveled in search of places to practice their religions without interference from the English.

Racism as a political policy was confirmed in spirit if not in law in 1910 as part of the policy of appeasement adopted by the British following the Anglo-Boer wars of the turn of the century. The British conferred full political rights on their former Boer enemies and, at the same time, colluded with the Boers to deny full political rights to Africans. The Boers recognized the need to create a class of workers for the developing mining industry. Exploitation and progressive segregation of blacks was confirmed in a series of legislative acts, most notably the 1927 Native Administrative Act and its subsequent amendments, which further deprived blacks of land and political rights.

African resistance to these developing racial policies arose coincidentally with British action. The establishment of Calvinist mission education and the creation of the mission presses assisted in the creation of a politicized black community, which led ultimately and successfully to the creation of the African National Congress (ANC), the Pan-African Congress (PAC), and the Black Consciousness Movement. The ANC was founded in 1912 and the PAC in 1914. These political bodies aimed at providing opposition to progressive institutionalized racism. They were little more than a holding operation and their efforts were thwarted in 1948 when the National Party came to power. After 1948 life in South Africa was dominated by two factors: a policy of refining the proscriptions of apartheid and further alienation of Africans from their land. Racial segregation that was elaborated into a formal policy of apartheid was proposed with the election win of the Daniel Francois Malannled National Party in 1948. Apartheid means, in Afrikaans, "apart-ness," the state of being made separate. After 1948, apartheid came to mean a racial policy of enforced segregation based on skin color. The classifications were "white," "colored," "native," "Bantu," or "African." Apartheid meant a number of things beyond segregation by color. It was extended to include a ban on social contacts between segregated groups, a ban on interracial marriage, and the creation of separate residential areas, leading eventually to the creation of the notorious "homelands," the consequent emergence of "shanty towns," separate businesses and the creation of signposted separate public facilities—parks, public transport, and washrooms for each colored group. A "pass" system was instituted whereby people traveling outside designated residential areas were required to prove their racial class. Apartheid guaranteed that whites were privileged: the best educational and employment opportunities were available to whites and denied to blacks and coloreds who become essentially a servant class, underpaid and unprotected from the harsh laws that encompassed their lives.

In the 1950s, 1960s, and early 1970s, apartheid was refined and made more harsh and despotic. The odious nature of South Africa's racial policies was brought to worldwide attention by the Sharpeville massacres of 1960. A gathering of unarmed Africans came together in Sharpeville, a community near Johannesburg, to mount a peaceful protest against the pass law. They were fired on by police: 70 were killed and some 200 wounded. This led to South Africa's expulsion from the Commonwealth and eventually brought about diplomatic and economic boycotts by western nations.

South Africa continued its racial policies into the 1970s and 1980s under a series of political leaders. Political opposition was silenced and went underground. The African National Congress, the most prominent opposition party, was outlawed, and its leaders, most prominent among them Nelson Mandela, were put in prison or sent into exile.

The absolute harshness of apartheid was shown in the events in Soweto, a township created to restrict and contain the movement of blacks, in 1976. Students in the township marched *en masse* to protest against apartheid. More than 600 were killed and many more wounded when police, in unrestrained reaction, opened fire on the marchers. The antiapartheid movement received another serious blow when Steve Biko, the leader of the Black Consciousness Movement, was killed while in police custody.

Harsh conditions continued for blacks even when there was some easing of restrictions against recalcitrant whites—those who protested against apartheid—coloreds, and Asians. If anything, despite these reforms and mounting international boycotts, suppression of opposition continued. For instance, in response to growing internal opposition in the form of strikes, boycotts of the pass laws, and denial of domestic services, a state of emergency was declared in 1985. This lasted until 1990, when the designation was lifted. Following that, under the prime minister, F. W. de Klerk, working together with Nelson Mandela, apartheid was gradually dismantled and bans of several decades on the African National Congress and the South African Communist Party were lifted. Considerable unrest continued through the transitional period between 1990 and 1994 and a racial war threatened, especially when two prominent leaders in the opposition died. Chris Hani, the leader of the South African Communist Party, was assassinated. Oliver Tambo, the chairman of the African National Congress, died of a stroke. Peace, however, was maintained. In April 1994 an open election was held and Nelson Mandela was elected the first president of a democratic republic.

In 1960 the ANC, the PAC, and the South African Communist Party (SACP) were banned as political parties. This resulted in the Defiance Campaign of 1952, an anti–pass law campaign that culminated in the tragic events of Sharpeville in 1960 and the Soweto school riots in 1976.

Oppressive conditions worsened. Members of banned organizations faced greater and greater repressive measures. Many went into exile, where they continued their political activism. Eventually, as a result of the activities of the ANC, PAC, and SACP, together with increasing external pressure in the form of sanctions, boycotts, and disinvestment, the bans on the ANC, PAC, and SACP were lifted in February 1990. Nelson Mandela and other political prisoners were released from their extended periods of confinement. President F. W. de Clerk made a formal apology to the black people of South Africa for the policies and procedures of apartheid. In 1994 a negotiated nonracial democracy was accomplished in South Africa.

This is the political and social background against which writing in English develops. This writing more or less coincides with the arrival of English-speaking immigrants from Britain in the 1820s. The English occupied the Cape in 1796 and had become firmly established by 1806. English administration, law, and education—that is, English culture—became entrenched with the arrival of some 5,000 settlers in 1820 and then with more groups in 1824 and 1849–50.

The imposition of English administration on the Cape and the Eastern Cape prompted the Great Trek of 1836–38 by Boer communities. These folk moved into what became known as the Orange Free State, the Transvaal, and Northern Natal as independent Boer republics. These occupations led, in turn, to an escalation, beginning in 1811, of the more or less constant frontier wars and skirmishes with indigenous African peoples, particularly the Zulus under Dingane; the Matabele under Mzilikitze; and, later in the century, the Pedi. These wars continued until 1879.

The tension between the Boers and the British that existed from their first encounters erupted into war when diamonds were discovered in 1868 near the confluence of the Vaal and Orange rivers, and when gold was discovered in 1886 on the Witwatersrand. This resulted in the rapid development of a wage-based, industrial economy that quickly supplanted agriculture. It further resulted in the fragmentation of the African nations through further alienation from their lands when whites saw the need to create an easily exploitable labor force. Some Africans colluded with the whites in the process. Another consequence of the exploitation of Africans as a labor force was that cities came into being and, with them, black ghettos where poverty and disease, most notably tuberculosis and alcoholism, became rampant.

In the mines, blacks were ruthlessly exploited by white owners. The seeds of apartheid, proceeding from the collapse of tribal unity and integrity, together with the callous and exploitive racism of the whites, were sown in these early years.

The English world in South Africa, in fact and in literature, was a self-contained world. It was a racial minority, but one that possessed political power based on wealth, which allowed it to exert an influence and to foster a literature out of proportion to its numbers. Writing in English in South Africa, it is generally agreed, dates from the publication of poetry by Thomas Pringle. And in the intervening years, spanning nearly 200 years, only some

70 authors have attracted the attention of readers, critics, and scholars. Of these, perhaps a dozen are of interest both for their place in a developing literary tradition and the intrinsic merit of their writing.

Now that apartheid, with its strict censorship that forced writers into specific molds and curbed their literary sensibilities, has been abandoned, there will be a literary output similar to, say, Nigeria.

This literary community is part of the English literary world, its writing a central feature in any discussion of writing in English. South African literature in English, small as it is in quantity, is large in quality. It has inherited a literary tradition and exploits it in ways such as other writers, both white and black, have done from other parts of the Empire turned Commonwealth turned independent nations. And that fact was not altered despite the fact that President Hendrik Verwoerd took South Africa out of the Commonwealth in 1960.

In the beginning, all literary forms appeared in South Africa—drama, poetry, prose fiction, short stories, and literary criticism—at about the same time. As was typical with other parts of Africa, local publication drew on imported models as authors. Those serious and committed worked at finding a voice, a vocabulary that would authenticate the new and strange land they found themselves in.

Three strands of writing are apparent from the outset. First, there is a large body of adventure literature and frontier reminiscences, which find their counterpart in European encounters with East and West Africa. H. Rider Haggard is the most prominent writer in this class. Much of this kind of writing was aimed at boys and is couched in an appeal to the exotic and to the taming of the wild frontier, overcoming both hostile "natives" and a hostile land. This kind of writing was popularized in more than 100 novels by G. A. Henty, who sets his fiction in all parts of the developing empire. Those set in Africa—in West and South Africa—tell of improbable and often terrifying adventures in a realistic manner through which Henty celebrates the Victorian virtue of honest hard work and the success that is gained through honoring it. This strain of writing continues to the present day. Wilbur Smith is its major South African exponent. A subgenre of the adventure story comprises books about wars and skirmishes between Africans and whites. Shaka, the Zulu leader, is the most prominent figure in this body of writing.

Second, there is a literature that cultivates a stereotype of Boers as racist, cruel, ignorant, and yet sanctimonious in the narrowness of their religious beliefs and practices. The subtext in this writing is a justification of the British annexation of the land, their confrontation with the Boers, and their eventual triumph in the Anglo-Boer War of 1899–1902.

Third, there is an expressed concern, deriving from the English Romantic movement with its emphasis on human values, for the human rights of African peoples. This new sensibility is juxtaposed with the social Darwinism of the Victorian period, which was used to justify the subjugation of the African people and which was disguised, but nevertheless unadulterated racism. Liberal concerns eventually prevailed dating from the time of Olive Schreiner and continuing through the poetry of Roy Campbell and William Plomer into the 1950s in the writing of Alan Paton, followed by Nadine Gordimer and Ezekiel Mphahlele, from the 1950s to the present, and a constantly expanding body of writing by both blacks and whites. The writing becomes more and more focused on the devastating consequences, in human terms, of the increasing repressiveness of the political regime, alleviated eventually in the rapid and comprehensive reforms of the last decade.

While this book is concerned principally with fiction, passing mention must be made of the developing theater movement in South Africa for the prominent place it has in the reaction against apartheid. Theater, in the form of touring companies, played a part in garrison life once British hegemony was established on the Cape in 1795. Plays from London's West End theaters toured the Cape. But the first original play to be written and produced in South Africa was *Kaatjie Kekkelbek, or, Life among the Hottentots*, a satirical farce written by George Rex and Andrew Bain and published in 1846. From that time until the mid-1930s, a series of actor-managers formed local theater companies that produced drawing-room dramas and social satires. Most prominent among these writer-producers was Stephen Black, a prolific writer of plays (as well as radio plays, film scripts, and fiction). In 1939, H.I.E. Dhlomo wrote and published the first play by an African writer, *The Girl Who Killed to Save* in 1936.

Dramatic production experienced a lull because of World War II and the increasing popularity of motion pictures. But in 1947, the state-supported National Theatre Organization (NTO) was founded. Its mandate was to develop local theater to meet the cultural needs of South Africans and to supply work for people of the theater—actors, playwrights, producers, directors, and technical personnel. The NTO was replaced in 1961 by four state-supported regional Performing Arts Councils (PACs), with the same mandate of the NTO—to cater to the needs of the white community.

Reacting against the political and cultural policies of the NTO and PAC, an authentic theater came into being. Athol Fugard's *No Good Friday* was staged in 1958 and *The Blood Knot* in 1963, marking for the first time the use of theater as a potentially subversive political weapon. The state responded to this by passing the Publications and Entertainment Act in 1963, which provided for censoring undesirable productions, and the Group Areas and Separate Amenities Act in 1965, which specified that no racially mixed casts or audiences were permitted at theatrical events. An international boycott of South Africa in 1963 and an Equity (actor's union) ban on performers working in South Africa in 1966 had a stifling effect on the theater. With the growth of the Black Consciousness Movement in the 1970s, alternate theater became highly politicized and a genuine force for social and political change. Cape Town's Space, Theatre Workshop, The People's Experimental Theatre, The Company, and Junction Avenue Theatre all flourished in the period for varying lengths of time.

It should not be surprising , then, that black writing in English, not unlike drama, reflects a highly politicized cultural landscape. Such writing finds its first expression in the work of Solomon Plaatje, H.I.E. Dhlomo, and Thomas Mofolo. Its beginnings are in the mission schools and presses. It is, in some respects, compromised by the Christian standards imposed on these writers. It is nevertheless a record of the disenfranchisement, both culturally and politically, of black peoples, especially those who sought survival in the growing towns and suffered the consequent racism, poverty, repression, and ultimate alienation they found there.

The Boer Wars were the subject of novels by Olive Schreiner, Douglas Blackburn, and Richard Dehan (a pseudonym for Clothilde Grace), among South African writers. A large number of overseas writers, most notable among them Rudyard Kipling, Sir Arthur Conan-Doyle, A.E.W. Mason, G. A. Henty, and Edgar Wallace, used the war as a metaphor for the growth of boys into manhood. The writing was patriotic in purpose, jingoistic in tone, and partisan in treatment.

The topic of relations between the races was introduced in such books as *Margaret Harding* (1911), by Perceval Gibbon, and *Turbott Wolfe* (1926), by William Plomer; the latter book proposes miscegenation as a possible solution to South Africa's racial problems. Most notable among these writers is Sarah Gertrude Millin, who published a series of novels beginning with *God's Stepchildren* (1924), in which she shows the disastrous consequences to successive generations if a policy of mixed race marriages is adopted or allowed.

Political issues have been part of South African writing from its beginnings, from Pringle's comment on the incipient racism of early settler attitudes, through the white-black relationships displayed in the books of Rider Haggard, John Buchan, and Sir Percy Fitzpatrick.

Once the issue of race relations and of the circumstances of Africans is addressed in literature it becomes a constant in South African writing up to the close of apartheid and even into the present. Writers such as Daphne Rooke, Dan Jacobson, Nadine Gordimer, and Andre Brink are the most prominent writers treating the subject in novels and short stories. As noted, it is also found in the writing of black writers such as Plaatje and Dhlomo, continuing through the writing of such authors as Peter Abrahams and Richard Rive and into the present. R.R.R. Dhlomo published *An African Tragedy* in 1928 and Modikwe Dikobe published *The Marabi Dance* in 1973, based on his experience of living through the 1930s. Peter Abrahams's *Mine Boy* and Alan Paton's *Cry, the Beloved Country*, both published in 1948, offer variations on the theme of the place of Africans in the developing racist state. They tell of a young man or woman, sometimes both, who, dispossessed of their rightful land, seek employment in the city—for the man work in the mines, for the woman domestic employment. For various reasons, these people fall victims to the pressures of living in the cities.

Peter Abrahams sets the tone and direction of writing in the 1950s, 1960s, and 1970s. His focus on the life of his African characters in the slums of Johannesburg connects with the autobiographical and semiautobiographical writing of such authors as Ezekiel Mphahlele in *Down Second Avenue* (1959), and Can Themba in *The Will to Die,* published posthumously in 1972 but describing life in Sophiatown in the 1950s, Todd Matshikiza in *Chocolates for My Wife* in 1961, and Bloke Modisane in *Blame Me in History* in 1963.

With the growth and refinement of apartheid, violence in the country increased. Its representation in fiction likewise increased, especially after the Defiance Campaign in 1952, which challenged segregation in all its forms. The challenge and responding violence escalated after the Sharpeville massacres in 1963. After the Sharpeville massacres and the Soweto riots that followed, politics becomes the dominant theme in South African writing. These events prompted a literature of even greater protest as writers responded to the quickly deteriorating conditions for black people, for coloreds, and even for segments of the Asian community. The political novel dominates writing in English from Richard Rive's *Emergency* (1964) through Nadine Gordimer's *The Late Bourgeoise World* (1966), *The Conservationist* (1974), and *July's People* (1981); Jack Cope's *The Dawn Comes Twice* (1969); C. J. Driver's *Elegy for a Revolutionary* (1969); Mary Benson's *At the Still Point* (1969); the novels of Alex La Guma beginning with *A Walk in the Night* (1962); the novels of Andre Brink beginning with *Looking on Darkness* (1974); Miriam Tlali's *Muriel at the Metropolitan* (1975) and *Amandla* (1980); Sipho Sepamla's *The Root Is One* (1979) and *Ride on the Whirlwind* (1981); Mongane Wally Serote's *To Every Birth Its Blood* (1981); Mubelelo Msmane's *My Cousin Comes to Jo'Burg and Other Stories* (1981) and *Children of Soweto* (1982).

This writing reflects how literature is increasingly being used as a means of achieving political ends through militant action. Because of the increased security and vindictiveness of the apartheid regime, the difficulty of achieving these aims also increased, making life hazardous for writers. Rive's *Emergency,* Abrahams's *A Night of Their Own* (1956) and La Guma's *In the Fog of the Season's End* (1972) are novels about the activities of the underground movement and about police reprisals in the 1960s. Abrahams dedicated his book to "Walter Sisulu, Nelson Mandela, and all others, the captured and the still free, who are at war against the evil of this night of their own" (Abrahams 1956, n.p.). La Guma's book is dedicated to "Basil February and others killed in action, Zimbabwe, 1967" (La Guma 1972, n.p.) and puts forward the belief that only though guerilla warfare will inequality in South Africa be abolished. Recent events have not borne out this conviction, apposite as it was when the book was written. But it remains a compelling account of the nature of subversive activities and the complexity of motivations that compelled guerilla actions. Nadine Gordimer, unlike La Guma, is a disinterested writer who suggests in "Some Monday for Sure" that on some perfectly ordinary day, for sure, black South Africans will free themselves and rule themselves—a prophecy fulfilled in the course of events. History has borne out her belief, yet the observation that the day was ordinary is true only in the sense that the guerilla activity of more than a decade, with its consciousness-raising effect, made possible the peaceful celebrations of the four days of May in 1994.

A subgenre of prison writing develops in the late 1960s as writers are arrested and sentenced under various repressive laws. Robben Island in Table Bay becomes a synonym for prison, and prison, in turn, becomes a synonym for life in South Africa. Dennis Brutus's *Letters to Martha and Other Poems from a South African Prison* (1968), D. M. Zwelonke's *Robben Island* (1973), and Athol Fugard's *The Island* (1973) are notable examples of literature that protests against political injustice and solitary confinement. Alex La Guma describes the internal apartheid of solitary confinement—separate cells for blacks, coloreds, and whites, and the mixing of hardened criminals and nonviolent political prisoners. La Guma suggests how these circumstances can be put to advantage by propagating communal feeling in the prison and thus increasing opportunities to promote political awareness.

Short fiction kept pace with the growth of the novel, poetry, and drama in tracing the changing fortunes of South Africans. Writers from the time of Olive Schreiner and W. C. Scully to later writers like Herman Charles Bosman, Pauline Smith, Alan Paton, Nadine Gordimer, Dan Jacobsen, Jack Cope, Lewis Nkosi, Ezekiel Mphahlele, Mtutzeli Matshoba, James Matthews, Jabulo Ndebele, and Ahmed Essop have used the form to elaborate on and expound the substance of their writing in other forms.

Prose fiction, however, gives ground to poetry as writing in the 1970s and 1980s was subjected to progressive censorship. Black writers found new means both for exposing the appalling conditions of apartheid and at the same time avoiding the strictures of the censorship laws. The uses of poetry in the 1980s represents the culmination of a line of development that has its origins in the experiences of the poets of the 1930s and their connections with the English literary tradition. Francis Carey Slater published *Drought: A South African Parable* in 1929. He edited two influential anthologies, *The Centenary Book of South African Verse* (1925), and *The New Book of South African Verse* (1945), which reflect connections with the English Romantic tradition. This tradition was, however, rendered obsolete by the joint efforts of Roy Campbell and William Plomer, who, together and separately, shook South African society out of its complacent colonial attitudes through their joint editing and publishing of *Voorslaag* (1926). In this work they sought to reveal and commend the unique nature of the South African landscape. Campbell and Plomer were sensitive to the problems of incipient racism and, in poems like "The Serf" and "The Zulu Girl," Campbell suggests the possibility of a confrontation between whites and blacks. This engendered resentment and anger on the part of whites, as did the long satirical poems *The Wayzgoose* (1928), and *The Georgiad* (1931). Plomer had already made plain his sensitivity to the worsening plight of African peoples in *Turbott Wolfe* (1926), and his poetry continues in this vein. Both Campbell and Plomer left South Africa, disaffected by the resentment their writing aroused in their countrymen.

The characteristic sentiments of their writing, however, continued to find expression in poets of the 1940s, poets committed to the cultivation of liberal and humane values, such as truth, justice, and equality. David Wright, Anthony Delius, and Guy Butler fought in World War II to defend humanist values. After the war, they sought in their writing to import these values. However, with the election of the National Party in 1948, the insistent growth of apartheid, and the eventual declaration of a republic in 1961, they saw the values for which they stood eroded. Wright and Delius left South Africa; Butler, along with Alan Paton, remained, prompted by the belief that he could work "on the ground" for reconciliation and amelioration of the injustices inflicted on Africans by apartheid. Other poets of the period, most prominent among them Ruth Miller and Douglas Livingstone, look inward and, by adopting the proscriptions of modernism, record their personal angst resulting from their recognition of their isolation and the fears this engendered.

In the 1970s, a "black" voice emerges. Inspired by the Sharpeville massacres, the Soweto riots, and the Black Consciousness Movement, poetry of protest against apartheid and an assertion of African integrity and aspiration came into being. This is a militant and revolutionary poetry written by blacks. The suggestion that racial equality might be gained through negotiation and accommodation is no longer heard. Poets of the 1970s—Oswald Mtshali, Mongane Wally Serote, and Sipho Sepamla—by implication and assertion, advocate confrontation.

The Black Consciousness Movement came into being because of the disaffection of blacks and other organizations that took up their cause. Such organizations as the Liberal and Progressive parties, and the national Union of South African Students, essentially conservative in approach, proved ineffectual in effecting changes in the laws governing segregation and discrimination. The South African Students Organization, which eventually developed into the Black Consciousness Movement, was organized to better reflect and represent black interests. Eventually and quickly, however, it articulated the plight of all oppressed peoples. It operated on its own terms, independent of of the ANC and PAC. It was not until 1974 that it established formal relations with these political parties.

Black Consciousness was short-lived. It was banned in 1977 and its founder, leader, and most articulate spokesman, Steve Biko, was put in jail where he died in mysterious circumstances. However, in its brief existence, the Black Consciousness Movement became one of the most influential forces in South Africa, its influence as great as that of the ANC and PAC. Its aim was to raise the consciousness of black people through a positive assertion of black history and culture. It was successful in achieving these aims and its influence was felt long after it was officially banned.

Writing after the advent of the Black Consciousness Movement is different in character than writing of the 1960s. It is openly political, hortatory, didactic, and assertive. It is about black experience and "racial pride," defined through a consideration of various subjects and issues that engage writers and inform their literary output. It is precisely focused on those circumstances that compromise or affirm blackness. Part of the commitment of Black Consciousness, therefore, was to discredit the negative images of Africans, historical figures, peoples, and cultures promulgated in educational texts adopted for general use in the schools, to rewrite the stories of these discredited peoples and cultures and, while doing this, find correspondences with contemporary issues.

The major thrust of the writing of the Black Consciousness poets— Oswald Mtshali, Dennis Brutus, Keorapetse Kgoitsile, Mbulelo Mzmane, James Matthews, Casey "Kid" Motsis, Mongane Wally Serote, Njabulo Ndebele, Mandla Langa, Dom Mattera, Modikwe Dikobe—is to describe township poverty and violence (the two being intimately related); internal disparities in privilege and potential; suffering, humiliation, and despair; educational and economic deprivation; political oppression; the irrationality of the disparity between blacks and whites; the opposition between the depleted arid homeland and the equally arid and abusive city/ghetto. All these conditions stood opposed to the general conditions of whites in South Africa.

Running parallel to the poetry associated with the Black Consciousness Movement, a popular theater developed, which had its origins in the 1950s and 1960s and gained its greatest prominence in the 1970s. Lewis Nkosi's *Rhythm of Violence* and Athol Fugard's *The Blood Knot* are the most prominent examples of the plays from the 1960s. These plays proposed the possibilities of a *rapprochement* between the races. With liberalism discrediting itself in the 1970s, plays like those gave way to a theater dealing with the day-to-day concerns of people—with race relations, victimization by the authorities, corruption in its various forms, drink, crime, and sex. These were issues exploited in popular successes—*King Kong, Sikalo, Zwi, Lifa* and *Ipi Tomba*—plays that enjoyed great success overseas and, ironically, reinforced the stereotypes of race and culture against which the ANC, the PAC, and the Black Consciousness Movement were campaigning.

Radical theater groups—The Serpent Players, The Phoenix Players, and Workshop '71—presented plays that involved the efforts of various peoples from South Africa and suggested the possibility of reconciliation in performance not possible in the day-to-day existence of the audience members who attended them. Fugard is the seminal force in the theater of the time, and plays like *Siswe Bansi Is Dead*, *"Master Harold" and the Boys*, *The Island*, and *A Lesson from Aloes*, expose in their various approaches the exploitation, oppression, and dehumanizing effects of the political system.

Literary and political issues are intimately bound together in the writing of novelists, poets, and playwrights of the 1980s. Most of this writing continues the business of consciousness raising, of resistance to racist policy, and of the adoption of radical revolutionary actions, whether explicitly or implicitly. The balance between political statement and aesthetic concerns varies, but when the two conditions achieve a balance, a body of writing was produced which will endure as literary artifact as much as will a historical document.

A central figure in the movement of the 1980s is Njebulo Ndebele, who believes that the manner of expression should be of equal concern to the artist as the matter described. As one of his characters in a short story says, "too much obsession with removing oppression in the political dimension soon becomes a form of oppression." Ndbele's writing works by implication while displaying the belief that "apartheid will wear itself out in the end" (Ndbele 1984, 23).

This is, of course, what happened in the end, although the complexity of pressures that brought about the lifting of the ban on political parties and the release of political prisoners has not yet been fully recorded in the writing.

There were predictions up until 1989 that, because of the greater and greater repression in the form of laws enforced by progressively vindictive security forces, nothing short of violent revolution and guerilla warfare with outside support has any realistic chance of overthrowing apartheid. These predictions proved wrong as events leading up to the four days in May 1994 showed. In the end, a gradualist and negotiated approach prevailed. It is plain, however, that the main predications and assertions of the militants, reflected in the writing of the Black Consciousness Movement, prompted the increase of the pace of negotiations that took place between Nelson Mandela and F. W. de Klerk in March 1989.

Now that South Africa has entered the postapartheid period, South African writing to date will be submitted to greater literary analysis, and reasons for its effectiveness in its own time will be demonstrated for its continuing interest in the present and beyond. The need for a radical literature directed at ameliorating the appalling applications of apartheid has passed with apartheid. What follows remains to be seen.

The events of May 1994—the first general election in South Africa—saw the triumph of the ANC in forming the national government, representative of popular preference, leading to the death of apartheid. With the elections of May 1994, South Africa entered the postcolonial era and achieved a kind of parity with other former colonies of the anglophone world.

South African authors are doubtless elated with the reversal of circumstances against which they campaigned relentlessly and single-mindedly for 45 years. However, there may well be a dark side to the euphoria. The end of apartheid will not necessarily enhance the liberation of the artistic imagination that for so long was tempered by repression. Dissident and exiled writers now have a new part to play. It may take some time to discover what that part may be. But judging from the postapartheid writing of three South African writers, that will not be the case. Nadine Gordimer and J. M. Coetzee have made the transition smoothly and without any diminution of their powers.

SOUTH AFRICAN LITERATURE

Olive Emilie Albertina Schreiner is South Africa's first authentic novelist. She published three novels: *The Story of an African Farm* (1883), and *From Man to Man,* and *Undine* (the latter two published posthumously, in 1926 and 1929). *The Story of an African Farm* is the most famous of her fictions because it represents a clear break with the English colonialist tradition of writing. In the novel, Schreiner follows her own advice "to paint what lies before you": that is, to turn away from English models and to present the reality of the landscape in which the writer finds herself. The novel tells the story, in a fragmented structure with solid interpolations of political and religious matters, of three children growing up in the Karoo region of South Africa in the 1860s. Schreiner paints a rounded picture of South African rural life in the period of her novel. The fragmentary structure of the novel might be said to reflect the largely unordered social organization of the embryonic community she depicts in the work.

Equally important is Schreiner's depiction of the status—or lack of status—of women in the period. Her concern is dual: first, she implicitly advocates the need for women to achieve equality with men. Second, she expresses a concern about the position of nonwhite women where white women are privileged. As well as the implicit comment in the novel, Schreiner articulates her feminist thoughts and beliefs in *Woman and Labourer* (1911). In this book, she deals with questions of education, of the exploitation of women in labor, their sexual exploitation, and of women and questions of their relations to war.

Trooper Peter Halket of Mashonaland (1897) and *An English South African's View of the Situation* (1899) are about the pointlessness of the impending Anglo-Boer War, predicting that the war seems inevitable while expressing the hope that it can be avoided. In *The Political Situation* (1896), she is prescient in predicting that a burgeoning South African capitalism will depend more and more on racist policies that exploit necessary labor. In this way, Schreiner anticipates the main concern of the century before her. *Closer Union* (1909) develops this theme further in articulating racial segregation and its relations to monopoly capitalism. Here, Schreiner proposes that South Africa should create a federalist state.

Schreiner's writing stands at the beginning of an authentic literary tradition in English in South Africa and, taken together, her writing adumbrates all of those themes and issues that inform the work of writers who come after her.

William Charles Scully is known for his fiction, poetry, short stories, and autobiographical reflections. His writing shows a wide-ranging response to the South African landscape and a deeply sympathetic understanding of African peoples, especially as their lives and cultures experience the relentless impact of imperial annexation. Scully's writing reveals an essential duality in imperial practices. He is, on the one hand, a supporter of imperialism and believes in its many credos. Yet, at the same time, he deplores the jingoistic excesses of its more strident exponents who practice an exploitative racism under the guise of a benevolent paternalism. Scully treats the subject fully in *The Harrow* (1921), a retrospective recreation of Boer suffering in the Anglo-Boer War of 1899–1943.

Scully further represents the position and condition of Africans living in both the rural and urban settings in *Daniel Vananda: The Life of a Human Being*. The novel was published in 1923 but deals with the period 1880–1920. Scully pursues his sympathetic interest in the lives and cultures of African peoples in three collections of short stories—*Kaffir Stories* (1895), *The White Hetacomb and Other Stories* (1897), and *By Veldt and Kopje* (1907).

His other publications include *The Wreck of the Grosvenor and Other South African Poems,* published anonymously in 1886, and *Poems* (1892). *Between Sun and Sand* (1898) is about the lives of nomadic people in Namaqualand, and *Lodges in the Wilderness* (1915), also about Namaqualand, describes the spiritual connection Scully finds with that landscape.

Scully also published three volumes of autobiographical reminiscences that amplify his concerns about the country—*A Visit to Johannesburg* (1912), *Reminiscences of a South African Pioneer* (1913), and *Further Reminiscences of a South African Pioneer* (1913).

Douglas Blackburn worked for 15 years as a journalist and his seven novels are drawn from those years. His novels include the trilogy *Prinsloo of Prinsloosdorp: A Tale of Transvaal Officialdom, by Sarel Erasmus* (1899), *A Burgher Quixote* (1903), and *I Came and Saw* (1908). The trilogy deals, at first with gentle satire and as the series progresses with greater naturalism, with the experiences of a young Boer farmer, Sarel Erasmus, as he feels increasing pressures through British encroachment. Blackburn was antiim-perialist and uses these books to expose the more absurd kinds of British behavior.

Richard Hartley, Prospector (1905) again reveals Blackburn's antiimperal-ist and antiexpansionist beliefs. Here he chooses a form and manner that sat-irizes the adventure/romances of such popular writers as Rider Haggard. *Leaven: A Black and White Story* (1908) exposes the fallacy of the so-called noble (pliable) savage as found in the romances of popular writers while at the same time anticipating a major theme in South African writing—the dis-placement of Africans from rural areas as they become exploited labor in the gold mines of the Witwatersrand. *Kruger's Secret Service by One Who Was in It* (1900) debunks the militant imperialism of Cecil Rhodes. *Love Muti* (1915) is about the question of love between the races, anticipating a theme that would figure prominently in the South African literary tradition.

Blackburn was, then, a humanist who used irony and satire as his princi-pal literary weapons in exposing what he saw as the cruelties and injustices of imperial capitalist expansion in South Africa. Reginald Perceval Gibbon (1878–1926) was, like Douglas Blackburn, a visitor to South Africa. And, like Blackburn, he remained in South Africa long enough—from 1897 until 1903—to feel a close identification with the country and to write about it in four widely known and provocative novels. Like Blackburn, he foresaw the social imperatives that would come to dominate and divide South African society.

Souls in Bondage (1904) is about miscegenation and the devastating effects of racism, a racism based upon the social Darwinism of the late Victorian period. *The Vrouw Grobelaar's Leading Cases* (1905) is again about racism. The story is told from the point of view of a rural Cape Dutch woman. *Flower of the Peach* (1911) was republished under the now more familiar title, *Margaret Harding*, in 1983. It is set on a colonial farm and near to a TB sanitarium. It deals with a variety of related human issues, most notably with the possibilities of black-white relations. Perceval deals with his themes in a realistic manner and thus complements the ironic stance of Blackburn.

Sir Percy Fitzpatrick is best known for his novel *Jock of the Bushveld* (1907), a story set in the gold fields of the Eastern Transvaal and based on the author's experiences there. It is the story of the bond between a boy growing to maturity and his terrier pup set against a background of pio-neering life and characters. The book is a classic of children's literature but is as well enjoyed and revered by adult readers for its lack of sentimentality.

Fitzpatrick's other published work includes *Through Mashonaland with Pick and Pen* (1892), *The Outspan: Tales of South Africa* (1897), and *Transvaal from Within: A Private Record of Public Affairs* (1899). This lat-ter book argues the case for the Uitlanders at the outbreak of the Anglo-Boer War. For his sentiments toward the Boers, Fitzpatrick was charged with treason for his association with the Jameson Raid, the ill-fated attempt of the Rand mining concerns, backed by the British, to seize control of the gold fields of the Witwatersrand. Fitzpatrick published his account at the end of a three-year silence that was imposed on him. From this period forward, Fiztpatrick was an advisor to the British government on South African affairs. He was knighted for his service in 1902 and remained an influential figure in effecting the unification of the South African colonies in 1910.

Sarah Gertrude Millin (1889–1968) published 17 novels, a collection of short stories, two autobiographies, two biographies, six war diaries, and three reference works on South Africa, making her by far South Africa's most published author to date. In her fiction, she has adopted and modified a theory of biological determinism based on pseudoscientific nineteenth-century concepts of the racial degeneration that would occur should miscegenation be practiced. She demonstrates her convictions in a trilogy of novels—*God's Stepchildren* (1924), *King of the Bastards* (1940), and *The Burning Man* (1949). Four of her novels, *The Coming of the Lord* (1928), *What Hath a Man?* (1938), *The Wizard Bird* (1962), and *Goodbye, Dear England* (1965) dramatize her conviction of the disastrous effects that will inevitably occur if an alien and imported culture is imposed on an indigenous people. These novels, viewed from a certain perspective, adumbrate the segregation of cultures that inevitably led to the policy of apartheid.

Millen's biographies of Cecil Rhodes and Jan Christian Smuts; her social commentaries, *The South Africans* (1926, 1934) and *The People of South Africa* (1951); and her autobiographies *The Night Is Long* (1941) and *The Measure of My Days* (1955) achieved considerable popularity in their day with both white South Africans, mainly Boers, and with an international audience.

Millin's contemporary, William Charles Franklyn Plomer, published the landmark novel *Turbott Wolfe* in 1926. The story centers on the advice given by the eponymous hero of the novel to a beautiful white woman: he encourages her to marry a black man. The novel engages in an open discussion about sexual relations, unique in its time for suggesting that black-white marriage be accepted in South African society. The novel, therefore, also contains an attack on racial prejudice. The novel presents a number of opposing points of view. It nevertheless outraged white society. Plomer introduced a theme that was to become central to much white South African writing that followed, most notably in books by Sarah Gertrude Millin, Alan Paton, Nadine Gordimer, and Andre Brink

Plomer's short story, "Ula Masondo," introduced a theme that was to become as prominent as miscegenation. The "Jim comes to Jo'burg" theme, as it came to be known, tells the story of the young man who travels from his village to the city in search of work, in this case the gold mines in Johannesburg. Plomer shows the myriad difficulties experienced by his hero, a portrayal that came to be typical in writing that followed—the antipathy between whites and blacks and the escalation of this antipathy, resulting in the creation of apartheid, the creation of segregated townships, and the events of Sharpeville and Soweto. Plomer was well aware of the prophetic nature of his novel and short story.

Plomer, with Roy Campbell and Laurens van der Post, founded the literary journal *Voorslaag,* a bilingual journal devoted to publishing writing in South African languages other than English—as well as English—and a journal that was especially critical of a burgeoning racial prejudice. Reaction to *Voorslaag* was hostile and Plomer left South Africa in 1926. He moved to Japan and remained there until 1929. He then moved to England where he remained for the rest of his life. He was a reader for Jonathan Cape publishers and helped to establish the writing careers of such literary luminaries as Arthur Koestler, Langston Hughes, John Betjeman, Vladimer Nabokov, John Fowles, and Alan Paton.

Plomer continued to write, turning more and more to poetry. He collaborated with Benjamin Britten on four musical projects. He published two volumes of autobiography, *Double Lives* (1943) and *At Home* (1958). These two volumes were combined as *The Autobiography of William Plomer* (1975). Sections of these books dealing with South Africa were published in 1984 as *The South African Autobiography.* Plomer published a collection of short stories, *I Speak of Africa* in 1927, and a biography of Cecil Rhodes in 1933.

Plomer remains a central figure in the South African literary canon because of *Turbottt Woolfe.*

Pauline Smith achieved a fame equal to Plomer's, although she published only one novel, *The Beadle* (1926), one collection of short stories, *The Little Karoo* (1925), and *Platkops Children,* a book for children (1935). Her literary sensibility was shaped by the journeys she took with her father, Dr. Herbert Urinson Smith, through the arid and dry Karoo. From early childhood, she came to understand the effects, both social and psychological, of the hard existence of the men and women of the Karoo—English, Afrikaner, and African. Her writing conveys a deeply sensitive nature that is able, in only two adult publications, to catch the colonial, political, sexual, and racial issues of her time and to convey the plight of those suffering under hardships to prevail. She is able to reveal the inner nature of her characters while placing them firmly in the realities of their environment. She is especially sensitive to the conditions of women in a patriarchal society. Her work endures because of its sensitivity, compassion, and charity.

Rolfes Robert Reginald (R.R.R.) Dhlomo earned a living by writing, under various pseudonyms, newspaper pieces and reportage, both educational and comic, mostly in *Sjambok,* a satirical magazine funded by Stephen Black that ran from 1929 to 1931. Dhlomo has a central place in South African literature because he published the first novel written by a black South African writer. *An African Tragedy* (1928) is the first of a series of novels that deal with the temptations of the city for a young man who travels there from the country in search of work.

Dhlomo also published stories in the newspaper *Bantu World;* the stories were collected and published in *Africa1* in 1975. From 1935 until his death, Dhlomo wrote in Zulu and published historical novels about the lives of the great Zulu leaders of the nineteenth century—Dingane, Shaka, Mpande, Cetshewayo, and Dinizulu.

As well known on the international literary scene as in South Africa, Sir Laurens Jan van der Post published *In a Province* in 1934. Influenced by Plomer through their connection with *Voorslaag,* the novel is one of the first to denounce race relations, specifically the "color bar" as the incipient apartheid policy was called at the time. The novel anticipates a long list of writing on the subject. Van der Post's principal interest, one which informs his later writing, as well as the film documentaries he prepared later in his career, is in the differences between belief systems of blacks and whites. His point is that by recognizing differences and accepting them, cultural unity in the country might be obtained. Equally, he shows the destructive consequences to African life when white systems are forcibly imposed on Africans.

Other novels set in South Africa by van der Post are *Flamingo Feathers* (1955), *The Hunter and the Whale* (1967), *A Story Like the Wind* (1972), and its sequel, *A Far-Off Place* (1974). Van der Post is also known for his nonfiction writing. His books that record his search for the descendants of the Bushmen of the Kalahari Desert became the television series *The Lost World of the Kalahari* (1958). Van der Post wrote two further books related to the Kalahari, *A Mantis Carol* (1976) and *Testament to the Bushmen* (1984). Van der Post's other works include *Jung and the Story of Our Time* (1976), recording his friendship with Carl Jung, *Yet Being Someone Other* (1982), a record of his experiences of living in Japan; *A Walk with a White Bushman* (1986), and *About Blady: A Pattern Out of Tune* (1991). He also published an inspirational cookbook, *First Catch Your Eland* (1977), in which one finds as much cultural as culinary lore.

The most popular writer of the period is Stuart Cloete. Taken together, Cloete's novels form a fictionalized history of South Africa. Altogether he published 14 novels in the sequence, all in the form of the adventure story His first novel, *Turning Wheels* (1937), was published in the centenary year of the Great Trek. The novel was subsequently banned until 1947 because of its alleged defaming of its Boer characters. Other novels that followed and contributed to Cloete's international reputation are *Watch for the Dawn* (1939), about the frontiers of the Karoo; *The Hills of Doves* (1941), about the Anglo-Boer conflict; and *The Mask* (1957), about a young Afrikaner and his life on the frontier. Cloete was a popular novelist because he knew what expectations were regarding the historical periods that were the subject of his books and wrote to fulfill those expectations.

Peter Abrahams, still the most prolific colored writer from South Africa, left South Africa in 1939, going into voluntary exile in England. Despite the fact that all of his writing has been done overseas—in England and Trinidad—he gained international reputation for the large body of writing he published expressing various concerns about South Africa and the state of the black and colored peoples. His first publication was *Dark Testament* (1942), a series of short pieces that have as their context a political struggle and record the experiences, both public and personal, of a young colored writer. *Song of the City* (1945) is Abrahams's first novel; set in South Africa, it deals with the debate over whether or not South Africa should enter World War II. It is about the political allegiances that obtained at the time. Like some of his predecessors, Abrahams factors the complicated issue of race into his fictional analysis of the time.

Abrahams finds his authentic voice with his second novel, *Mine Boy*, in 1948. The novel deals with the nature of the progressive urbanization that comes about as the industrial base of South Africa develops and as the need for work in the mines accelerates. Abrahams's characters are at once representative figures in the landscape and yet are highly individualized. They collect around Leah who runs a shebeen, an illegal drinking establishment. Leah is streetwise and expert in the art of survival in the city. The people who frequent her shebeen are all in various ways victims of the incipient racism of South Africa. Daddy, for whom Leah cares with compassion, is an alcoholic when we meet him, a man who devoted his life to the political struggle for equality and who is eventually broken by the system he seeks to change. Eliza is a schoolteacher who yearns for the rewards of living in the white world, a yearning that is unfulfilled because of her skin color. Johannes is a gentle giant who works in the mines and suffers from a bipolarism induced by the white world. When sober, he is gentle and compassionate; when drunk, he is aggressive in response to the conditions that threaten to destroy his life.

Xuma is the novel's central character, the Mine Boy of the book's title. Through Xuma's story, Abrahams makes his central point about the condition of the working class in South Africa. Through Xuma, we experience the physical and psychological danger of the poorly paid mine work. *Mine Boy* is a novel about the class struggle, about the contention between owners and workers. What is more, it is a novel that seeks to present reform of the conditions it dramatizes. There is some hope for solidarity at the novel's close, when white, Irish-born supervisors and black workers unite in a protest strike.

In *The Path of Thunder* (1948), Abrahams deals with the affair between a colored man and a white woman who try to bridge the color bar. Abrahams uses their relationship to display the disastrous consequences to anyone who tries to flout racist determinants. The harsh setting of the novel, the arid Karoo, is a leitmotif for the human experiences in the book. Lennie Swartz

and Sarei Villiers, their love denied, die in a gun battle with white suprema-
cists, but not before Lennie has killed three of their oppressors. Abrahams's
liberal convictions are obvious in the human drama of the book.

Wild Conquest (1950) is a historical novel about the Great Trek of 1834,
one of a very large body of writing on the subject that continues to capture
the imagination of South African writers. The novel is not judged one of
Abrahams more successful works, it being an almost perfunctory performance as if he felt obliged to contribute to the literature on the subject.

Return to Goli (1953) and *Tell Freedom* (1954) are both autobiographical
works about Abrahams's political beliefs, the former occasioned by a visit to
South Africa sponsored by the London *Observer* newspaper. These books
deal with political and social developments in South Africa from the 1930s
forward. They are marked by a plainness and exactness of writing.

A Wreath for Udomo (1956) is a prophetic novel that dramatizes with
uncanny accuracy how the first African colony will gain its independence
from Britain. It anticipates Ghanaian independence by one year. The novel
describes, through conversations and actions, the various local interests that
compete for the large rewards they believe independence will offer, and the
myriad, and, ultimately in this case, overwhelming issues the first leader will
have to face. The novel ends in a head-on confrontation between African
conservatism and modern western political policies.

Udomo is the leader of the group of politically interested expatriate
Africans. Mhendi is Udomo's counterpart from a neighboring country who
sees the needs of his country as different from Udomo's. For reasons of
political expediency, Mhendi is sacrificed. Selina is a rich market woman who
finances Udomo's campaign. She stands for African conservatism and
expects Udomo to support her demands. She is responsible for Udomo's
murder when, once in office, he shows his policies at extreme odds with
hers. Adehboy is a western-trained doctor who nevertheless supports Selina
against Udomo. He, too, stands for African conservatism although his
motives are purely self-serving. The novel is prophetic not only in terms of
showing how independence can be gained but also in showing how fragile
it is once achieved.

A Night of Their Own (1965) uses the framework of a love affair between
a black man and an Indian women, both political outcasts, to examine the
role of the artist in an underground political movement.

In *This Island Now* (1966), Abrahams examines the politics of race relations in a Caribbean setting, again displaying the difficulties inherent in the
transition from colonial dependency to independence. In *The View from
Coyaba* (1985), Abrahams broadens his perspective to consider the question
of Africa, the Caribbean, and America in the context of 150 years of black
history. A forerunner of African writers, Abrahams's literary successes as well
as his treatment of political and racial themes have provided encouragement
to black writers who have come after him.

Es'kia (formerly Ezekiel) Mphahlele published a short-story collection, *Man Must Live,* in 1946, which anticipates in form and subject matter collections of short stories to follow; his primary subject is the oppressive nature of life for Africans in the context of apartheid, leavened to some extent by the resiliency of blacks to extract decency and even humor from their binding circumstances. Possibly still his best-known work is the autobiographical *Down Second Avenue* (1959), which pays tribute to the strong women who influenced his life and, as well, the conditions that eventually caused him to go into exile in 1957. *Africa My Music: An Autobiography 1957–1983,* a sequel to *Down Second Avenue,* was published in 1984 on Mphahlele's return to South Africa. Mphahlele's other short-story collections are *The Living and the Dead* (1961), *In Corner B* (1967), *The Unbroken Song* (1981), and *Renewal Time* (1988).

The Wanderers (1971) is an autobiographical novel set in countries resembling Nigeria and Kenya, where Mphahlele lived and worked, and the novel *Chirundu* (1979) deals with corruption in independent Zambia.

Mphahlele's collections of essays on literary and general cultural subjects and issues, *The African Image* (1962, revised 1974) and *Voices in the Whirlwind* (1972), retain a contemporary relevance as well as having historical interest.

Prominent among women writers of this period, Daphne Rooke published her first novel, *The Sea Hath Bounds,* in 1946; it was reprinted in 1950 as *A Grove of Fever Trees.* Her other novels are *Mittee* (1951), *Ratoons* (1953), *Beti* (1959), *A Lover for Estelle* (1961), *The Greyling* (1962), *Diamond Jo* (1965), and *Margaretha de la Porte* (1974).

Mittee brought Rooke international recognition. It is set in the period prior to and during the Anglo-Boer War in the Transvaal. *Beti* is set in India, while her other novels are set in New Zealand and Australia—where Rooke lived for periods of time and where she eventually retired with her husband.

The Greyling was banned in South Africa because of its treatment of the issue of color. Rooke was regarded initially as a writer of popular romances and romance themes do dominate in her fictions. But political issues, as well as issues of gender and race relations, work as subtexts deftly and accurately integrated into her stories. Recognition of her place in South African writing proceeds from her unusually sensitive treatment of these issues. Critics latterly mention her in the same breath as Olive Schreiner and Nadine Gordimer.

Jack Cope, Rooke's exact contemporary, was a prolific writer and publisher. He published more than 100 short stories, three volumes of poetry, and four novels. Cope's main preoccupation was white-black relations, particularly the destruction of black culture as a result of white intervention and the attempts of blacks to reclaim their culture and their dignity. His work reveals his close acquaintance with and understanding of black, especially Zulu, culture, and his profound sympathy with these peoples derives from that understanding.

His point of view in these matters is established in his first novel, *The Fair House* (1955), which is based on the Zulu rebellion of 1906, and re-formed in the novels that followed—*The Golden Oriole* (1958), *Albino* (1964), and *The Rain Maker* (1971). Cope was an influential figure in the formation of the South African literary tradition as writer, editor, and publisher. He was also a central figure in the struggle against apartheid.

Daniel Jacobson has published 19 volumes—novels, short stories, and literary commentaries. His writing career coincided more or less with the beginnings of apartheid, and thus develops along lines parallel to the progressive refinements of that racist policy and with the abuses of power and public responsibility it represented. We should not be surprised, then, that Jacobson's first published work, *The Trap* (1955), is a novella about the influence of environment on character. There, he looks at racism and greed and how both whites and blacks are affected by them. Jacobson's preoccupation with racism extends his interest in how Jews are affected by South African racism, a subject he treats fully in two subsequent novellas, *The Price of Diamonds* (1957) and *The Beginners* (1966). The settings of this writing are variously the Karoo, Kimberley, and Johannesburg. *The Beginners* is Jacobson's most ambitious novel both in terms of subject matter and length. It is the story of three generations of Jewish immigrants to and emigrants from South Africa, tracing a pattern from Russia to South Africa to Israel and thence to England. The members of these Jewish families fall victim to the racist policies of South Africa in the same way as blacks and coloreds. Thus, Jacobson's fiction documents their flights from South Africa, some to England and some to Israel, to escape the racism that circumscribes their lives.

The Evidence of Love (1960) is Jacobson's first full-length novel and deals with the theme of miscegenation. It tells the story of the impossible relationship of Isobel, a white South African woman, and Kenneth, a colored South African man. Their relationship develops in London, free to do so without restraints on mixed relationships, and is destroyed on their return to South Africa.

The Beginners is Jacobson's last work with a South African setting. His later writing is set in different places and times, mostly London. But his writing about South Africa has a central place in South African literature for the record it provides of the ways in which human lives are restricted by formal policies of racial discrimination.

Herman Charles Bosman is a central figure in South African literature. He saw through his work as editor on various journals and magazines the potential of creating an authentic South African literary tradition. Equally, he recognized that such a tradition would have to free itself from colonial literary influences if it were to succeed. To illustrate his convictions, Bosman wrote poetry, fiction, short stories, and plays. His two novels, *Jacaranda in the Night* (2000) and *Willemsdorp* (not published until 1984, after his death in

1977), are attacks on Afrikaner Puritanism as this revealed itself in the pro-scriptions of the National Party after its rise to power after 1948, especially as the policy of apartheid was developed. Associated with these attacks are Bosman's concerns over the system of forced labor and his responses to the Immorality Act, which forbid mixed relationships. Bosman was a complex figure who displayed in his writings a wide range of responses to the situation he dealt with. Essentially an anarchist, he could be populist or elitist, compassionate or acerbic, romantic or satirical, tolerant or intolerant as cir-cumstances demanded in his examination of relations between the races in South Africa.

Like Stuart Cloete in an earlier generation of South African writers, Wilbur Smith is South Africa's most widely published novelist. He is a pop-ular writer of the romance thrillers and family saga genres. He has published 25 novels to date, their settings equally in the present and the past, most dealing with aspects of South African themes. His first novel, *When the Lion Feeds* (1964), introduces the Courtney family and traces their development in the context of the political, social, and economic history of South Africa over a 100-year period. Smith has also written novels about British-Boer relations, especially in the period of the Boer War; the history of Southern Rhodesia to its eventual emergence as Zimbabwe; the politics of Mozambique; the Independence War (which he calls the Mau Mau Rebellion) in Kenya; and the emergence of militant black action against the racist regime of apartheid. Smith's novels pander to popular taste, which he is a master of judging. They add nothing to an understanding of the com-plexity of South African life and the issues surrounding its racial policies before independence.

Andre Brink is a protean figure in South African literature. He is a pro-fessional academic and from that base works as a novelist, essayist, transla-tor, playwright, and theater director. Brink writes both in Afrikaans (his native tongue) and English. (It is his work in English that concerns us here.) His fiction deals almost exclusively with the political and social realities of South Africa, ranging through historical periods to the present day. He is especially concerned with race relations as these are shaped by the political imperatives of the National Government, which held sway from 1948 until 1994. He is also concerned with the role and responsibility of the artist in his or her society.

Brink's first published novel is *Looking on Darkness* (1974), which deals with the near impossibility of taking direct political action in a repressive regime. The novel focuses on the relationship between Joseph Malan, a Cape colored, and Jessica, a white woman. Malan is accused of her murder and for this he will be hanged. The novel is told retrospectively. Brink claimed that his novel was one of the first to confront directly and unam-biguously the apartheid system. Because it deals with a mixed-race relation-ship, it was banned when first published.

An Instant on the Wind (1976) is set in the eighteenth century. A white woman, Elizabeth Laarson, the wife of an explorer and naturalist, is widowed when her husband dies on an expedition into the bush. She meets an escaped slave, Adam Mantoor, who says he will lead her back to civilization if she, in return, will arrange for his freedom. They encounter many difficulties on their journey, eventually arriving in Cape Town. Mantoor has kept his part of the bargain. Elizabeth, bowing to intense social pressure, betrays him. Brink's novel is a rewriting of the story of Eliza Fraser, a colonial woman who was shipwrecked and helped by an escaped slave. The contradictions in race relations of the novel's historical period suggest similar contradictions and moral issues of the present.

Rumours of Rain (1978) is cast in the form of a diary written in London by Martin Mynhart, an Afrikaner South African business executive. The diary is a record of the measures Mynhart will go to to achieve personal success. He sacrifices love and loyalty and betrays his father, his wife, his mistress, and his black assistant. The novel is a devastating exposure of Afrikaner sensibility. Mynhart is a thoroughly reprehensible character.

In *A Dry White Season* (1979), an anonymous narrator examines the papers of an old friend, Ben du Toit, who has been killed in a road accident. The narrator unfolds Ben's story, through the progressive sacrifices he has made—the love of his wife and daughter (his son remains loyal to him) and his job—in his quest to discover what has happened to the son of Gordon, a cleaner at the school where Ben teaches. He learns that the son has been killed by the security police in the aftermath of the Soweto riots. Gordon is subsequently arrested, tortured, and murdered. Ben is betrayed by his daughter to the security police and his murder by road accident is arranged. Ben's story is eventually told by the writer to whom he has entrusted his papers.

A Dry White Season is perhaps the most terrifying indictment of the apartheid system, its methods, and the agents who implement it. Brink reveals powerfully the physical and psychological damage wrought on a whole society by this inhumane system of governance.

In *A Chain of Voices* (1982), Brink exploits a number of voices—black and white, female and male—to tell a story of a slave revolt in Cape Colony in 1825. The narrative employs various languages to advance the story—primarily English and Afrikaans—and to make the metaphoric point that the lack of understanding among the various characters is equivalent to the lack of intelligibility in present-day South Africa. Problems cannot be solved because voices and the values they announce cannot be heard.

In *The Wall of the Plague* (1984), Brink uses an inquiry into the causes and consequences of a plague in medieval Europe as a metaphor for apartheid. The story devolves around the relationship between Andrea Malgas, the colored heroine, Mandla Mgayisa, a black activist living in exile, and Paul Joubert, for a time Andrea's fiancé. Andrea achieves political awareness through her researches and through her discussions with Mandla. She comes to see, as Brink wants his readers to see and understand, that the disease, the putrefaction engendered by the plague, finds a contemporary equivalent in the disease of apartheid.

The narrative structure of *States of Emergency* (1988) is complex in its treatment of various intersecting themes. Conventional realistic narrative is balanced against a metafictional treatment. There is an autobiographical element. The principal narrator is both an academic and novelist struggling to establish a reputation in other areas of endeavor. There is an Orwellian element in that the action of the novel is set in a locale where state control is absolute. Characters drawn from real life are placed in verifiable historical moments and intersect with the lives of imaginary characters. The principal character, an author persona, struggles to complete a novel that becomes the title of Brink's next published work, described as "The Lives of Adamastor" in *States of Emergency*. There is a dual meaning in the title: both the writer and the world he lives in are in a state of emergency. The novels thus deal with different kinds of intersecting emergencies, political in the state and authorial as the writer struggles with his texts—story, form, authorial point of view, and depiction of personal relations.

An Act of Terror (1991) is a reworking of themes dealt with more compellingly in Brink's earlier work. *On the Contrary* (1993) returns to Cape Colony in the 1730s and, invoking historical figures, argues the case for the unreliability and indecipherability of both historical reconstruction and fictional imagining as just witnesses to human relationships and conduct.

Brink has also published *Mapmakers: Writers in a State of Siege* (1983), a collection of essays, and *The Ambassador,* in Afrikaans in 1963 and in English in 1967 as *File of a Diplomat.*

Brink's colleague at the University of Cape Town, John Maxwell (known as J. M.) Coetzee, was awarded the Nobel Prize for Literature in 2003. Coetzee is a postmodernist writer—his first novel, *Dusklands,* was called the first postmodern novel from South Africa by one its earliest critics. Coetzee has done advanced work on linguistics and he acknowledges his debt to such European literary and cultural theorists as Jacques Derrida, Michel Foucault, and Jacques Lacan. His novels are experimental, often founded in parables and parodies and frequently drawing on and modifying established literary texts.

Taken together, Coetzee's novels, literary criticism, and autobiographical writing form a cultural history of South Africa. The ideological framework in which he functions as a writer is described in his collection of essays, *White Writing: On the Culture of Letters in South Africa* (1988).

His first published fiction is *Dusklands* (1974). The book comprises two novellas. "The Vietnam Project" is a study of how a specialist in psychological warfare comes to a state of emotional collapse by the methods he attempts to use on others. "The Narrative of Jacobus Coetzee" is about a megalomaniac frontier farmer who makes two journeys into the interior of the country in a fruitless quest for ivory. Here he meets members of the indigenous population with whom he deals harshly when they do not share his vision of himself as god.

Coetzee's *In the Heart of the Country* (1977) explores the psychology of two related themes—father/daughter relations and master/servant relations. The narrator of the story is Magda, who lives with her father and their two servants, Hendrik and Klein-Anna, on an arid wilderness farm. Magda alternates in her moods as at times she seeks the approval of her father and at other times fantasizes about killing him. At times Magda has visions of being raped by Hendrick and at others she appeals to Klein-Anna to call her, Magda, by name so that she may discover who she is. This is a complicated and complex novel in its structure and in the psychological base on which it builds an inquiry into the difficulty of establishing personal relationships in a harsh landscape that emulates like conditions in the country as a whole.

Waiting for the Barbarians (1980) is set in an indeterminate time in an indeterminate locale, described simply as the western province of an unnamed empire. Here, liberalism, as practiced by the Magistrate, and fascism, the practice of a political power and represented by Colonel Voll, are in opposition. Coetzee poses the question of who are the barbarians for whom the people of the outpost wait. Are they a force for evil or disruption to the stable life of the community and country? Alternately, might the barbarians be civilizing agents? The quest for an answer to this question causes Voll to mount a fruitless search into lands beyond the frontier post. The book shows a progression from tedious but useful bureaucratic administration to a state of totalitarian control, symbolized by Voll's torture and mutilation of a barbarian woman. The Magistrate is also the victim of Voll's wrath when he is tortured for alleged but unspecified offenses against the state. The novel is not about South Africa per se but there are clear analogies with the methods of state security forces in the 1970s.

Life and Times of Michael K (1983)—the correspondences with Kafka's novel is obvious—is about the ability to survive one's differences from others: Michael K has a cleft palate, which sets him apart from his fellow citizens. The story tells of Michael K's attempts to honor his dying mother's wish that she die and be buried in her own country. It is a time of civil war, but even so Michael K sets off with his mother on a perilous journey. The mother dies on the journey. Michael buries her ashes on a deserted farm. Michael then devotes his life to growing pumpkins. But he is suspected of providing food for the enemies of the state and is taken to a military camp where he refuses to eat and refuses the ministrations of the camp physician. He survives this ordeal, eventually making an escape from the camp. Michael K's experience with the soldiers is a allegory for the treatment meted out to outsiders in South Africa (but the country is not named) and his rendering of the harsh dealings of the camp as well has his character's desire to make a new beginning function as a metaphor for the human capacity to endure, survive, and prevail.

Foe (1986)—again the debt to a classic of English literature is deliberate—is a reworking of Defoe's *Robinson Crusoe*: Susan Barton, the narrator, after surviving a mutiny on a ship that is taking her to find her daughter, is cast up on Crusoe's (here spelled "Cruso") island. She, Cruso, and Friday are rescued. Cruso dies on their return journey to England. Susan and Friday seek out the author, Foe, who will tell their story. Susan is able to tell her story but Friday is not: his tongue has been cut out. Their positions in relation to the business of telling the story suggest that the truth of a story and the telling of a life can never be fully known because they can never be fully reconstructed. Friday is silent and thus his story can never be told, but telling is an important dimension of the totality of experience, the knowable part revealed in Susan's ability to tell of her experience. In metafictional terms, their quest for whole truth adumbrates the impossibility of ever finding it and telling it. The novel is about the open-endedness of the writer's quest.

Age of Iron (1990) is in the form of a long letter written by Elizabeth Curren to her daughter who lives in exile in America. The novel is set in the closing years of apartheid, an age characterized by duality: on the one hand the claims of the state that they hold power and, on the other, the iron will of the resistance of black militants who seek to wrest it from them. This conflict is made specific in the story of the narrator/letter writer, a retired lecturer in classics who is now dying of cancer. Coetzee suggests that the cancer that is killing her is a metaphor for the cancer that is killing the state, that the humanist tradition embodied in the classics has been progressively killed by the antihumanist measures employed by the state. Another and larger issue is implied in the novel, namely the direction the state will take once apartheid has been abolished.

The Master of Petersberg (1994) is set in Russia in 1869. Dostoevsky returns to Russia from exile, concerned to discover the cause of the death of Pavel, his stepson. The son has been involved with a radical student political movement. Is his death a suicide as some claim? Has he been murdered? If so, by whom: the state authorities—or perhaps even by elements within the political cadre? His search is twofold: it is an inquiry, through meetings with the state police and the leader of the student movement, into the events in which his son has been involved. It is, as well, a journey of self-discovery as Dostoevsky, beset by doubt and debt—he fears he will be hounded by his creditors—and subject to attacks of epilepsy, looks for meaning in his life, assesses his achievements, and considers his future. Numerous contacts shape his inquiry—his son's landlady, Anna Sergeyevna and her daughter, Maximov, the police commissar, and Sergei Nacheyev, the anarchist student leader. The novel examines a number of related issues: parent/child relationships as these adumbrate outward into conflicting relations within the state; and the question of whether either of the political forces at work in the state—the current totalitarianism or the anarchy proposed by the adversarial political movement—is likely to make for peace and harmony. Coetzee puts the issue before his readers, but proposes no solutions. The world that Coetzee evokes with terrifying clarity in *The Master of Petersberg* is a world of hunger, sickness, and poverty created for the masses by the ministries of the Tsarist regime and merchant banks. It is a world analogous in many ways to Coetzee's South Africa, whose conditions were only relieved in the year Coetzee writes his book.

Disgrace (1999) tells the story of how close to the surface of the lives of ordinary people lies the social and psychological fact of racial violence in the postapartheid state. The novel tells the story of David Lurie, a semiretired university lecturer in Romantic poetry and communications at the Cape Technical University. Lurie lives a modest and contented life . His sexual needs are met by weekly visits to a prostitute. But his life takes a disastrous turn when he becomes obsessed with one of his students, whom he seduces. When Melanie, the student, wants to withdraw from the relationship, Lurie, in his obsession, continues to pursue her. Melanie and her father bring a complaint against him, he appears before an academic committee where he admits his guilt but is not repentant for his actions. He is scorned by his former wife, threatened by Melanie's boyfriend, and ridiculed by students in the university. Forced to resign his post, Lurie leaves Cape Town and seeks refuge with his daughter in his country farm. There he tries to understand the nature of changing relations between races in the postapartheid state and to restore relations with his daughter. One day, three black men visit the farm and ask to use the telephone. Lurie and his daughter are subjected to an afternoon of violence which leaves them badly shaken and at further odds with each other. Lurie returns to Cape Town and finds his home has been vandalized. He returns to his daughter, who has been made pregnant by one of the black attackers. Lurie, his self-esteem completely corroded, takes a job in an animal clinic: his job is to destroy diseased and abandoned dogs. Lurie's state and that of his daughter offer an epitome of the uncertainties and confusion that inform the South African state in the aftermath of a half century of racial rule.

The Lives of Animals (1999) proceeds from two lectures given by Coetzee as the 1997–98 Tanner Lectures at Princeton University. These are incorporated in *The Lives of Animals* as fictional pieces read before the university community of Appleton College by an aging Australian novelist, Elizabeth Costello. For her, the uses to which animals are put and the treatment they are given in the contemporary world constitute a stupefying crime. Her convictions about crimes against animals constitute her two lectures. The lectures evoke a variety of responses on the part of her listeners and these are most revealed in interchanges with her son, a professor at Appleton College, who is careful in setting forth his adversarial arguments—more careful than

Elizabeth's daughter-in-law, who dismisses her arguments as mere moral superiority.

The arguments—based on the revelation of the horrors wrought on animals in abattoirs, in zoos, and in laboratory experiments—are articulated in the fictional part of the book—and elaborated further in the nonfictional sections, the "Introduction" and the "Reflections." The "Introduction" is written by Amy Gutman, Laurance S. Rockefeller Professor at Princeton University and founding director of the University Centre for Human Values. The four "Reflections" are by distinguished academics who offer comment on the Coetzee/Costello lectures from radically different vantage points. The academics are Wendy Doniger, professor of the History of Religions at the University of Chicago; Marjorie Garber, professor of English at Harvard University and director of Harvard's Centre for Literary and Cultural Studies; Peter Singer, professor in the Centre for Human Bioethics at Monash University, Australia; and Barbara Smuts, professor of Psychology and Anthropology at the University of Michigan.

Youth (2002) is set in South Africa and England in the 1960s. The life of the first-person narrator, identified as John, in many ways resembles Coetzee's life. He is a white Afrikaner in a troubled South Africa, and a student of mathematics at the University of Cape Town. He is also an aspiring poet, troubled by which literary models he should follow, electing for Pound and Eliot among the moderns. When he moves to London in his quest for a life in art, to sustain himself he works as a computer programmer, first in London and then in Aldermaston. He engages in a number of casual sexual affairs but finds no comfort or commitment in them.

His life is compromised in two ways. First, as a South African, white and Afrikaner, he is never able to rid himself of the knowledge that "the ground beneath his feet is soaked with blood and the vast backward depth of history rings with shouts of anger" (17).

The massacre of Sharpeville and the protest marches shape his sensibility and intrude on his quest for a life in art. He knows that South Africa is headed for revolution and that Sharpeville has signaled the beginning of massive change. He predicts, when asked at his interview for a job with IBM, that the revolution will take place in 5 years—he is right in his prediction but about 30 years off in his timing.

His life is circumscribed by his failure to be what he wants to be—a successful artist, first as a poet, and when he feels that will elude him, as a novelist. Here, too, he searches for models. But he writes little. Success escapes him. His life in London—the London of the 1960s with its last great London Fog, London of the 1962 freeze-up, a desolate landscape which mirrors his own overwhelming loneliness—is characterized by his acknowledgment that misery is his constant companion. In the end, he is forced to admit that he will never be a poet or an artist, that he is a computer programmer and not an exceptional one at that. He will be overtaken by younger and brighter people than himself and his fate may be that of an Indian colleague who, unable to adapt to the ways of the world he lives in, dies of starvation, starvation of the body emanating from starvation of the soul.

Coetzee paints an honest if bleak world, offering neither false hope for the future nor consolation in the present. Coetzee here infuses ordinariness with a frightening and bleak intensity.

Elizabeth Costello (2003) is a collection of eight "Lessons" that make up a partial autobiography of an internationally recognized Australian novelist. Now in her declining years, Costello puts together a series of encounters with various peoples and places in her past, which she reviews for the purposes of determining what her life and achievements actually add up to. Coetzee moves from fiction to fact and back again and much of what is attributed to Costello in this novel is a reworking of materials given by Coetzee as lectures in other times. The "Acknowledgments" page at the book's close says that six of the "Lessons" have been published elsewhere as earlier versions of what is published in *Elizabeth Costello*. The subject matter of the Lessons is divided between talks on literary subjects—"Realism," the "Novel in Africa," "The Humanities in Africa"—and on the question of animal rights—the Appleton lectures which were first published as *The Lives of Animals*. Two Lessons are philosophical inquiries into the "Problem of Evil" and "Eros." The final Lesson, "At the Gate," dramatizes Costello's encounters with a panel of judges who ask that she define "belief" and describes the sheer difficulty of doing so, as she seeks permission to enter whatever lies beyond the gate. The correct answer to the question—if there is one—will allow her entry into the land which lies beyond the gate because it will sanction her achievement. Much of the novel is given over to the uncertainties about her life and her achievement, her worth as she sees it, as she recalls encounters from her past and tries to sum them up. These recollections and musings suggest that, however successful one is judged by the criteria that are current, there is always doubt and the knowledge that there is more to be learned and achieved, while at the same time one must accept that the time for doing more has passed. The novel is a powerful and provocative inquiry into abstract philosophical questions to which Coetzee offers partial answers through the life and musings of his writing.

Miriam Mesoli Tlali is the first black woman to have a novel published in South Africa. *Muriel at the Metropolitan* (1975) describes a series of events that take place in a white-owned hire purchase store, called the Metropolitan Radio, as these events affect the eponymous heroine who works in the store. Black-white relations are displayed in a variety of contexts, specifically pointing out the disparity between the races reflected in the policies of the store which are a reflection of the wider racial policies of South Africa at the time when the novel was written and published.

Tlali's second work, *Amandla* (1980), takes its title from the Zulu word meaning "power." "Amandla" was the cry of the people and the novel deals with the Soweto riots. It was banned in South Africa. *Mihloti* (1984) presents a woman's perspective on the oppression of black people under apartheid, one of dozens of books by black and white writers to suffer a similar fate under the apartheid regime.

Stephen Gray published his first novel, *Local Color*, in 1975. Five novels have followed—*Caltrop's Desire* (1980), *Time of Our Darkness* (1987), and *War Child* (1991). Gray is also known as a poet, playwright, and literary critic. So Gray finds the subject matter for his writing in a geographic entity that is formed of South Africa, Lesthoso, Botswana, Swaziland, Zimbabwe, and Namibia, countries which are attached to South Africa—the Cape Province, the Orange Free State, Natal, and the Transvaal—by historical precedents as well as geography. He writes about issues of race, class, politics, religion, and sexual orientation.

Sheila Roberts has published three novels, two collections of short stories, and a volume of poetry. *He's My Brother* (1977), *Johannesburg Requiem* (1980), and *The Weekenders* (1981) are novels which, in various ways, deal with the conduct and beliefs of the working classes in South Africa. Her realistic portrayals and frankness, especially regarding sexual activity, have drawn harsh criticism from some critics; one novel, *Johannesburg Requiem,* was banned.

Ahmed Essop writes about the Johannesburg Asian/Indian community. Like writers of Asian/Indian background in other countries—for example, V. S. Naipaul in Trinidad and M. G. Vassanji in Tanzania and Kenya—Essop writes about how members of his community respond to their marginalized position. Usually members of a mercantile class, Essop's characters struggle to accommodate themselves to their alien position while at the same time retaining their cultural values and practices.

In his novels *The Visitation* (1980) and *The Emperor* (1984), Essop presents a cast of characters ranging from members of the professional and educated class (teachers and philosophers) through the middle classes (journalists, clerks, shopkeepers) to fringe characters (soldiers, gangsters, pimps, and prostitutes) revealing different responses to the social and legal codes that contain them in the apartheid state.

Christopher Hope has published in a wide spectrum of literary forms: prose fiction, poetry, children's books, radio plays, and autobiography. His novels (like his other writing) employ a wide variety of approaches—satire and irony, caricature, exaggeration, surrealism—to attack and expose the moral ambiguities and hypocrisy of apartheid. His first novel, *A Separate Development* (1980), sets a thematic pattern, the ramifications of which are explored in subsequent novels—*Black Swan* (1987), *Kruger's Alp* (1984), *The Hottentot Room* (1988), and *Serenity House* (1992).

Menan du Plessis has published two novels, *A State of Fear* (1983) and *Longlive* (1989). The materials of these books are drawn from her social and political activities among the poor and dispossessed, especially the children of Cape Town. Menan dramatizes the lives of a wide range of people living on the fringes of South African society and powerfully evokes the presence of the city in its variety—racially, socially, and linguistically—to make an implied appeal to the social conscience and consciousness of responsible citizens to the plight of her subjects. Her aim, as with most of the writers of her generation, is to effect the eradication of racial discrimination in South Africa.

Mongane Wally Serote's first published work was two volumes of poetry—*Yakhal Inkomo* (1973) and *Tsetlo* (1974)—which were timed to coincide with the beginnings of the Black Consciousness Movement. He continues to be best known as a poet. His novel, *To Every Birth Its Blood* (1981), is unique in South African fiction for the form it adopts in portraying apartheid. The novel is in two distinct parts. The first is the story of a newspaper reporter who, falsely apprehended, is taken into custody and submitted to the full range of horrors that the agents of apartheid have at their disposal. The second part of the book is about the attitudes, values, and actions of a number of people who become involved in political resistance activities. Their resolve to take direct political action against the apartheid regime is an exact reflection of the mood of the 1970s, when Serote began to write his novel.

ADDITIONAL READINGS

Abrahams, Peter. 1942. *Dark Testament.* London: Allen and Unwin.
———. 1943. *Song of the City.* London: Dorothy Crisp.
———. 1948. *Mine Boy.* London: Dorothy Crisp.
———. 1948. *The Path of Thunder.* New York: Harper.
———. 1950. *Wild Conquest.* London: Faber and Faber.
———. 1953. *Return to Goli.* London: Faber and Faber.
———. 1954. *Tell Freedom.* London: Faber and Faber.
———. 1956. *A Night of Their Own.* London: Faber and Faber.
———. 1956. *A Wreath for Udomo.* London: Faber and Faber.
———. 1965. *A Night of Their Own.* London: Faber and Faber.
———. 1966. *This Island Now.* London: Faber and Faber.
———. 1985. *The View from Coyaba.* London: Faber and Faber.
———. 1969. *At the Still Point.* London; Chatto and Windus.
Benson, Mary. 1969. *At the Still Point.* London: Chatto and Windus
Blackburn, Douglas. 1899. *Prinsloo of Prinsloosdorp: A Tale of Transvaal Officialdom, by Sarel Erasmus.* London: Dunbar.
———. 1900. *Kruger's Secret Service by One Who Was in It.* NPD.
———. 1903. *A Burgher Quixote.* London: Dunbar.
———. 1905. *Richard Hartley, Prospector.* NPD Edinburgh: William Blackwood.
———. 1908. *I Came and Saw.* NPD. Alston Rivers.

————. 1908. *Leaven: A Black and White Story*. London: Alston Rivers.

————. 1915. *Love Muti*. NPD.

Bosman, Herman Charles. 1984. *Willemsdorp*. Cape Town, South Africa: Human and Rousseau.

————. 2000. *Jacaranda in the Night*. Edited by Stephen Gray. Cape Town, South Africa: Human and Rousseau.

Brink, Andre. 1974. *Looking on Darkness*. London: W. H. Allen.

————. 1976. *An Instant on the Wind*. London: W. H. Allen.

————. 1978. *Rumors of Rain*. New York: Morrow.

————. 1979. *A Dry White Season*. New York: Morrow.

————. 1982. *A Chain of Voices*. New York: Morrow.

————. 1983. *Mapmakers: Writing in a State of Seige*. London: Faber and Faber.

————. 1984. *The Wall of the Plague*. New York: Summit Books.

————. 1988. *States of Emergency*. New York: Summit Books.

————. 1991. *An Act of Terror*. London: Secker and Warburg.

————. 1993. *On the Contrary*. Boston: Little Brown.

Brutus, Dennis. 1968. *Letters to Martha and Other Poems from a South African Prison*. London: Heinemann.

Campbell, Roy. 1928. *The Wayzgoose: A South African Satire*. London: Cape.

————. 1931. *The Goergiad: A Satirical Fantasy in Verse*. London: Boriswood.

Chapman, Michael. 1996. *Southern African Literatures*. London: RKP.

Chinodya, Shimmer. 1982. *Dew in the Morning*. London: Heinemann.

————. 1984. *Farai's Girls*.

————. 1989. *Harvest of Thorns*. London: Heinemann.

Cloete, Stewart. 1937. *Turning Wheels*. London: Collins.

————. 1939. *Watch for the Dawn*. London: Collins.

————. 1941. *The Hills of Doves*. London: Collins.

————. 1957. *The Mask*. Boston: Houghton Mifflin.

Coetzee, J. M. 1974. *Dusklands*. Johannesburg: Ravan Press.

————. 1977. *In the Heart of the Country*. London: Secker and Warburg.

————. 1980. *Waiting for the Barbarians*. Harmonsworth, Middlesex: Penguin.

————. 1983. *Life and Times of Michael K*. London: Secker and Warburg.

————. 1986. *Foe*. London: Secker and Warburg.

————. 1988. *White Writing: On the Culture of Letters in South Africa*. New Haven, Conn.: Yale University Press.

————. 1990. *Age of Iron*. New York: Random House.

————. 1994. *The Master of Petersberg*. London: Secker and Warburg.

————. 1999. *Disgrace*. London: Secker and Warburg.

————. 1999. *The Lives of Animals*. Princeton, N.J.: Princeton University Press.

————. 2002. *Youth*. London: Secker and Warburg.

————. 2003. *Elizabeth Costello*. London: Secker and Warburg.

Cope, Jack. 1955. *The Fair House*. London: MacGibbon and Kee.

————. 1958. *The Golden Oriole*. London: MacGibbon and Kee.

————. 1964. *Albino*. London: Heinemann.

————. 1969. *The Dawn Comes Twice*. London: Heinemann.

————. 1971. *The Rain Maker*. London: Heinemann.

Dangaremgba, Tsitsi. 1988. *Nervous Condition*. Seattle: Seal Press.

Dhlomo, R.R.R. 1928. *An African Tragedy.* Johannesburg: Lovedale Institution Press.

Dikobe, Modikwe. 1973. *The Marabi Dance.* London: Heinemann.

du Plessis, Menan. 1983. *A State of Fear.* London: Pandora.

———. 1989. *Longlive.* London: Pandora.

Driver, C. J. 1969. *Elegy for a Revolutionary.* London: Faber and Faber.

Essop, Ahmed. 1980. *The Visitation.* Johannesburg: Ravan Press.

———. 1984. *The Emperor.* Johannesburg: Ravan Press.

Fitzpatrick, Sir Percy. 1892. *Through Mashonaland with Pick and Pen.* London: Heinemann.

———. 1897. *The Outspan: Tales of South Africa.* London: Heinemann.

———. 1899. *Transvaal from Within: A Private Record of Public Affairs.* Toronto: W. Briggs.

———. 1907. *Jock of the Bushveld.* London: Longman, Green and Co.

Fugard, Athol. 1973. *The Island.* Harlow: Longman.

Gibbon, Perceval. 1904. *Souls in Bondage.* NPD.

———. 1905. *The Vrouw Grobelaar's Leading Cases.* NPD.

———. 1911. *Flower of the Peach.* NPD.

———. 1983. *Margaret Harding.* Capetown, South Africa: David Philip, South African Paperbacks.

Gordimer, Nadine. 1966. *The Late Bourgeoise World.* London: Gollancz.

———. 1976. "Some Monday for Sure." In *Short Stories.* London: Heinemann.

———. 1974. *The Conservationist.* London: Cape.

———. 1981. *July's People.* London: Cape.

Gray, Stephen. 1975. *Local Color.* Johannesburg: Ravan Press.

———. 1980. *Caltrop's Desire.* Oxford: Africa Book Centre.

———. 1987. *Time of Our Darkness.* London: Muller.

———. 1991. *War Child.* London: Serif.

Hope, Christopher. 1980. *A Separate Development.* Johannesburg: Ravan Press.

———. 1984. *Kruger's Alp.* London: Heinemann.

———. 1987. *Black Swan.* New York: Harper and Row.

———. 1988. *The Hottentot Room.* London: Heinemann.

———. 1992. *Serenity House.* London: Macmillan.

Hove, Chenjerai. 1988. *Bones.* Harare, Zimbabwe: Baobab Books.

———. 1991. *Shadows.* Oxford: Heinemann International.

———. 1994. *Shebeen Tales.* Harare, Zimbabwe: Baobab Books.

———. 1996. *Ancestors.* Harare, Zimbabwe: Baobab Books.

Jacobson, Daniel. 1955. *The Trap.* London: Weidenfeld and Nicholson.

———. 1957. *The Price of Diamonds.* London: Weidenfeld and Nicholson.

———. 1960. *The Evidence of Love.* London: Weidenfeld and Nicholson.

———. 1966. *The Beginners.* London: Weidenfeld and Nicholson.

Jan van der Post, Laurens. 1934. *In a Province.* London: Leonard and Virginia Woolf.

———. 1955. *Flamingo Feathers.* New York: Morrow.

———. 1958. *The Lost World of the Kalahari.* London: Hogarth Press.

———. 1967. *The Hunter and the Whale.* London: Hogarth Press.

———. 1972. *A Story Like the Wind.* London: Hogarth Press.

———. 1974. *A Far-Off Place.* London: Hogarth Press.

————. 1976. *Jung and the Story of Our Time*. London Hogarth Press.

————. 1976. *A Mantis Carol*. London: Morrow.

————. 1977. *First Catch Your Eland*. London: Hogarth Press.

————. 1982. *Yet Being Someone Other*. London: Hogarth Press.

————. 1984. *Testament to the Bushmen*. London: Viking.

Kachingwe, Aubrey. 1966. *No Easy Task*. London: Heinemann.

Kayira, Legson. 1965. *I Will Try*. Garden City, N.Y.: Doubleday.

————. 1968. *The Looming Shadow*. Garden City, N.Y.: Doubleday.

————. 1969. *Jingala*. Garden City, N.Y.: Doubleday.

————. 1971. *The Civil Servant*. London: Heinemann.

————. 1974. *The Detainee*. London: Heinemann.

Killam, G. D., ed. 1984. *The Writing of East and Central Africa*. London: Heinemann.

La Guma, Alex. 1962. *A Walk in the Night*. Ibadan, Nigeria: Mbari Publications.

————. 1972. *In the Fog at the Seasons End*. *London: Heinemann*.

Mandela, Nelson. 1994. *Long Walk to Freedom: The Autobiography of Nelson Mandela*. Boston: Little, Brown.

Maphahlele, Ezekiel. 1959. *Down Second Avenue*. Berlin: Seven Seas.

————. 1961. *The Living and the Dead*. Ibadan, Nigeria: Ministry of Education.

————. 1962. *The African Image*. London: Faber and Faber.

————. 1967. *In Corner B*. Nairobi, Kenya: East African Publishing House.

————. 1971. *The Wanderers*. New York: Macmillan.

————. 1972. *Voices in the Whirlwind*. New York: Hill and Wang.

————. 1979. *Chirundu*. Johannesburg: Ravan Press.

————. 1981. *The Unbroken Song*. Johannesburg: Ravan Press.

————. 1984. *Afrika My Music: An Autobiography 1957–1983*. Johannesburg: Ravan Press.

————. 1988. *Renewal Time*. Columbia, La.: Readers International.

Marechera, Dambudzo. 1978. *House of Hunger*. New York: Pantheon.

————. 1984. *Mindblast; or, The Definitive Buddy*. Harare, Zimbabwe: College Press.

————. 1990. *The Black Insider*. Harare, Zimbabwe: Baobab Books.

————. 1992. *Cemetery of the Mind: Collected Poems of Dambudzo Marechera*. Edited by Flora Veit-Wild. Harare, Zimbabwe: Baobab Books.

Matshikiza, Todd. 1961. *Chocolates for My Wife*. London: Hodder and Stoughton.

Millin, Sarah Gertrude. 1924. *God's Stepchildren*. New York: Grosett and Dunlop.

————. 1926. *The South Africans*. London: Constable.

————. 1927. *The People of South Africa*. London: Constable.

————. 1928. *The Coming of the Lord*. London: Constable.

————. 1938. *What Hath a Man?* London: Constable.

————. 1940. *King of the Bastards*. London: Heinemann.

————. 1941. *The Night is Long*. London: Faber and Faber.

————. 1949. *The Burning Man*. London: Heinemann.

————. 1955. *The Measure of My Days*. London: Faber and Faber.

————. 1962. *The Wizard Bird*. London: Heinemann.

————. 1965. *Goodbye, Dear England*. London: Faber and Faber.

Modisane, Bloke. 1963. *Blame Me in History*. New York: Dutton.

Moleah, Alfred T. 1993. *South Africa: Colonialism, Apartheid, and African Dispossession*. Wilmington, Del.: Disa Press.

Mopeli-Paulus, A. S. with Peter Lanham. 1951. *Blanket Boy's Moon*. New York: Crowell.

———— with Miriam Basner. 1956. *Turn in the Dark*.

Msmane, Mbulelo. 1981. *My Cousin Comes to Jo'Burg and Other Stories*. Harlow: Longman.

————. 1982. *Children of Soweto*. Harlow: Longman.

Mulaisho, Dominic. 1971. *The Tongue of the Dumb*. London: Heinemann.

————. 1979. *The Smoke that Thunders*. London: Heinemann.

Ndebele, Njabulo. 1984. "Turkish Tales and Some Thoughts on South African Fiction." *Staffrider*.

————. (Njabulo Simakahke) 1991. *Rediscovery of the Ondinony*. Johannesberg, South Africa: Congress of South African Writers.

Ngara, Emmanuel. 1985. *New Writing from Southern Africa: Authors Who Have Become Prominent Since 1980*. London: Heinemann.

Omer-Cooper, J. D. 1994. *History of South Africa*. 2d ed. London: James Currey.

Paton, Alan. 1948. *Cry, the Beloved Country*. New York: Scribners.

Plomer, William. 1926. *Turbott Wolfe*. London: The Hogarth Press.

————. 1927. *I Speak of Africa*. London: The Hogarth Press.

————. 1943. *Double Lives*. London: Cape.

————. 1958. *At Home*. London: Cape.

Rive, Richard. 1964. *Emergency*. London: Faber and Faber.

Roberts, Sheila. 1977. *He's My Brother*. Johannesburg: Ad. Donker.

————. 1980. *Johannesburg Requiem*. New York: Taplinger.

————. 1981. *The Weekenders*. Johannesburg: Bataleur.

Rooke, Daphne. 1946. *The Sea Hath Bounds*. Boston: Houghton Mifflin.

————. 1951. *Mittee*. Boston: Houghton Mifflin.

————. 1953. *Ratoons*. Boston: Houghton Mifflin.

————. 1959. *Beti*. Boston: Houghton Mifflin.

————. 1961. *A Lover for Estelle*. Boston: Houghton Mifflin.

————. 1962. *The Greyling*. New York: Reynal.

————. 1965. *Diamond Jo*. New York: Reynal.

————. 1974. *Margaretha de la Porte*. New York: Reynal.

Ross, Robert. 1993. *Beyond the Pale: Essays on the History of Colonial South Africa*. Middletown, Conn.: Wesleyan University Press.

Rubidari, David. 1967. *No Bride Price*. Nairobi, Kenya: East African Publishing House.

Schreiner, Olive. 1883. *The Story of an African Farm*. London: Hutchinson.

————. 1896. *The Political Situation*. London: T. F. Unwin.

————. 1897. *Trooper Peter Halket of Mashonaland*. London: T. F. Unwin.

————. 1899. *An English South African's View of the Situation: Words in Season*. London: Hodder and Stoughton.

————. 1909. *Closer Union*. London: Fifield.

————. 1911. *Woman and Laborer*. London: T. F. Unwin.

————. 1926. *From Man to Man*. London: T. F. Unwin.

————. 1929. *Undine*. London: Benn.

Scully, William Charles. 1886. *The Wreck of the Grosvenor and Other South African Poems.* NPD

———. 1892. *Poems.* NPD.

———. 1895. *Kaffir Stories.* NPD.

———. 1897. *The White Hetacomb and Other Stories.* NPD.

———. 1898. *Between Sun and Sand.* NPD.

———. 1907. *By Veldt and Kopje.* NPD.

———. 1912. *A Visit to Johannesburg.* NPD.

———. 1913. *Reminiscences of a South African Pioneer.* NPD.

———. 1913. *Further Reminiscences of a South African Pioneer.* NPD.

———. 1915. *Lodges in the Wilderness.* NPD.

———. 1921. *The Harrow.* NPD.

———. 1923. *Daniel Vananda: The Life of a Human Being.* NPD.

Sepamla, Sipho. 1979. *The Root Is One.* London: Collins.

———. 1981. *Ride on the Whirlwind.* London: Heinemann.

Serote, Mongane Wally. 1981. *To Every Birth Its Blood.* London: Heinemann.

Serote, Mongane Wally. 1972. *Yakhal Inkomo.* Johannesburg: Renoster Books.

———. 1974. *Tsetto.* Johannesburg: Renoster Books.

———. 1983. *To Every Birth Its Blood.* London: Heinemann.

Slater, Francis Casey. 1929. *Drought: A South African Parable.* London: E. Benn.

———. 1925. *The Centenary Book of South African Verse.* London: Longmans, Green.

———. 1945. *The New Book of South African Verse.* London: Longmans, Green.

Smith, Pauline. 1925. *The Little Karoo.*

———. 1933. A. B. "A minor marginal note." London: J. Cape.

———. 1926. *The Beadle.*

———. 1935. *Platkops Children.*

Smith, Wilbur. 1964. *When the Lion Feeds.* London: Heinemann.

Themba, Can. 1972. *The Will to Die.* London: Heinemann.

Tlali, Miriam. 1975. *Muriel at the Metropole.* London: Longman.

———. 1980. *Amandla.* London: Longman.

———. 1984. *Mhiloti.* Johannesburg: Skotaville Publishers.

Van der Post, Laurens. 1986. *A Walk with a White Bushman.* New York: William Morrow and Co.

———. *About Blady.* 1991. London: Chatto and Windus.

Zwelonke, D. M. 1973. *Robben Island.* London: Heinemann.

Chapter 7
Nadine Gordimer: Burger's Daughter (1979) and The House Gun (1998)

Nadine Gordimer published her first novel, *The Lying Days*, in 1953. Since then she has published 12 novels. With the exception of *A Guest of Honour* (1970/71), all of her novels are set in South Africa. And all of the novels describe the varied social, political, and even, indirectly, fiscal implications of South Africa seen from a multitude of perspectives. However much historical antecedents are interpolated into her text, the life of the novels is in the present.

Gordimer is essentially a political writer in the sense that she is concerned with how political arrangements affect, contain, and compromise the lives of citizens, denying them, whatever their color, full enfranchisement. Nadine Gordimer is also a writer of the apartheid and postapartheid period in South Africa's history. She grew up in the apartheid state. She was born in 1923 in the mining town of Springs, near Johannesburg in the Transvaal. Her father, a jeweler, had immigrated from Lithuania. Her mother came from England. She had little formal schooling. Her mother taught her at home. She had one year at the University of Witwatersrand. She early became interested in writing, read widely, and began writing short stories. Her first short story was published when she was 16. Her first collection of short stories, *Face to Face*, was published in 1949 and a second collection, *The Soft Voice of the Serpent*, in 1952.

Her first novel, *The Lying Days*, based on her experience of growing up in South Africa, records the increasing dissatisfaction of the heroine, Helen, with the claustrophobic atmosphere of a small town, and records the beginnings of the social and psychological implications of an increasingly divided racial society. Her first responses to the deepening divide forced on society by racialist policies is more satiric than angry in the two novels that followed: *A World of Strangers* (1958) and *Occasion for Loving* (1963). Her growing concern and anger over the progressive development of racial policies first finds its expression in *The Late Bourgeois World* (1966), in which the subject matter and conditions that shape the rest of her writing are adumbrated. In the seven novels that follow *The Late Bourgeois World,* with one exception, Gordimer exposes apartheid in all its ramifications.

A Guest of Honour (1970) is the one novel by Gordimer that is not located in South Africa. Set in an imaginary country that bears resemblances to both West and East Africa, the novel dramatizes the problems that face an African state once British colonial rule is withdrawn. The central issue is what political program, capitalist or socialist, will create the best conditions for the people of the newly independent country. The novel is drawn from Gordimer's travels across the middle belt of Africa when she visited a number of African countries facing the same political choices as those that shape her novel. The novel offers both an accounting and a prophecy of the chaos that can result if differences between contending political agendas are not reconciled quickly.

Burger's Daughter (1979) is a pivotal novel in the Gordimer canon. It describes changing circumstances in the apartheid state, in spite of harsh restrictive measures imposed on opponents of apartheid. After the Soweto uprising, a different kind of urgency than was felt heretofore informs the political scene. The defiance of the students who give their lives in protest suggests a movement at the grassroots level that will not be denied.

July's People (1981) is set in a future period when a revolt by an oppressed people creates anarchy and chaos in society and places the chance of survival for a conventional South African white family in the hands of a former servant. The novel reveals how little whites in South Africa understood the complexities of the system, particularly the master-servant relationships they casually fostered, and how ill-prepared they were to cope with the predicted total breakdown of that system.

A Sport of Nature (1984) and *My Son's Story* (1990) contemplate what the problems for families and individuals might be in the postapartheid state. *None to Accompany Me* (1994) dramatizes the sense of both urgency and confusion that will be experienced by both black and white South Africans whose adult lives have been shaped and contained by apartheid. In *The House Gun* (1998), the causes and consequences of violence of a kind different than that which characterized the apartheid state are examined through a murder trial. In her latest novel to date, *The Pickup* (2001), Gordimer tells the story of a love affair that develops from the chance encounter of a white woman and an Arab man who is an illegal immigrant to South Africa. A love relationship between people of different colors (and thus different cultures) is seen as no less difficult than such a relationship was in the apartheid state. Here, as in her other work, Gordimer focuses a remorseless yet compassionate eye on the dilemma faced by two lovers from vastly different cultures in a state where race relations are still, to some extent, determined by the segregationist policies of the former South African regime.

Burger's Daughter (1979)

Burger's Daughter describes and dramatizes the infinite complexity and interrelationships of dozens of people whose lives are circumscribed by and involved in the attempt to dismantle apartheid. Rosa Burger is the main character in the novel and everything that happens is filtered through her experiences. Gordimer adopts a number of narrative voices, points of view, and time frames in the book. But everything in it issues from and returns to Rosa. She is a 14-year-old girl when we first meet her. From that time forward, we live her life through her direct experiences and her musings on their implications. She is the daughter of Lionel Burger, whose professional life and political activities dominate her life. Lionel is a medical doctor whose mission in life is to stand boldly against apartheid and work toward seeing it dismantled. He has a double healing mission. Lionel has been arrested several times for his political activities and public statements; he has gone to prison several times and eventually dies there. Rosa's mother, Cathy, Lionel's second wife, has been equally active and she, too, dies in prison. Clustered around these three characters are men and women involved in the struggle who, while agreed on their immediate aim, often express conflicting beliefs about how the struggle should be conducted.

The novel has three parts. Part one is set in South Africa and describes Rosa's life from age 14 until she leaves South Africa to escape the intense scrutiny and demands made on her as Lionel Burger's daughter. Through various perspectives we come to know Rosa, Lionel, and Cathy. We come to understand the difficulty Rosa has in discovering who she is as a person and not merely, as she is persistently seen, as an adumbration of her father and mother and their lives in politics. Can she become simply "Rosa" and not "Burger's daughter"? That is her quest. Her life is circumscribed by her knowledge that she is, along with those with whom she associates, under constant surveillance by agents of the state.

Seeking escape from the intensity of this scrutiny, Rosa leaves her country and in part two of the novel, set mostly in the south of France, she is absorbed into a colony of disaffected expatriates (some of them from South Africa), central among whom is Lionel's first wife, Katya. For a time, Rosa finds pleasure and briefly, love, living an indolent life. But because of a chance encounter with an African friend from her childhood days who besmirches her father's name and his political activities by attacking Rosa, her father's surrogate, Rosa returns to South Africa.

Part three of the book describes life after her return to South Africa. She works in a children's hospital and sees first hand the awful consequences of the Soweto riots. Because of her connections with her father's former political activists, she is accused under the Treason Act, arrested, tried, and put in prison. By the close of the novel, she has come to an understanding of the importance and commitment of her parents to foster change in South Africa. She has come, as well, to understand herself as an individual, as Rosa and not "Burger's daughter."

Through Rosa's various encounters with people who respond differently to the South African situation, Gordimer develops a complex narrative pattern in order to bring collaborating and competing positions into play and focus. These positions range from the personal to the disengaged, through the enunciation of intellectual but unengaged stances, to the public declaration of the need for direct militant action. Gordimer is at pains to reveal the social, psychological, and intellectual forces at work in the political climate of South Africa. These components mix easily enough at the discursive level but contend when practical implementation is considered.

The story of Lionel's involvement from an early age in the activities of the Communist Party in South Africa, the various attempts at gaining political position and influence through a series of crucial public actions, all specified and dated, are described. (There are no chapter demarcations in the book.) The influence of Leninist arguments is central here. The first stage of Lionel's political activism and that of the Communist Party—the end of a whole political era in South Africa—came to an end in May 1948 with the election of the Malan Party to power. Ironically, this is the month and date of Rosa's birth. This is the year in which the policy of apartheid was first formulated. Rosa's life, then, is dominated by apartheid from the policy's intimidating beginnings to its darkest, most oppressive period.

Lionel Burger's position is one of full engagement with the struggle against racial oppression. Gordimer fully humanizes him through his relations with family, with political comrades, with those destitute people he takes into his home without concern for their color, and through his work as a medical doctor. Lionel's defense of his political beliefs and actions is fully articulated at his trial, during which his voice is heard in public for the first and last time. His repudiation of the current police state is based on his acceptance of the argument, the core of Marxist/Leninist political and economic analysis, that the contradiction between "the form of social control and the economy" must be eliminated. Only then will "discrimination on grounds of the color of skin" (25) be obliterated. Gordimer places Lionel within the broad political context of those parties and movements whose aims and objectives he represented—not only the Communist Party, but the ANC and "other movements."

In conflict with the proscriptions and activities of the Communist Party and the ANC are the beliefs and actions of the Black Consciousness Movement. The Communist Party and the ANC each had a long history, dating back to the 1930s. With their banning, the Black Consciousness Movement, a phenomenon of the 1970s, became the dominating expression of black repudiation of apartheid. It stood opposed to the multiracial composition of the earlier movement's membership. The Black Consciousness Movement had its origins in South Africa's segregated universities. The movement promoted the rediscovery of African heritage in South Africa's black peoples, those whose education and experience had been adversely affected by white culture. Black Consciousness repudiated these influences as embodied in the activities of the Communist Party and the ANC. The purposes of the Black Consciousness Movement were to reassert black culture and, working through various organizations—the South African Students' Organization, the Black Peoples' Convention, the Black Women's Federation, and the South African Students' Movement—to combat apartheid. Black Consciousness saw South Africa divided into two distinct communities, the whites who had power, wealth, and privilege and the blacks who were penalized and disenfranchised on the grounds of racial stereotypes. Diffuse as the membership was, Black Consciousness proposed a militant agenda that aimed at reestablishing pride in blackness, creating solidarity among blacks and delegitimatizing apartheid. The Soweto uprising was the most notable political assertion of Black Consciousness, an assertion of militancy that Gordimer exploits in two central places in *Burger's Daughter.* The first is the heated exchange between Orde Greer and Duma Dhladhla. Greer expounds the Marxist position of militant interracial collaboration in opposing the South African government, while Dhladhla expounds the position of Black Consciousness. For the latter, the struggle is "not a class struggle for blacks; it's a race struggle" (163). And further, "all collaboration with whites has always ended in exploitation of blacks" (159).

The second assertion of Black Consciousness is an exchange in London between Rosa and Zwelinzima Vulindlela. Called "Bassie" when he was a boy, he lived in Burger's household and had seen Burger's beliefs translated into action. But for Bassie, Burger's actions and the fame they brought him had overshadowed the sacrifices made by many blacks, his own father among them, in their heroic opposition to apartheid. For Vulindlela, Burger's conduct, his treatment of blacks admitted into his own family, is nothing more than a kind of paternalism. Vulindlela's indictment of her father shatters Rosa and, though she is hard pressed to define precisely why it prompts her return to South Africa, where she takes up the legacy of her father and mother in the struggle against racial discrimination.

Nadine Gordimer interpolates into her novel the political positions of a number of thinkers, mostly unattributed, whose ideas taken together form parts of the intellectual and active opposition to the insanity of apartheid.

She does this to display the then current political situation in South Africa and as well to show how ideas distill in the minds of characters engaged in the dialectic about how best to bring about the destruction of an unacceptable because inhumane regime. She reveals a profound understanding of the complexities of political positions, their often oppositional natures. And she remains disinterested in creating her fictional dialectic.

The second part of the novel describing Rosa's time in France is crucial to an evocation of the complexity of attitudes that operate in South Africa. In this part of the novel we have a group of people, disaffected revolutionaries, who recollect their participation in a struggle that is now remote from the easy and decadent lives they currently live. For a time, Rosa is comfortable among them. But after her encounter with Bassie, she knows that her time away from the scene of her father's struggle and his subsequent martyrdom, is merely an interlude, her attempts to excuse her absence merely a rationale for postponement.

Burger's Daughter shows how literature can be a tool of engagement. Encompassed in a narrative structure that displays the endless complexities of personal engagements possible in a specific historical context, *Burger's Daughter* is Gordimer's most overtly political novel in which public displays of belief are balanced by personal ruminations on personal commitments. In an important sense, Rosa's story is the story of South Africa from the initiation of apartheid, which dominated all aspects of the lives of South Africans to the mid-1970s when the policy had reached its ultimate refinement. In its day, *Burger's Daughter* was a powerful indictment of apartheid. It remains a historical document crucial to anyone who would seek an understanding with its time and place in South Africa.

The House Gun (1998)

The House Gun (1998) is the second of three novels set in the postapartheid period in South Africa. As a group, these three novels dramatize in various ways the problems of adjustment faced by citizens from various constituencies in the new South Africa. The novels reflect official government policy following the elections of 1994 that allowed full democratic participation by blacks for the first time. Discriminatory policies and practices were abandoned and all government institutions, as well as the police and the military, were integrated. But Gordimer's novels reveal the gaps—economic, social, cultural, and psychological—that still exist between policy and practice. The legacy of apartheid lingers and there are disparities between whites and blacks in housing and earning power, for example, as South Africa strives for full equality between the races.

None to Accompany Me (1994) is set in the year of transition, 1994. It encompasses the final formal dismantling of apartheid, the electoral triumph of the African National Party, and the election of Nelson Mandela as the first prime minister in the new South Africa. The novel operates at two levels. It tells of the personal quest of Vera Stark to create a new life for herself against the backdrop of a country's quest to find the same solutions to problems at the public level as Vera does in her private life.

The background is a country hard pressed to address the legacy of apartheid—inadequate housing for Africans, violence in the streets, and persistent political rivalries between the ANC and Kwa-Zulu that threaten to undermine stability. Gordimer, here as in her other books, is unflinchingly honest. She has said of this book, "I hope [readers] will take away a sense of the true realities of South Africa, of the wonderful achievements of freedom in [a] few short months; and also understand that there are enormous tasks for people to tackle. . . . "

None to Accompany Me is divided into three sections—"Baggage," "Transit," and "Arrivals"—ubtitles that suggest the issues that confront Vera, the legacy of the life she has lived, the journey of self-discovery she feels she has to make, and the position she eventually achieves. Vera is a civil rights lawyer who feels forced to examine her life—to discover what she has achieved to date and where her life might go. Her self-scrutiny is prompted by the changes she sees in South Africa and in the lives of a large number of acquaintances in various social and political situations. Vera's husband is Bennett, an aspiring sculptor and the agent for a line of prestige luggage; her son, Ivan, is a banker in London; her daughter, Annie, is a gay South African doctor. Didymus and Sibongile (also called Sally) are black revolutionaries who return from their forced exile to continue their political work. Their daughter is Mpho. And while she is half Zulu and half Xhosa, her personality and behavior resemble that of the Londoners she has lived and grown up among when her parents were in exile. Oupa is Vera's colleague who had been detained on Robben Island. She continues to work toward building a new free state. Zeph Repulana, a final principal character, has the power and will to bring a new and better South Africa into existence.

Vera is at the center of this group and her quest is to find personal freedom which, as the story begins, means freedom from the obligations and demands imposed on her. The novel thus becomes an examination of public versus private responsibility. Gordimer delineates the psychological consequences of Vera's quest and her ways of resolving it, while she portrays the intersection of and competition between public and private values. The struggles of the various characters becomes a metaphor for the condition of South Africa in the period in which the novel is set.

The Pickup (2001) is equally complex in describing the positions of men and women in the postapartheid state. The novel describes the chance encounter between Julie, a white South African woman, and Ibrahim. Ibrahim, a one-time student of economics turned motor mechanic, is an illegal immigrant in South Africa. Their innocent encounter (when he repairs a problem with Julie's car), turns into a love affair and this allows Gordimer to examine, in fictional terms, the contrasts in their cultural, social, religious, and economic backgrounds. Issues of race and politics that have been in the foreground of concerns in Gordimer's earlier novels are not at issue in *The Pickup*. She is especially concerned to examine the motives of Julie and Ibrahim in reconciling the essential differences in the values and attitudes they hold, proceeding as they do from vastly different backgrounds. Abstract issues about cultural imperatives are defined in the examination of personal motives that inform their relationship. The novel is a continuing questioning of cross-cultural values in a community that now, at least on the surface, admits, if not wholly approves of, a mixed-race encounter.

The House Gun (1998) falls between *None to Accompany Me* and *The Pickup* and is much more narrowly focused. Here the background is postapartheid South Africa. Race is not at issue here except to show in public display how the racial imperatives of apartheid have disappeared. New racial relations are presented here in neutral terms. Whites and blacks easily intermingle. Gordimer places personal relationships in the foreground in a carefully controlled narrative in which an authorial voice dominates.

The novel is about murder, motive, and punishment as these affect a single family. It opens when Harald and Claudia Lindgard receive the devastating news that their son, Duncan, has been arrested and charged with the murder of his friend, Karl. Duncan is an architect who lives with his girlfriend, Natalie, in a cottage on the grounds of a large house occupied by gay friends. Duncan has had a homosexual relationship with Karl. And when he discovers Natalie and Karl making love, he takes revenge on what he sees as her betrayal by shooting Karl with "the house gun," a weapon left casually about in the room where Karl and Natalie make love. While Duncan admits to killing Karl, the motives for his actions are never made fully clear. In fact, Duncan is not allowed to speak for himself until the last third of the novel, in courtroom scenes where charges against Duncan are prosecuted and where a verdict is brought down and a sentence passed.

The central inquiry about their son's action is made by his parents. Their comfortable, middle-class existence is shattered by Duncan's actions. They have been passive liberals throughout the apartheid period, their lives to some extent shaped by those political events that troubled the country, events in which they did not participate. They have made a successful transition into the new dispensation. Harald sits on the board of a major insurance company, his professional life concerned with negotiating insurance contracts related to housing projects. He is a devoutly religious man who ponders metaphysical questions related to religious beliefs. Claudia is a pragmatist. She works as a doctor in a medical clinic and has an objective, compassionate view of human suffering as she finds it in her work.

The complacent world of each of the parents is shattered by their son's act and they are driven to question all of the factors that had gone into the shaping of Duncan's values and personality. At first, they are almost driven apart as contending points of view come into collision, his based on religion and literature, hers on science. But as the trial of their son approaches and as they sit through the proceedings of the court, they achieve a kind of renewed solidarity. Their inquiry is based on the things they recall in Duncan's growth toward manhood, on entries in his diaries, on the recollections and opinions of his friends, in the testimony at his trial about his relationship with Natalie.

Duncan's defense is conducted by a black lawyer, Hamilton Motsamai, a man who has risen to the top of his profession from an almost poverty-stricken birth and who has overcome the vicissitudes of apartheid, including banishment from South Africa. Motsamai's success represents the extent to which blacks, in their relationships with whites, both professionally and personally, are integrated into the new society.

The central question of the novel—why did Duncan murder his friend?—is never answered. The trial is formulaic, conducted within the framework of conventions. What makes the trial ominous, to some extent, is a question that hovers over it, a question occasioned by an inquiry concurrently conducted by the Constitutional Court of South Africa: will the death penalty be confirmed or be rescinded? The decision of the Constitutional Court will affect the sentencing in Duncan's trial. The inquiry of the Constitutional Court takes place in the Old Fever Hospital where, ironically, legal and not medical questions of health and sickness, life and death are raised. The implications of Duncan's case will adumbrate outward in postapartheid society where violence on the streets is endemic and always anticipated. So abstract questions about truth, justice, retribution, and punishment inform the text as Harald and Claudia move through a spectrum of responses to their son's deed. In this regard, however personal their experiences, Harald and Claudia can be seen as representative figures in the new South Africa, which has to contemplate and reassess its past in order to discover its future.

The novel raises and defines questions about the legacy of the old regime and the extent of its reach as many of its terms are transmuted into a new reality. Violence is the dominating metaphor in the novel and the various responses possible to it form the core of Gordimer's novel. The fact that Duncan cannot give an accounting for his actions is not a failure on Gordimer's part to resolve her plot. Rather, it is an exact reflection of the inability of the society to explain fully the reasons for its violence and the inability of officialdom to contain and remove it. However successful individuals are in making adequate responses to the new society, they are circumscribed by violence and their lives compromised by their alertness to its presence.

Gordimer, in *The House Gun,* presents a picture of the state in transition. And the transition is not an easy one. The habitual attitudes toward a brutal past still find voices in the present, despite sweeping changes. Reform cannot move fast enough even though those undertaken are on view—a total revision of race relations in education, in employment, in a different functioning of state authority. There are no easy solutions to pressing problems in the world of the novel and the real world it reflects. One is left at the novel's close thinking that Gordimer, in describing complex relationships in the equally complex society of current South Africa, is optimistic about the eventual construction of a just society, a society that all her writing, in all its variety, has been aimed at achieving over a 50-year period.

ADDITIONAL READINGS

Gordimer, Nadine. 1953. *The Lying Days.* London: Cape.
———. 1958. *A World of Strangers.* London: Gallancy.
———. 1963. *Occasion for Loving.* London: Gollancz.
———. 1967. *The Late Bourgeois World.* London: Gollancz.
———. 1970. *A Guest of Honour.* London: Cape.
———. 1979. *Burger's Daughter.* London: Jonathon Cape.
———. 1981. *July's People.* London: Cape.
———. 1984. *A Sport of Nature.* New York: Viking Press.
———. 1988. *The House Gun.* New York: Farrar, Straus & Giroux.
———. 1990. *My Son's Story.* London: Bloomsbury.
———. 1998. *The House Gun.* New York: Farrar, Straus and Giroux.
———. 2001. *The Pickup.* London: Bloomsbury.
Head, Dominic. 1995. *Nadine Gordimer.* Cambridge: Cambridge University Press.
King, Bruce, ed. 1993. *The Later Fiction of Nadine Gordimer.* London: Macmillan.
Smith, Rowland, ed. 1990. *Critical Essays on Nadine Gordimer.* Boston: G. K. Hall.

Chapter 8
Alex La Guma: In the Fog of the Season's End *(1972) and* Time of the Butcherbird *(1979)*

Alex La Guma was caught up in the political life of South Africa from his earliest years. He was born in Cape Town in 1925. His father, Jimmy La Guma, devoted his life to working for the civil rights of the African and colored people of South Africa. He was a union organizer, a secretary to the Cape Town Branch of the African National Congress (ANC), President of the South African Coloured Peoples' Congress, and a member of the South African Communist Party.

Alex La Guma followed in his father's footsteps. He was 21 years old when he organized a strike of workers in a factory where he was employed. In 1947, he joined the Young Communists League. In 1948, when, after its election the Boer Nationalist Party began to formulate its policy of apartheid, La Guma joined the Communist Party and remained a member until the party was officially banned in 1950. In 1956 he was charged with treason, one of many South Africans charged at the same time. The infamous treason trials lasted for nearly five years and saw, in the end, the acquittal of all those charged.

The government further compromised the rights of South Africans in 1960 as a result of the Sharpeville massacres. La Guma was arrested for a second time in 1961. From this time until he and his family took permanent exit visas and left South Africa for England, La Guma was systematically harassed by agents of the government. In 1962, with the passage of the Sabotage Act, he was placed under house arrest: he was confined to his home for 24 hours a day, a ban that lasted until 1966 and was only interrupted when he was imprisoned in solitary confinement. He was arrested again in 1966, but chose to leave South Africa, never to return.

From London, La Guma continued his work for the oppressed peoples of South Africa. He worked with the ANC and traveled widely. He visited and gave talks in Chile, Vietnam, the Soviet Union, and Tanzania. He was writer-in-residence for a time at the University of Dar es Salaam. In this period, as well, his writing began to attract attention. In 1977, he became secretary-general of the Afro-Asian Writers Association. In 1978, he moved to Cuba and became the ANC representative for the Caribbean and Central and South America. He died in Havana in 1986.

La Guma's writing career ran parallel to his political activities. He had worked from the 1950s until 1962 as a staff writer for the *New Age*, a Cape Town newspaper. During this period he published 14 short stories, the first four of which were published before his first novel, *A Walk in the Night* (1962). The novel was taken out of South Africa by Ulli Beier, a founding editor of *Black Orpheus: A Journal of African and Afro-American Literature*, and published by Mbari Publications in Ibadan, Nigeria. Four novels followed: *And a Threefold Cord* (1964) and *The Stone Country* (1967), both first published in Berlin; *In the Fog of the Season's End* (1972), first published in New York; and *Time of the Butcherbird* (1979), published in London. La Guma was writing a sixth novel, *Zone of Fire*, at the time of his death.

La Guma's literary output is relatively small, not surprising when one considers it was accomplished in the midst of a demanding public life. But this small body of writing placed La Guma among the most prominent African writers of his day, the peer of Chinua Achebe, Wole Soyinka, J. P. Clark, and Nadine Gordimer, to name but four. And it remains important for its literary values, for its profound humanity, for its political persuasiveness, and for its historical record of a society that existed before the free elections in 1994 in South Africa, a society whose problems still inform contemporary South African life.

A Walk in the Night is set in the slum area of Cape Town. The main characters are Michael Adonis, Willieboy, and Constable Rault. Michael Adonis, a colored South African, is filled with anger over the loss of his job because of a trivial offense. In the street after being fired, he is stopped by two policemen who insult and humiliate him simply because of his color. His anger increases as he drinks in a public house and then it is translated into a frustrated and murderous rage when he accidentally kills an old Irish roomer in the slum accommodation where he lives. The Irishman, Uncle Doughty, is a failed actor. Doughty supplies the novel's title by citing lines from Shakespeare's *Hamlet*. Michael Adonis ironically equates the old white actor with the foreman who has humiliated him and fired him from his job.

In a second irony is the story of Willieboy, an innocent who visits Adonis after the murder with the hope of getting a loan of money. Willieboy, an unemployed panhandler, lives on the bounty and generosity of others. He finds the dead Uncle Doughty, is recognized by another tenant in the building, is wrongly accused of murder, arrested and taken into custody, and dies when he is beaten by the sadistic Constable Rault, in whose values and actions are embodied the legalized brutality of the apartheid state.

A Walk in the Night is a powerful indictment of South Africa at the time of its writing. La Guma shows that brutality and murder are an inevitable consequence of the relentless racial policies of the state. He understands that all members of the society are the victims of its laws. Physical and psychological violence make everyone, potentially, a Michael Adonis, doomed for a time to walk in the night. La Guma, as author, does not intrude into the novel. No authorial invasion of the text is necessary to show the consequences to human life of the inescapable poverty, human degradation, and public/police brutality the novel dramatizes.

And a Threefold Cord, La Guma's second novel, is also set in a slum. La Guma describes the worst kind of living conditions for a dispossessed class of people—where there is putrid water, little electricity, no relief against overcrowding, and the imminent threat of disease. Nowhere does one find a more bitter indictment of a callous and uncaring government. The only defense against this general poverty—of spirit as well as of material needs—is violence, social and psychological, and prostitution and alcohol. None of the characters in the novel is able to prevail over the conditions in which he or she lives. The lives of the people in the novel convey La Guma's message that it is only by uniting and opposing such conditions that they will change. There is the need for organized and militant action.

The Stone Country draws on La Guma's experience of South African prisons. While drawing on the events in his own life, La Guma incorporates the stories of others who have suffered both for their political activities and from their consequent internment in prison. The story deals with the attempts of George Adams to unite prisoners in the jail to create a united front to sustain their demands for better treatment. Adams wants to oppose injustice wherever he finds it, inside as well as outside prisons. The prison, the Stone Country of the title of the book, is therefore a metaphor for the country as a whole.

Adams finds that prison officers and authorities promote, successfully, a policy of setting individual prisoners against each other. This general policy is represented in the fight to the death between Butcherboy and Yusef the Turk. Adams is deeply frustrated by this event, sees it as typical of the failure of victims to understand clearly that only by uniting against and opposing the wretched conditions in which they live will these conditions be alleviated and their lives made tolerable.

In describing the moral, spiritual, and physical destitution wrought by apartheid and the failure of oppressed groups to unite and move against their oppressors, La Guma's point of view in his first three novels is largely negative. He puts forth in ideological terms what must be done. In *The Stone Country*, the people of the slum experience hardships and suffering to the point of inanition. In *And a Threefold Cord*, Adams in unable to enjoin inmates of the prison to take collective, concerted action, the only means by which they will achieve relief from their oppressors and the policies they administer. He hopes that in vividly evoking the conditions that overrun humane behavior, he will prompt reforming action. But, drawing on his own observations and experience, with characteristic honesty, he dramatizes the self-interest and confusion that mitigates against this kind of resolution.

In the Fog of the Season's End (1972)

La Guma's stance alters entirely in the two novels that follow *The Stone Country* and *And a Threefold Cord*. In the *Fog of the Season's End*, La Guma's description of the setting is the same as in the first three novels. He makes plain his opinion of what kind of action is required to change society for the greater good of all of its members. He also makes plain the price, in human terms, that will have to be paid. In his fourth novel, the atmosphere is one of almost unrelieved tension and fear. The brutal reality in which blacks and coloreds live in South Africa, including the threat of apprehension by the police and of possible betrayal by one's co-conspirators functions as a leit-motif. The prologue exposes the cynical reality of treatment administered to political prisoners. An anonymous prisoner, just brought into custody, puts the case—his and La Guma's case—for resistance to the regime. For making a speech, defending his actions in human terms against oppression and vic-timization, he is mercilessly beaten, urinates on himself, and is left hanging in his cell from hand-cuffed hands.

There are two principal characters in the novel—Beukes and Elias Tekwane—and a number of less-prominent characters all of whom, as well as being fully realized personae, stand for positions taken within the apartheid state. Beukes is legally defined as "colored." He has been happily married and has a family. He recalls this period of his life from time to time throughout the novel, sometimes in the form of flashbacks, sometimes in the form of nostalgic reminiscences. Political motivation prompts him to sacrifice this life and to join a secret and subversive underground political movement aimed at destroying apartheid. Beukes knows that only a nonra-cial society will provide conditions for permanent happiness. His job in the movement is to arrange for the distribution of pamphlets that urge militant action against the state. Beukes lives in constant fear of apprehension by the police and of betrayal from within the cadre of supporters as he moves from place to place meeting with various sympathizers of the movement. Through Beukes's travels, mostly by night, La Guma is able to display comprehen-sively the oppressive political, economic, and personal problems engendered by the vicious system of apartheid. Where La Guma foregrounded these conditions in his earlier novels, here he makes them the background to personal sentiments and values, as well as the activities of those who adopt an aggressive stance taken by various characters against the regime. There is Isaac, a young African, who has organized a cell of resistance that he operates with cool confidence. There is Tommy, a dancer, who defines himself and life in general through the titles of an endless number of popular songs, but who makes a small but vital contribution to the cause by carrying messages between various cell members. There is Polsky, who overcomes his almost debilitating fear in order to distribute pamphlets. There is Bennett who describes himself as sympathetic to the cause but whose contribution is compromised by a dominating wife.

We see more of Beukes in the novel than we do Tekwane. But we know more of Tekwane. We do not know until the closing horrific scenes of the novel that the unidentified person arrested and tortured to death by the police is Tekwane. But we learn why he is so feared by the police through a series of scenes interwoven with those devoted to Beukes and his present activities. In chapter 6 we learn of Tekwane's father's death in an unsafe mine accident. We learn more about his experiences as tighter and tighter controls are placed on black and colored peoples, and we learn how their lives and sensibilities are circumscribed by servitude. La Guma describes how apartheid functions through the implementation of pass laws that affect all nonwhite South Africans, restricting mobility and therefore employment opportunities as well as personal freedom.

Chapter 12 tells more of Tekwane's life, in particular his life as a young man forced to live in sordid barracks in black "locations." When he applies for a pass to travel to the city to find work (to earn money to care for his family), he is humiliated by having to strip before bureaucrats and have his genitals examined by white officers, an incident which suggests the near castration of blacks by whites. Tekwane is only 17 years old when this happens to him. But he is given the age of 20 on official records. La Guma dramatizes these two events to signify the absolute control of blacks by whites. Even his name, Elias, is assigned to him by a priest who cannot pronounce his African name. Tekwane learns early in his life about the way racism is practiced in South Africa as a way of controlling the work force, exploiting labor with poor wages to create a greater profit for those who own and control industry. His interest in the movement and its aims is grounded in the desire to see both equality in race relations and an equal distribution of wealth.

Tekwane's experiences are highly personalized but they account for his complete commitment to the movement and can be taken as typical of others who have adopted the cause. He is a man who knows that active opposition to exploitation and terrorist tactics is the only way to achieve a just society. The torture he receives at the hands of the police is presented by La

Guma with a detailed and brutal honesty. Tekwane dies in horrible circumstances but he does not betray his comrades. And, as he dies, he has a vision of joining his ghostly ancestors, "their spears sparkling like diamonds in the exploding sun" (175).

That the personal violence vented on Tekwane is typical of that imposed on the general population of nonwhites is revealed in chapter 9. Constructing an event obviously based on the Sharpeville massacres of 1960, La Guma gains effect by having victims of the police attack presented anonymously as "outlaw," "Child," "bicycle messenger," and "washerwoman," thus suggesting that any nonwhite might experience the indiscriminate violence of the agents of state oppression.

And La Guma achieves additional drama by interpolating in sequence throughout his text the progress of a trial against a woman who has systematically poisoned her husband to the point where she can strangle him. The implications of this substory are several and related. First, the story sustains the overwhelming atmosphere of violence and cruelty endemic in the society. Secondly, the story suggests that violent means are needed to overcome oppression. Third, given the attention of the press in response to their avid readership, the story exists as a fascinating episode in a culture where violence is commonplace.

The novel ends with a group of men, all of whom have been compromised and betrayed and who fear imprisonment or worse, crossing the border into Botswana, there to train as freedom fighters and insurgents. They represent a future where there is hope, however distant it is at the moment of the novel's close.

La Guma pulls together into a comprehensive pattern all of the elements, historical and contemporary, that inform and shape the society against which he protests so vehemently. He provides in synoptic form a historical background lacking in the earlier novels. There are allusions to South African settlement, the antagonism between Boers and British, the Great Trek, and the support for Hitler and the Third Reich by Boers/Afrikaners during World War II. The contemporary situation is what concerns him most—the nocturnal activities, full of tension and fear, Beukes, the ugly death of Tekwane, an almost archetypal figure, the responses of other characters associated with Beukes—all of these descriptions extend the text beyond its physical limits.

Time of the Butcherbird (1979)

Time of the Butcherbird moves from the urban to the rural setting La Guma's implied recommendations about the means through which resistance against apartheid can be successful and the kind of temperament required to effect those means. La Guma takes his title for the novel from South African folklore. In reality, the butcherbird feeds on ticks that live on livestock. They perform a cleansing function. Transmuted to the level of allegory, the butcherbird can be seen as an agent for cleansing society, destroying human parasites that threaten to bleed it dry. In *Time of the Butcherbird*, the parasites are those whites who threaten the destruction of the African community by dispossessing it of its ancestral land. The symbolic butcherbird in the novel is Mma-Tau, the sister of a traditional chief, Hlangeni. By white edict, Hlangeni has seen his title of "chief" reduced to "headman," thus denuding him of traditional authority. He gives in to white pressure and renders himself ineffective as leader of his people.

Mma-Tau assumes the role of her brother, organizes her people, and informs government that her people will "not go from the land" (20). The rebellion she mounts is successful, at least in the short term, breeding confusion in white ranks as Africans attack their oppressors with a barrage of thrown stones. What is important to La Guma is the success of the specific resistance shown by Mma-Tau and her people, but, more importantly, the kind of militant organized action required to rid the community of the parasitic "ticks" that feed off it. The story of Mma-Tau is the principal interest of the novel. At the close of the book, Mma-Tau and her followers retreat to the hills and await the inevitable reprisal of the whites, but they remain determined to continue their resistance against the racist regime.

La Guma writes into his text two other stories, one of which runs parallel on a personal level with the public rebellion of Mma-Tau. This is the story of Shilling Murile, who returns to the place of his birth after spending time in prison. His single-minded mission is to avenge the death of his brother, Tim, by the white farmers, Jaap Opperman and Hannes Meulen. Oppperman, who in a brutal reprisal against Murile and Tim, had tied them both to a tree as punishment for opening a sheep pen and allowing the sheep, belonging to the white farmers, to wander off. The night was bitterly cold and Tim dies of exposure to the weather. Murile strikes out against Opperman and Meulen, slashing the arm of the former. For this attack, Murile is sent to prison. For their part in Tim's death, Opperman and Meulen are merely given a public rebuke by a white magistrate. Opperman is dead when Murile returns from prison. He kills Meulen with one of his own shotguns, afterward escaping to seek shelter with the militant band of Mma-Tau. He is not, he asserts at first, interested in the collective effort of the Africans to seek justice.

The symbolism implicit in Murile's story is clear. Meulen and Opperman represent three generations of Afrikaner farmers and, thus, the dominating political power in the land. Afrikaner historical involvement with the land and Meulen's personal relation with it are briefly but succinctly outlined in the text through references to the celebrations of Dingane's Day, and the day of Blood River of Afrikaner disaffection from British domination—all celebrations of days in which Boer notions of racial supremacy were progressively secured. Meulen is a university graduate and the local candidate for election to the national government. For La Guma he is the "tick," the parasite that sucks the life blood out of the community. Murile is the butcherbird that rids the land of a parasite. There is no sense at the close of the story that Murile will join Mma-Tau's renegades. But he does carry Meulen's shotgun with him, saying he has a few shells left and that he may find a use for them.

The third story concerns an Englishman named Stokes. Stokes is a traveling salesman, moving from place to place, selling baubles in a land and among a people whom he privately views with contempt, even while putting on an affable manner. Stokes is by his own admission a failure, trapped in a job with few rewards. His sorry condition is reinforced by his unsatisfactory marriage to Maisie, whose values are shaped by those she finds in Hollywood romantic films. When Stokes fails to produce the glamorous life he had promised her, Maisie engages in a number of affairs that provide at least a small measure of the life she had hoped to live. Murile mistakenly shoots and kills Stokes when he kills Muelen. Stokes is another kind of "tick" who feeds off the land, all the while despising it. Murile provides a double function, then, as butcherbird, ridding the land of two kinds of parasites.

Time of the Butcherbird is open to the charge of being too neatly organized and of creating characters more symbolic than realistic. But when one remembers that the political situation the novel evokes requires that individuals stand for something that prompts either action or its opposite, one sees that the personal and the public coincide. There are no soft alternatives. Given La Guma's purpose in alerting the generality of people to the forms and causes of their oppression, and his conviction that collective militant action is the way to end oppression, the symbolism in the novel is well contained by the personal experiences of the people in the book.

La Guma is a revolutionary writer and his novel proceeds from the same source of human concern as the writers Sembene Ousmane or Ngugi wa Thiong'o or Ayi Kwei Armah. He believes that literature can be used as an instrument in the battle to overcome oppression and can prompt people, through words and thought, to action. His writing will retain its position in African literature not only for its historical record and relevance but also as a reminder, and even a warning, of how systems of oppression work, what the cost of yielding to them is, and how they must be confronted.

ADDITIONAL READINGS

Abrahams, Cecil A. 1985. *Alex La Guma*. Boston: Twayne.
Balutansky, Kathleen. 1990. *The Novels of Alex La Guma: The Representation of a Political Conflict*. Washington, D.C.: Three Continents Press.

Coetzee, J. M. 1974. "Man's Fate in the Novels of Alex La Guma." *Studies in Black Literature* 5 (1): 16–23.

La Guma, Alex. 1962. *A Walk in the Night*. Ibadan, Nigeria: Mbari.

———. 1964. *And a Threefold Cord*. Berlin: Seven Seas Publishers.

———. 1967. *The Stone Country*. London: Heinemann.

———. 1972. *In the Fog of the Season's End*. London: Heinemann.

———. 1979. *Time of the Butcherbird*. London: Heinemann.

Rabkin, David. 1973. "La Guma and Reality in South Africa." *Journal of Commonwealth Literature* 8 (1): 54–61.

Scanlon, Paul A. 1979. "Alex La Guma's Novels of Protest: The Growth of the Revolutionary." *Okike* 16: 39–50.

Chapter 9
Alan Paton: Cry, the Beloved Country *(1948)*

Alan Paton published *Cry, the Beloved Country* in 1948. This was the year that the Afrikaaner National Government was elected to power. This was the year in which the minister of justice, Henrick Verwoerd, introduced the policy of apartheid. Paton describes and dramatizes the situation of the black people of South Africa in his novel—their poor working conditions, poor pay, poor housing, and inadequate medical services for the quantity of illness suffered by those living in designated areas and squatter camps. Pass laws were already in place. These are the conditions institutionalized by government policies, conditions that would worsen with each refinement of apartheid policy. African resistance to these conditions is already beginning at the time of Paton's earliest writings in the form of boycotts and strikes by blacks.

The tragic circumstances the novel dramatizes are therefore the direct result of government policy. South Africa, epitomized by life in Johannesburg, is a country dominated by fear where civility, compassion, and love survive only in the hearts of a few, and where hope is all but stifled.

Cry, the Beloved Country is a novel of protest, one of the first in what would become a burgeoning publication of fiction describing South Africa's racist society. Nadine Gordimer, Alex La Guma, Andre Brink, and latterly J. M. Coetzee are but the most prominent of those writers who exposed the apartheid state, whose writing added weight and substance to the growing resistance movement represented by the African Nationalist Congress and the Black Consciousness Movement. In *Cry, the Beloved Country,* Paton offers an implicit prediction of what will come if racist policies are not dramatically amended. He knows that what he describes will breed hatred for whites and prompt a debilitating civil war if government policies are not amended and made more humane. He was prescient. Only the actions of F. W. de Clerk, working in close concert with Nelson Mandela, and only Mandela's persuasiveness could have avoided the kind of internal chaos Paton knew could eventuate if the conditions he describes in his novel were not drastically altered. Paton knew at first hand the effect of these conditions on the black population.

Alan Stewart Paton was born in Pietermaritzburg, Natal Province, South Africa on January 11, 1903. He had his secondary school education at Maritzburg College and his university education at Natal University College (which became the University of Natal). From the completion of his formal education until his death on April 12, 1988, Paton was deeply involved in the political, educational, and cultural life of South Africa. He is known in South Africa and well beyond for *Cry, the Beloved Country,* which was translated into 20 foreign languages; adapted as a Broadway musical, *Reach for the Stars,* by Maxwell Anderson and Kurt Weill; and produced as two film versions, each with the novel's title. Paton also wrote and published poetry and two further novels, *Too Late the Phalarope* (1953) and *Ah, but Your Land Is Beautiful* (1981); a short-story collection, *Debbie Go Home/Tales from a Troubled Land* (1961); and the play *Sopono* (1965). He published three biographies, *Hofmeyer* (1964), and an abridged version of the volume, *South African Tragedy: The Life and Times of Jan Hofmeyer* (1965), as well as *Apartheid and the Archbishop: The Life and Times of Geoffrey Clayton, Archbishop of Cape Town* (1973). He also published three volumes of autobiography—*For You Departed* (1969), the British title was *Kontakion for You Departed, Towards the Mountain* (1980), and *Journey Continued* (published posthumously in 1988). His other publications are *South Africa in Transition* (with Dan Weinen in 1956), and *Instrument of Thy Peace* (1982). His collected writings were published as *The Long View* (edited by Edward Callan in 1968), *Knocking on the Door: Shorter Writings of Alan Paton* (edited by Colin Gardener in 1975), and *Save the Beloved Country* (edited by Hans Strydon and David Jones in 1987).

Paton's life beyond writing was equally full. After university and a brief but fruitful career as a secondary schoolteacher at Ixopo High School where he taught chemistry and mathematics, he became in 1935 principal of Diepkloof Reformatory for African Boys. He became fully engaged in this work and brought about many reforms, mitigating the harsh treatment and conditions in which the boys were held. His reforms were later negated as apartheid policies were consolidated. He wrote numerous articles on crime, punishment, penal reform, and the relations between church and race.

Paton helped found the Liberal Party, became its vice president in 1953, and its president in 1956. He continued to work with the Liberal Party, a nonracial party opposed to apartheid, until it was outlawed in 1968. Paton suffered the punitive action of the police state: his passport was revoked in 1961 and not restored until 1970. Honors began to accumulate in 1971 as Paton's literary reputation and his work on behalf of humanity in South Africa gained international recognition. He was awarded honorary degrees from the universities of Harvard, Edinburgh, Toronto, Kenyon College, Michigan, and Trent.

In 1946, Paton took a leave of absence from Diepkloof Reformatory and traveled widely in Europe, the United States, and Canada, visiting penal and correctional institutions. It was on this tour that Paton, lonely for and nostalgic about his native land, began writing *Cry, the Beloved Country* in Trondheim, Norway. He finished the book in San Francisco at the end of his tour. It was published in New York in February 1948, three months before the election of the National Party, which saw the beginnings of the policy of apartheid. What was informal if insistent in matters of racial separation before this election became formalized and eventually institutionalized with the advent of the new government.

Nadine Gordimer has said that with the publication of *Cry, the Beloved Country*, South African literature in English made a new beginning. The novel is the cornerstone of an edifice of writing about the racial, political, social, cultural, and economic life of South Africa. *Cry, the Beloved Country* embraces all of these issues. Even though conceived out of travel weariness and nostalgia for a South African homeland, the novel is not a nostalgic or sentimental book despite its lyrical language and the anguish experienced by all its characters. The multiplicity of themes the book examines and dramatizes is belied by its simplicity of style.

Paton deals with a variety of relationships in contention with each other—relationships between siblings, between parents, between children and grandchildren, between different ideologies; between the Christian church and an incipient labor movement—all leading to personal desolation. Under the human drama that informs the book's surface is the quest on the part of all of the characters for personal redemption and forgiveness.

The personal concerns the novel explores are set in a country in the throes of confused reconstruction with the almost total collapse of the rural economies and the migration of black agricultural workers to the city to find work in the mines. Here they are poorly paid while they labor to create great wealth for their employers, and so are forced into squalid living conditions in designated areas and squatter slums. Against these conditions the only opposition available is the power of the Christian church with its message of love and its appeal to the humanity of the powerful. Public political confrontation, in the form of an incipient union movement, is evident in the novel and Paton seems to support its aims and methods. But his ambiguous response to one of its leaders seems to compromise his position—or to create a novelistic problem that he did not quite solve.

Cry, the Beloved Country is the story of the Reverend Stephen Kumalo, a priest in an Anglican parish in the village of Ndotsheni in Zululand. A letter arrives from a fellow priest in Johannesburg telling Kumalo that his sister, Gertrude, is ill and enjoining Kumalo to travel to Johannesburg. Gertrude is one of three members of Kumalo's family who has left her ancestral home, gone to Johannesburg, and lost contact with Kumalo. The others are his brother John and, more importantly, his son, Absolom. Kumalo travels by train to Johannesburg and sees for the first time the endless and varied landscape of the country, redolent with history, and of wars and punitive actions that subdued the country. He sees, as well, the desecrated landscape wrought by the development of the gold mines.

Kumalo's quest is to find his sister, his brother, and his son. And, as he pursues his quest, assisted by the priest who wrote the letter, the Reverend Theophilus Msimangu, he discovers that his sister has become a prostitute in order to survive in the city and to provide for her infant son. He learns that his brother, John (an ambiguous character in the novel), has become a political figure of great power and influence, feared by the police for his oratorical skills in opposing the forces, political and economic, that exploit labor and suppress organized complaint. He discovers that his son has been involved in a series of petty criminal acts and is incarcerated in prison. His search for his son is arduous. Absolom has been released from prison on the compassionate grounds that he wants to care for a young woman who will bear his child. As Paton describes Kumalo's search, we are shown the conditions that shape the lives of Gertrude, John, and Absolom. Paton's is a panoramic view of the appalling conditions in which the generality of people barely survive as well as a view of the spirit that prompts their survival.

Kumalo eventually learns that Absolom has committed the worst of all possible crimes. He has committed murder. His victim is the son of a wealthy white farmer, Jarvis, from the same parish as Kumalo. Steven Jarvis, the victim, eschewing the rural life of his forefathers, has become an activist for the reform of laws that make for the oppressive racism of South Africa. The irony is that he is killed in a mindless act by someone whose life he is trying to improve. John Kumalo's sons, who have been with Absolom at the fatal shooting, are acquitted of the crime because of the defense prepared by a skillful lawyer.

The lives of Kumalo and Jarvis intersect as a result of the murder and the subsequent trial. Absolom is found guilty of a deliberate act to kill. His lawyer argues that the murder was not premeditated but resulted from the panic of being discovered. Absolom is sentenced to death. Kumalo and his brother are further alienated.

Before his execution, Absolom is reconciled with his father, who arranges a marriage between Absolom and the young woman he has made pregnant. She will travel with Kumalo to Ndotsheni. He also arranges to care for

Gertrude's child when Gertrude says she will repent of her life as a prostitute by becoming a nun.

Jarvis dominates the latter part of the story as he reads through his son's papers and discovers the extent of his passion for reform. Jarvis is brought for the first time to consider the complexities of his society, its racist policies, and its inhumanity. Moved by his son's beliefs and hopes, Jarvis builds a church in his son's memory and provides a fund of money toward establishing a legacy for his son's work. The novel thus ends on a note of hope and of tentative reconciliation.

Cry, the Beloved Country is a prophetic book. In its examination of the exploitation of labor, the horrendous conditions of living for the majority, the pass laws and police brutality, it anticipates the progressive refinement of apartheid laws, and their worsening results. Paton is prophetic in showing the elements and actions in the society that in due course will develop into a full-scale segregation based on institutionalized racism.

Apartheid was in its initial stages when Paton published his novel. The novel describes the creation of the segregationist "homelands," thus ensuring that any equal sharing of the products of labor would be denied the producers of wealth. But we see, as well, the beginnings of black activism as revealed in the organized and successful bus boycott and especially in the speeches of John Kumalo, already seen as a threat by the watchful police. Reference is also made to two other characters who articulate the need and nature of black resistance—Tomlinson and Dubula. To this point in the political and social context, nonviolent agitation is proposed as a means of effecting change. The variety of responses of the citizenry is articulated through a number of anonymous voices in chapter 9 of the novel, voices heard by Kumalo and Msimangu as they conduct their search for Absolom through the seemingly endless townships—Sophiatown, Claremont, Alexandra, Orlando, and Shanty Town.

In one sense, the characters may be seen as merely typical or representative of the various elements in the population, devoid of complexity. Absolom and Gertrude, for example, may be seen as typical victims. But such was the nature of the world in which they lived that the responses and attitudes of characters require an exact focus on the conditions that circumscribe and confound them. Yet each of the principal characters—Kumalo, Msimangu, Jarvis, John Kumalo, and Dubula all advocate different possible means for ameliorating the circumstances of black people. And while these various approaches represent distinct possibilities, they also represent a state of confusion and lack of accord among the protesting groups.

But in dramatizing the discoveries of Kumalo and Jarvis, whose tragedies embody those of the society as a whole, Paton writes with a profound sympathy, understanding, and compassion that removes the suspicion of stereotyping.

Paton advocates implicitly and through the beliefs and actions of Kumalo, Msimangu, and the Christian brothers, through Steven Jarvis and, in a less obvious way, through the actions of Jarvis, his belief in Christian practices that will promote love out of which will ultimately come collaboration between the races. This is a conviction that at least in part informed the policies of the Liberal Party, sentiments that disappear as apartheid policies become entrenched, as the militant policies of the ANC are articulated and practiced, and as the celebration of African-ness prompts the creation of the Black Consciousness Movement. In the postapartheid period the Christian humanism of Paton has reasserted itself in the rapprochement between races as affected by Nelson Mandela and his government, and in the inquiries of Bishop Desmond Tutu and his court, the ultimate aim of which was to find grounds for forgiveness.

The novel's closing line reads: "But when the dawn will come of our emancipation, from the fear of bondage and the bondage of fear, why, that is a secret." More than once in the novel Msimangu says, expressing his deepest concern, "I have one great fear in my heart, that one day when they turn to loving they will find we have turned to hating" (301). These are prophetic words that almost came to pass.

ADDITIONAL READINGS

Callan, Edward. 1982. *Alan Paton, Revised Edition.* Boston: Twayne.

Paton, Alan. 1948. *Cry, the Beloved Country.* New York: Scribner.

———. 1953. *Too Late the Phalarope.* New York: Signet.

——— with Dan Weinen. 1956. *South Africa in Transition.* New York: Scribner.

———. 1961. *Debbie Go Home/Tales from a Troubled Land.* London: Cape.

———. 1964. *Hofmeyer.* London: Oxford University Press.

———. 1965. *Sopono.* New York: Scribner.

———. 1968. *The Long View,* ed. Edward Callan. New York: Praeger.

———. 1969. *For You Departed.* New York: Scribner.

———. 1973. *Apartheid and the Archbishop: The Life and Times of Geoffery Clayton, Archbishop of Cape Town.* New York: Scribner.

———. 1975. *Knocking on the Door: Shorter Writings of Alan Paton.* Edited by Colin Gardner. Cape Town, South Africa: David Philip.

———. 1980. *Toward the Mountain.* New York: Scribner.

———. 1981. *Ah, but Your Land Is Beautiful.* London: Cape.

———. 1982. *Instrument of Thy Peace.* New York: Seabury Press.

———. 1987. *Save the Beloved Country.* Edited by Hans Strydon and David Jones. New York: Scribner.

———. 1988. *Journey Continued.* New York: Scribner.

Chapter 10
Bessie Head: When Rain Clouds Gather *(1968)*

Bessie Head is, with Flora Nwapa from Nigeria, Africa's first woman novelist. Often referred to by woman writers who come after her, Bessie Head's path to literary recognition and acceptance was arduous in the extreme, as was her life.

She was born on July 6, 1937, in Fort Napier Mental Institution in Pietermaritzburg, Natal Province, South Africa. Her mother was Bessie Amelia Emery, a member of a white landowning family whose name was Birch. Her father was a stable hand. Her mother remained in the mental hospital until her death in 1943.

Bessie Head lived in a number of foster homes until 1950, when she was placed in St. Monica's, an Anglican orphanage in Hillary, Durban. While there she completed high school, taking her Junior Certificate in 1953. She received the Natal Teacher's Certificate in 1957 that qualified her as an elementary school teacher. And from 1956 to 1958, she taught primary school in Durban. But teaching was not a congenial occupation and she resigned her position to attempt a career in journalism. She worked in Cape Town and Johannesburg for various newspapers and journals. She was one of many South Africans arrested and held briefly in jail in the aftermath of the Sharpeville massacres.

In 1960, she met and married another journalist, Harold Head. Troubled all her life by periods of mental illness, she attempted suicide in 1960. In 1962, her son, Howard, was born. In 1962, she moved with her husband and son to Port Elizabeth, where her husband found a job with the *Evening Post* newspaper. The family moved back to Cape Town in 1963. At this time, the marriage began to have difficulties that continued to develop until it was formally ended in 1964.

In 1964, Bessie Head left South Africa on an exit permit and took a primary school teaching position in Serowe, Botswana. In her first years in Botswana, she moved from job to job and from place to place, as teacher, as copy typist, and in odd jobs in Serowe, Radisele, and Francestown. It is in these early years in Botswana that her writing career begins to take shape. Literary pieces were published in *The New Statesman* and other journals and magazines. *When Rain Clouds Gather,* her first novel, was published in 1968. This was followed by *Maru* (1971) and *A Question of Power* (1974). During this period Bessie Head had two mental breakdowns, the second severe enough to keep her in the hospital for three months. Her third novel draws extensively on this period of her life.

In 1976, Bessie Head began to receive recognition for her writing and was invited to a gathering of writers and academics at the University of Botswana. This was to be the first of a series of invitations to literary gatherings and to academic institutions that took her to the United States, Germany, Denmark, Nigeria, Zimbabwe, and Australia. On her travels, she met fellow writers from Africa and beyond—Mary Benson, Stephen Gray, Sipho Sepamla, Mbulelo Mzamane, Andre Brink, Ngugi wa Thiong'o, Bruce Chatwin, Salman Rushdie, and Angela Carter. By the time her travels had ended, her literary reputation was secure.

In these years she attained Botswanan citizenship and saw the publication of *The Collector of Treasures and Other Botswanan Village Tales* in 1972; *Serowe: Village in the Rain Wind* in 1981; and *A Bewitched Crossroad: An African Saga* in 1984. Around 1985, Bessie Head began to drink heavily. She also ignored warnings from her doctor, who diagnosed hepatitis. She died on April 17, 1986. She was 49 years old.

Bessie Head's life was troubled from its beginnings to its end. Her fear of inherited madness, thrown at her by an unfeeling teacher when she was very young, stayed with her throughout her life and at times overtook her. In South Africa, she was a victim of worsening racial policies. Yet however much she felt herself and other colored and black peoples the victims of institutionalized racial policies, she was never able to make her experiences in South Africa the subject matter of her writing.

Equally, though she lived in Botswana from 1946 until her death, she was never fully able to come to terms with her adopted and adoptive country. The ambiguities in her life are reflected in her writing. Most profoundly, however much recognition and acclaim she was given as her books made their way in the literary world, she never escaped the sense of alienation, loneliness, and fear of rejection that plagued her life.

When Rain Clouds Gather is a symbolic title for a novel written in the realist tradition. People in a drought-ridden area see in the distant gathering of the clouds a hope for rain that will bring them and their land relief and rebirth. Similarly, the parched souls of individuals see in the clouds the symbolic possibility of spiritual renewal: "That is why all good things and all good people are called rain. Sometimes we see rain clouds gather even though not a cloud appears in the sky. It is all in our heart" (168). Bessie Head's quest for personal salvation is what prompted her to leave South Africa. In Botswana, she found not the fragmented society of her country of birth but a homogenous, traditional pastoral society that gave her, for a time, peace of mind. No generalizations are fully satisfying in describing and accounting for a writer's life and work. But it is safe to say that Bessie Head's writing, all of which was done in and about Botswana, transmutes her personal experiences into fiction.

In *A Question of Power,* the autobiographical element is almost inseparable from the fictional. The setting of the novel is Golem Mmidi. The village is in Botswana, a place characterized as "the worst tribal country in the world" (10). Golem Mmidi "acquired its name from the occupation the villagers followed, which was crop growing" (22). Golem Mmidi is not a traditional village but a place that "consisted of individuals who had fled there to escape the tragedies of life" (22). The land is the reason for their existence. Bessie Head characterizes Golem Mmidi in this way: " . . . the villagers did not differ so greatly from everyone else in their way of life. The men attended to the cattle business and helped with the ploughing, while the women were the agriculturalists or tillers of the earth . . . . [they] supplemented their incomes with wood carvings and basket making" (22). Life in the country is not static, however. Change is in the air: "The country was going through a year of self-government prior to complete independence" (19). There is a British colonial police officer, a vestige of the past. There is a member of the Pan Africanist Party, a representative of the anticipated independence. Traditional ways and modernists practices meet to form what one character calls a "cautious progressiveness" (19).

The novel proper begins with the arrival of Mahkaya Mateso in Golema Mmidi. Mahkaya is a Zulu whose name, translated into English, means "one who stays home," an irony because he has been active in subversive activities in various parts of South Africa, was caught and sent to prison for two years.

His personal credo now is "I just want to step on free ground. I don't care about people. . . . I want to feel what it is like to live in a free country and then maybe some of the evils in my life will correct themselves" (10).

When Rain Clouds Gather is constructed on a series of oppositions. There are traditionalists and conservatives and there are reformists, not revolutionaries, those who advocate a gradual changing of traditional practices, principally in agriculture. Traditionalists are represented by Paramount Chief Sekoto, an amiable figure more concerned to enjoy good food, fast cars, and illicit love affairs with his various concubines than to devote himself to any innovation in the land and the lives he traditionally mentors. He is an ineffective, if influential, anachronism.

His brother, Matenge, is a different kind of traditionalist. He administers Golem Mmidi as surrogate to Sekoto, banished there when a plot to assassinate Sekoto failed, a plot in which it is thought he might have been involved. Matenge is a force for punitive conservatism. Yet his harshest judgments against his "subjects" are consistently overruled by Sekoto. Matenge cannot see, as even Sekoto in his indolent way can, that change is taking place rapidly as the colonial administration prepares to depart, at which point a "new Africa" would be "the outcome of the natural growth of a people" (178–79).

Pan Africanism is represented in a corrupted form by Joas Tsepe. However noble the tenets, aims, and objectives of Pan Africanism may be, Tsepe perverts them. He is a political opportunist, supported by "some mysterious source," (47) a figure who would, had he the chance, "plunge the African continent into an era of chaos and bloody murder" (47). Head introduces Tsepe and the way he would use the rhetoric of Pan Africanism as a comment on the pitfalls of ideology. However, with reference to Pan Africanism, she poses no explicit alternative position to Tsepe's.

This position might be embodied in a limited and local way through the work of Gilbert Balfour. Balfour is an Englishman who has grown tired of his middle-class life in England. He brings his considerable training and experience as an agronomist to Golem Mmidi to foster a modest cooperative venture in the production of tobacco. His purpose is to bring cash into the agricultural system of the village and use this to improve living conditions in general—better housing, more and cleaner water, and a more varied source and supply of food. Balfour wins the support of Mahkaya and of Dinorego, a voice of traditional wisdom in the community who shares Balfour's notion of a limited development in the local economy. Balfour also gains the support of the women in the village led by Paulina, a villager with a haunted past, the mother of a son who dies a lonely death from tuberculosis and a daughter who becomes deeply involved in the work of the women who come together to labor for Balfour and their village.

Chapter 3 of the novel is given over almost in whole to displaying Gilbert Balfour's belief in what the land is capable of producing and how it should be nurtured. Balfour believes in what he calls "conservative progress. He believed that co-operative organization was similar to communal ownership of the land" (101). Here Head reveals an acute and detailed knowledge of agricultural practices and potential, drawn from her own work in collaborative farming in 1962. What Balfour proposes is a realignment of land use according to traditional practices.

The novel is framed by a descriptive account of the life of the village as it subtly alters, mostly through the work of Balfour and Mahkaya. Mahkaya is, in fact, reborn through his work with Balfour. His cynicism and aloofness are replaced by a relentless and almost joyous involvement with the villagers whose lives take on a new meaning. Through their work and through discussions among themselves, Head reveals a range of emotions about the characters' hopes, fears, and values.

And while a range of contending relationships is dramatized in the novel, there is little overt conflict until near the book's close. Matenge, deeply angered by Paulina's role in organizing the 100 women who manage the tobacco venture, summons her to his home to punish her. The villagers rally around her, directly challenging his authority for the first time. When this happens, his retainers desert him and Matenge hangs himself. Balfour, Mahkaya, and Paulina see that the success of their collaborative venture is secured by the solidarity of the villagers who support Paulina and defy Matenge, an icon of worn out conservatism—domination, enslavement, and coercion. Matenge's collapse is inevitable. In issues raised between him and Sekoto, the latter is always supported by the police commissioner, Ashley-Green, and thus it becomes clear that Matenge has been overruled.

Bessie Head is not concerned with examining through character and action the political abstractions that engage writers from other parts of Africa. She says that the great political proposals sweeping over Africa stop at the borders of Botswana. And despite her love-hate relationship with Botswana, expressed either directly or by implication in her writing, she plainly feels drawn to the collectivity dramatized in *When Rain Clouds Gather,* in which the goals of individuals are of greater importance than adhering to massive popular political movements. Her creation of Tsepe, the individual and the political icon, makes plain her opinion of these movements.

The main characters in the novel work out their personal problems against a public background. Life and living in rural Botswana is hard and at times very harsh. Children die from tuberculosis when there are not the facilities to offer adequate treatment; cattle die from drought and disease, wealth is lost; rain does not fall, crops cannot grow, and the possibility of famine and starvation is always lurking. But individuals endure and prevail and, in the end, a number of small triumphs in individual lives are won. Balfour and Mahkaya marry happily. The characters and what they stand for may seem too carefully representative of contending points of view, the alignment of good and evil too obvious. Perhaps this is no more than a reflection of a cultural reality of the time and place. Perhaps the ending is too contrived. But the book, if nothing more—and it is much more—is a historical document of great worth, wrought by a deeply sensitive writer, not fully in love with the land she evokes but deeply committed to the humanity she finds there.

ADDITIONAL READINGS

Abrahams, Cecil, ed. 1990. *The Tragic Life: Bessie Head and Literature in Southern Africa*. Trenton, N.J.: Africa World Press.

Head, Bessie. 1968. *When Rain Clouds Gather*. New York: Simon & Schuster.

———. 1971. *Maru*. London: Victor Gollancz.

———. 1974. *A Question of Power*. London: Davis-Poynter.

———. 1977. *The Collector of Treasures and Other Botswanan Village Tales*. London: Heinemenn Educational.

———. 1981. *Serowe: Village in the Rain Wind*. London: Heinemann Educational.

———. 1984. *A Bewitched Crossroad: An African Saga*. Johanesburg: Konker.

Biographies

West Africa

Chinua Achebe (1930–). Nigerian novelist, short-story writer, literary editor, literary and political critic. Achebe was born Albert Chinualumogo in Ogidi in the Eastern Region of Nigeria. His father was Isaiah Okafor Achebe, a chatechist in the Church Missionary Society. His mother was Janet Iloegbunam Achebe. Achebe got his primary education in the Ogidi village school and his secondary education at Government College, Umuahia. He was a member of the first class at University College Ibadan, a constituent college of the University of London. He planned to study medicine but, after a year, turned to English literary studies. He graduated with an Honors B.A. from University of London in 1953. He joined the Nigerian Broadcasting Corporation (NBC) in 1954, first as a talks producer, then as comptroller of the NBC for the Eastern Region of Nigeria and then as director of external broadcast programming, "The Voice of Nigeria," in Lagos. He left Lagos in 1966 when civil war threatened, returning to the Eastern Region. The Eastern Region of Nigeria seceded Nigeria as Biafra and civil war broke out in 1967. Achebe served the Biafra cause from 1967 to 1970 when the war ended and Biafra capitulated.

After the war, Achebe taught in various universities in Nigeria and the United States. He was seriously injured in an automobile accident in 1990.

Achebe has received numerous literary awards and honorary degrees. He currently teaches at Bard College in Upper New York State.

Ama Ata Aidoo (1942–). Ghanaian novelist, short-story writer, poet, play-wright, and literary critic. Aidoo was born at Saltpond, Ghana, and was christened Christina Ama Ata Aidoo. She graduated from the University of Ghana in 1964. She has held political office in Ghana and has traveled widely in Europe and the United States.

Timothy Mofolorunsa Aluko (1918–). Nigerian novelist. Aluko was born in Ilesha, Western Nigeria. He was educated at Government College, Ibadan, and Yaba Higher College, Lagos. From 1946 to 1950, he studied town planning and civil engineering at the University of London. Returning to Nigeria, he spent 10 years as a district engineer in various parts of the country. Following this, he was director of public works for Western Nigeria and then senior research fellow in municipal engineering at the University of Lagos. His final post was as state commissioner for finance in the ministry of finance in Ibadan.

Elechi Amadi (1934–). Nigerian novelist and playwright. Amadi was born at Aluu, near Port Harcourt, in Nigeria.. He got his secondary education at Government College, Umuahiah. He then studied mathematics and physics at University College Ibadan. He served in the Nigerian Army, rising to the rank of captain. He was twice taken prisoner by Biafran forces in the civil war He left the army in 1965 to become a teacher. As well as teaching, Amadi served the Rivers State government and the ministry of education.

Ayi Kwei Armah (1939–). Ghanaian novelist, short-story writer, and essay-ist, Armah was born in Takoradi, Ghana. He was educated at Achimota College and the University of Ghana before leaving for the United States where he did further studies at Groton School in Harvard University and in the Graduate School of Fine Art at Columbia University. He has worked as an editor and translator and university teacher in France, the United States, Algeria, Tanzania, and Lesotho.

Miriama Ba (1929–81). Ba was born in Dakar, Senegal, the daughter of a civil servant who became Senegal's first Minister of Health. She was a pri-mary school teacher and later an inspector of schools. She was married to a Senegalese parliamentarian with whom she had nine children. They later separated. Miriama Ba was active in apolitical womens' associations. She gained international recognition as an author with her first novel, *Une si longue lettre; So Long a Letter* (1981). Miriama Ba died in 1981 after a long battle with cancer. She did not live to see the publication of her second novel, *Un chant ecarlate (1981); Scarlet Song (1986).*

Syl Cheney-Coker (1945–). Cheney-Coker was born in Freetown, Sierra Leone. He had his primary and secondary education in Freetown before studying overseas in the United States at the University of Oregon, the University of California at Los Angeles, and the University of Wisconsin. Following university studies, Cheney-Coker worked as a dock worker and factory hand, freelance writer, broadcaster, and journalist. He has been a visiting professor in Nigeria and in the Philippines.

Cyprian Ekwensi (1921–). Nigerian novelist and children's writer, Ekwensi was born in Minna, Northern Nigeria, where he had his primary education. He got his secondary education in Ibadan. He later trained in pharmacy and forestry, worked as a broadcaster for the Nigerian Broadcasting Corporation and, later, as director of a publishing house, Star Printing and Publishing He also served in the Nigerian government's ministry of information.

Buchi Emecheta (1944–). Nigerian novelist and children's writer, was born in Lagos where she received her primary and secondary education. In 1962 she traveled to London, where she earned a B.A. in sociology at the University of London. She has worked as a librarian, teacher, and social worker, as well as a writer. She held a senior research fellowship in the University of Calabar. She lives in London.

Chukwumeka Ike (1931–). Nigerian novelist, teacher, and government education administrator, Ike was born in Ndikelionwu, near Awka in Eastern Nigeria. He had his secondary education at Government College, Umuahia and university education at the University of Ibadan and Stanford University. Nigeria's most prolific writer, Amadi has held many public appointments, as assistant registrar for student affairs at the University of Ibadan, registrar at the University of Nigeria, Nsukka, and chief executive officer for the West African Examinations Council.

Festus Iyayi (1947–). Nigerian novelist, born in Benin City, Nigeria, and educated at Annunciation Catholic College in Irrua, Nigeria; Government College, Ughelli, Nigeria; Kiev Institute of National Economy, Russia, and the University of Bradford, United Kingdom. He was for many years a lecturer at the University of Benin. His radical political views have often resulted in detention without trial.

John Munonye (1929–). Nigerian novelist, born in Akokwa, Eastern Nigeria, Munonye had his secondary education at Christ the King College, Ibadan, and university education at University College Ibadan where he earned a B.A. in Greek and Latin. He did postgraduate work in education at London University. He has worked in various capacities in education as a teacher, administrator, and author of educational texts.

Flora Nwapa (1931–94). Nigerian novelist and children's writer, Nwapa was born in Oguta, Eastern Nigeria. She was educated in Lagos and at Elelenwa Girls' Secondary School in Port Harcourt. She took her B.A. degree at the University College Ibadan in 1957 and a diploma in education from the University of Edinburgh. She worked as a teacher, an education officer, and registrar at the University of Lagos, and as a commissioner in Anambra State in Nigeria. She was managing director of the Tana Press, her own publishing company, at the time of her death.

Gabriel Okara (1921–). Nigerian novelist and poet, Okara was born in Bumoundi, Western Nigeria. He had his secondary schooling at Government College, Umuahia, and Yaba Higher College in Lagos. He has worked as a bookbinder and a print and television journalist. He was a government information officer for Eastern Nigeria and was director of cultural affairs for Biafra at the time of the Nigerian civil war.

Ben Okri (1959–). Nigerian novelist, poet, short-story writer, and critic. Okri was born in Minna in Nigeria's middle belt, the son of an Igbo mother and an Urohobo father. He lived in England from 1961 to 1968, when he returned with his family to Nigeria. He had his secondary schooling at Children's Home School in Sapele, Christ High School in Ibadan and Urobo College in Warri. He returned to England in 1978. He attended the University of Essex in 1980, worked as poetry editor for *West Africa* magazine from 1983 to 1986 and, at the same time, in the West African Service of the BBC. He lives in London.

Kole Omotoso (1943–). Nigerian novelist, poet, and literary critic, Omotoso was born in Akure, Nigeria, educated at King's College, Lagos, the University of Ibadan where he took a degree in Arabic with French as his subsidiary subject, and at the University of Edinburgh where he earned a Ph.D. He has worked as a teacher in schools and universities and as a broadcaster and a publisher.

Sembene Ousmane (1923–). Senegalese novelist and filmmaker. He was born in Ziquinchorin in Senegal. He was educated in Koranic schools in Casamance and, when he was 12 years old, in French schools in Dakar. He joined the French colonial army in 1942 and fought in Africa and Europe in World War II. On his return to Senegal after the war ended, Ousmane joined the famous Dakar-Niger railworkers strike in 1947–48. In 1948 he left Senegal for France where he now lives, while traveling widely throughout the world.

Kenule Saro-Wiwa (1941–95). Nigerian novelist, poet, short-story writer, screenwriter, teacher, publisher, and political activist, Kenule Saro-Wiwa was born in Bori, Eastern Nigeria. He attended Government College, Umuahia, and the University College, Ibadan, where he graduated B.A. Honors in English. He taught at the University of Nigeria in Nsukka. When Biafra seceded, he joined the University of Lagos. He was appointed interim governor of the Rivers State when those territories were regained from Biafra by Nigerian military forces. He served in the Nigerian federal government. Leaving politics, he became a novelist, television screenwriter, businessman, and publisher of Saros International Publishers.

Saro-Wiwa was indicted on a trumped-up charge of murder by the agents of General Sani Abacha's military dictatorship. He was found guilty of complicity in the murder of four Ogoni elders. His expression of public concern for his Ogoni people and his public contempt for their oppressors led to the charges against him and, after a long period of incarceration, to the trial that found him guilty of the charges brought against him. He was murdered by hanging in Port Harcourt on November 9, 1995.

Amos Tutuola (1920–97). Magic-realist novelist Tutuola was born in Abeokuta in the Western Region of Nigeria. His formal education was limited to the years between 1934 and 1939. He trained as a metalsmith and served in that capacity in the West African Air Corps, a wing of the Royal Air Force, in World War II. After the war he worked as a messenger in the Labour Department of the colonial government. He began his writing career in his spare time on this job. His writing was not respected at first by his fellow Nigerians but brought international acclaim. Eventually he was accepted as an important contributor to the growing body of writing from West Africa. His unique vision and style brought him many honors late in life, most notably a visiting fellowship in the University of Ile-Ife in Nigeria in 1979, and in the International Writing Program at the University of Iowa in 1983.

East Africa

Austin Bukenya (1944–). Ugandan novelist, short-story writer, and playwright. Bukenya was born in Masaka, Uganda, and educated at Entebbe, Uganda, and the University College of Dar es Salaam. He also studied in Madagascar, at York University in the United Kingdom, and at Stirling University in Scotland. He taught at Kenyatta University in Kenya.

Nuruddin Farah (1945–). Somalian novelist. Farah was born in Bardoa, Somalia (at the time under Italian administration), and grew up in Ogaden (then administered by Somalia). He got his education in Ethiopia, Mogadishu, the Punjab University in Chandigarh in India, and the

University of Essex in the United Kingdom. He has traveled and taught in many places—Europe, Africa, the United States, and Canada.

Abdulrazak Gurnah (1948–). Tanzanian novelist and critic. Gurnah was born in Zanzibar and moved to England when he was 18 years old to further his studies. His studies were interrupted from 1980 to 1982 when he taught at the University of Kano in Northern Nigeria. He received his Ph.D. from the University of Kent, Canterbury, United Kingdom, in 1982. He has taught at the University of Kent since 1985.

Samuel Kahiga (1943–). Kenyan novelist, short-story writer, and collaborator with his brother, Leonard Kibera. Kahiga was born in Uthiro Village in Central Province, Kenya.

Leonard Kibera (1942–83). Kibera was born in Kabete, near Nairobi, Kenya. He attended Kangaru High School in Embu; the University College, Nairobi, where he took his B.A. in English; Stanford University and the University of California at Berkeley. He taught at the University of Zambia from 1973 until 1975 and at Kenyatta University in Nairobi from 1976 until his early death in 1983.

Charles Mangua (1942–). Kenyan novelist. Mangua was born in Nyeri, Kenya, where he had his early education. Later he attended Makerere University College in Kampala, Uganda, and Oxford University.

Meji Mwangi (1948–). Kenyan novelist. Mwangi was born in Nanyuki, Nyeri District, in Kenya's Central Province. He attended Nayuki secondary school, Kenyatta College in Nairobi, and Leeds University, in the United Kingdom. He worked for a time for the British Council in Nairobi, and as a sound technician for French television. By the mid-1970s he had become a full-time writer.

Peter Nazareth (1940–). Nazareth was born in Kampala, Uganda. His parents were from Goa in India. His B.A. degree is from Makerere University College, Kampala, Uganda. He did graduate work at Leeds University in the United Kingdom. He worked for the Uganda government from 1965 to 1973. In 1973 he was awarded the Seymour Lustman Fellowship at Yale University. Following his time at Yale, Nazareth joined the State University of Iowa, first as an honorary fellow and then as professor of English and African American world studies. He has been a major figure in promoting the work of the International Writing Program at Iowa City.

Ngugi wa Thiong'o (1938–). Kenyan novelist, short-story writer, playwright, and literary, political, and cultural critic. Ngugi wa Thiong'o (he was christened James Ngugi) was born in Kamarithu, Kenya. He was educated at Gikuyu Karig'a School; Alliance High School, Nairobi; Makerere University College, Kampala, Uganda; Leeds University in the United Kingdom; and Northwestern University in the United States. He was a journalist for the *Sunday Nation* newspaper in Nairobi in 1964 and worked as a lecturer in the department of literature at the University of Nairobi in 1971, and as its acting head in 1972. Since then, he has lived in exile, mostly in the United Kingdom until 1978, when he took up full-time teaching in the United States.

Rebecca Njau (1932–). Kenyan novelist, short-story writer, playwright, teacher, editor, and textile artist. Rebecca Njau was born in Kangariri in the Kambu District of Kenya. She attended Alliance High School in Nairobi for her secondary education and Makerere University College, Kampala, Uganda, where she studied for a diploma in education. Njau is seen as a pioneer in representing the concerns of women in Kenya.

Okello Oculi (1942–). Ugandan writer. Oculi was born in Lang'o, Northern Uganda. His degree is in political science from Makerere University College, Kampala, Uganda. He did further studies in the subject for his Ph.D. at the University of Wisconsin in Madison. He is a university teacher of political studies.

Grace Ogot (1930–). Kenyan novelist and short-story writer. Grace Ogot was born in Asembo Kabondo in Western Kenya. His early education was at Ngiya and Butere Schools. She subsequently studied and practiced nursing in Uganda and London. She also taught nursing practice in Maseno Hospital in Kenya. She has had a wide and varied career. She wrote scripts for the BBC African Service, was chair of the Kenya Writers Association, a district development officer, an elected Member of Parliament, and an assistant minister in government.

Peter Palangyo (1939–). Tanzanian writer, teacher, and diplomat. Palangyo was born in Oferu District in Northwest Tanzania. He attended Old Moshi Secondary School in the Kilimanjaro region of Tanzania and then St. Olaf College in Minnesota. His degree was in biology and chemistry. He studied for the Diploma in Education at Makerere University College in Uganda. He followed this by earning an M.A. in literature from Ohio State University and a Ph.D. in literature from the State University of New York at Buffalo. For a time he was a school principal before he joined the Tanzanian diplomatic service, rising to the rank of ambassador.

Gabriel Ruhumbika (1938–). Tanzanian novelist. Ruhambika was born in Ukerewe Islands, Tanzania. He is a member of the Ukerewe ruling family.

His B.A. is in English from Makerere University College in Uganda and his Ph.D. is from the Sorbonne. His subject was African theater. He was first lecturer and later professor of literature in the University of Dar es Salaam. He has been visiting professor in universities in the United States.

Robert Serumaga (1939–80). Ugandan playwright and novelist. Serumaga was born in Uganda and educated at Makerere University College in Uganda and at Trinity College, Dublin, where he took an M.A. in economics. He was prominent in the development of professional theater in Uganda, for which he wrote several plays. He held posts in Ugandan government in the post-Amin period. He died of a brain hemorrhage in Nairobi, Kenya, in September 1980.

Moyez Gulamhussein Vassanji (1950–). Tanzanian novelist and short-story writer; editor, publisher, and astrophysicist. Vassanji was born in Nairobi, Kenya, and educated at the Aga Khan School in Dar es Salaam and at the Massachusetts Institute of Technology and the University of Pennsylvania. He worked as a research associate in the University of Toronto in Canada before embarking on a full-time literary career. He is founder and publisher of *The Toronto South Asian Review*.

South-Central Africa

Steve Chimombo (1945–). Malawian novelist and playwright. Chimombo was born in Zomba, Malawi, and attended the Zomba Catholic Secondary School, His B.A. is from the University of Malawi. He took a teaching diploma in English as a Second Language from the University of Wales. He has an M.A. and Ph.D. in education from Columbia. He is professor of English in Chancellor College, Malawi.

Shimmer Chinodya (1957–). Malawian novelist. Chinodya was born in Zimbabwe and educated at Goromonzi secondary school and at the University of Zimbabwe. He gained his M.A. in fine art from the University of Iowa. He has worked for the ministry of education in Harare, Zimbabwe.

Tsitsi Dangarembga (1959–). Zimbabwean novelist and filmmaker. Tsitsi Dangarembga was educated at the universities of Zimbabwe and Cambridge. She studied medicine and psychology. She is concerned with a variety of social issues—the status of women, prostitution, AIDS, and unemployment—from the perspective of women.

Bessie Head (1937–86). South African novelist, short-story writer, and historian. Bessie Head was born in Piertermaritzburg in Natal Province of

South Africa. Her mother was white, her father black. She was born in a mental institution, where he mother was placed by her own parents. She was placed with foster parents until she was 13 and attended mission schools until she was 18. She trained and worked as a teacher for four years. She then worked as a journalist for *Drum Magazine* and *Golden City Post*. She had a brief and unsuccessful marriage, which broke up after the birth of her son, Howard. She moved to Botswana in 1964 where she remained until her death in Serowe. Two volumes of her writing were published posthumously.

Chenjerai Hove (1956–). Zimbabwean novelist and poet. Hove was born in Gwern, Zimbabwe. He has been active in the promotion of Zimbabwean literature through his presidency of the Zimbabwean Writers Union and his activities as writer-in-residence at the University of Zimbabwe. He was visiting professor at Lewis and Clark College in Oregon. Hove writes in both Shona and English.

Legson Kayira (1942–). Malawian novelist. Kayira was born in Nthalire in the northern Karonga District of a country still called Nyasaland. He was educated in the Livingstone Mission in Nyasaland, and later at Skagit Valley College and the University of Washington in Seattle. He later undertook postgraduate studies at Cambridge University.

Dambudzo Marechera (1952–87). Zimbabwean novelist, poet, and playwright. Marechera was born in Rusape in what was then Southern Rhodesia. He was educated in Zimbabwe at St. Augustine's Mission in Penhalonga and began studies in the B.A. program at the then University of Rhodesia. He was expelled for taking part in student protest marches. He attended Oxford University in 1974. He was expelled for erratic behavior and academic dereliction. He returned to Zimbabwe in 1982 and died there in 1987.

Atwell Sidwell Mopeli-Paulus (1913–60). South African novelist and poet. He was born in Witzebroek in the Orange Free State of South Africa. He served in North Africa in World War II. He worked in Durban and Johannesburg after the war. He eventually returned to his place of birth where he became active in local politics. He wrote in both English and Sesotho. He is noted for his collaboration with Peter Lanham and Miriam Basner in two of his published works.

Dominic Mulaisho (1933–). Zambian novelist. He was born in Feira, Zambia. He was educated at Canisius College, Chalimbana, and later at the University College of Rhodesia and Nyasaland. After completing his education, he had a long and distinguished career in public service in the government of Kenneth Kaunda.

David Rubadiri (1930–). Malawian novelist and poet. He was born in Liule, Nyasaland, and then moved on to Makerere College, Uganda. He took further studies at King's College, Cambridge. He was Malawi's first ambassador to the United States and the United Nations. He broke with the regime of Dr. Hastings Banda, Malawi's first Prime Minister, and joined the University of Botswana as professor of education. When Banda fell from power, Rubadiri returned to the United Nations as Malawi's ambassador.

South Africa

Peter Abrahams (1919–). South African novelist. Abrahams was born in Vrededorp, Johannesburg. His formal education began at age 11. He attended a series of schools—Diocesan Training College at Grace Dieu, St. Peter's Ross Henville in Rosettenville. Early in his life he made the acquaintance of Ezekiel Mphahlele, the future novelist and literary critic, and Oliver Tambo, the future African National Congress leader. He also came in contact with the work of black American writers—the poets Countee Cullen, Claude Mackay, and Langston Hughes—and the writings of W.E.B. Du Bois, writing that shaped his own left-wing sensibility. He worked as a newspaper reporter and writer in Cape Town and Johannesburg. In 1939 he left South Africa, worked for a time as a seaman and later for British newspapers. In London he met a group of African intellectuals, some of whom in due course were leaders in the independence movements in Africa, most prominent among them Kwame Nkrumah, who led the Gold Coast to independence as Ghana in 1957. Abrahams reported to the London *Observer* newspaper on the color question in South Africa and Kenya. He eventually settled in Jamaica.

Stephen William Black (1880–1931). South African novelist and playwright. Black was born in Cape Town and had his education at the Diocesan College in that city. He was a well-known athlete and gained fame as a boxer. Later he worked as a sports reporter. Still later, he worked as an actor-manager in various stage companies, for some of whom he wrote plays. In fact, he is known as the founder of South African drama. Black lived in London from 1913 to 1915 and in France from 1918 to 1927. From 1929 until his death, Black edited a weekly paper, *The Sjambok*.

Douglas Blackburn (1857–1929). South African novelist. Blackburn was born in London. He lived in South Africa between 1892 and 1908 and published seven novels based on his experiences as a journalist traveling in the country. He is one of the first writers to explore in fiction the theme of miscegenation and the first to dramatize in his fiction the nature and the ensuing disastrous social consequences of the capitalist exploitation of Africans.

This latter in the form of the "Jim comes to Jo'burg" theme, which Blackburn introduced into the literature.

Herman Charles Bosman (1905–51). South African novelist, short-story writer, poet, and playwright. Bosman was born in Kuils River, near Cape Town. His first language was Afrikaans, but he attended English language schools and the universities of Witwatersrand and Johannesburg. Bosman was a central figure, through his literary output—novels, poems, and plays—together with the anthologies of literature and criticism he edited. Bosman was one of the first advocates for the establishment of a distinctive South African literature.

Andre Brink (1935–). South African novelist, playwright, literary critic, and academic. Brink was born in Vrede in the Orange Free State. He was educated at Lydenberg High School and Potchefstroom University. He took his M.A. in English in 1958 and an M.A. in Afrikaans—his native tongue—in 1959. He studied comparative literature in Paris at the Sorbonne from 1959 to 1961. He returned to South Africa to teach at Grahamstown University, where he became associated with a group of young South African writers who called themselves the "Sestigers"—the "1960ers"—whose aim was to introduce European modernist values into South African writing. Through his writing, first in Afrikaans and then his translations of his work into English, Brink became an outspoken critic of apartheid. Brink taught at Rhodes University, where he obtained his Ph.D., and later at Cape Town University where he still teaches.

Stuart Cloete (1897–1976). South African popular novelist and short-story writer. Cloete was born in Paris of South African parents. He was educated in the United Kingdom and served in the British army in World War I. After the war ended, Cloete visited South Africa for the first time and thereafter spent his time between South Africa and England. He died in Cape Town.

John Maxwell Coetzee (1940–). South African novelist. Coetzee was born in Cape Town. He took degrees in English and mathematics at the University of Cape Town in 1963. He worked in computers in London in the 1960s and then accepted a Fulbright Scholarship to the University of Texas at Austin where he earned his Ph.D., for a thesis on Samuel Beckett, in 1969. He has been a member of the faculty at the University of Cape Town and later at various universities in the United States.

Jack Cope (1913–91). South African novelist, short-story writer, playwright, poet, editor, and literary critic. Cope was born in Natal Province and began his writing career as a journalist. He worked in South Africa and in the United Kingdom.

Rolfes Robert Reginald Dhlomo (1901–71). South African novelist, short-story writer, and journalist. Dhlomo was born near Pietermaritzburg and educated at Ohlange Institute and Adam's Teachers Institute. He worked as a clerk in the Johannesburg mines before becoming a journalist. He contributed to *The Sjambok* and *Bantu World,* and later was editor of the *Ilanga lase Natal.* Dhlomo was active in local politics in Natal. Dhlomo wrote in both English and Zulu.

Modikwe Dikobe (1913–). South African novelist. Dikobe was born, an illegitimate child, at Seabe in the Northern Transvaal. He was christened Marks Rammitloa. But he wrote under his mother's name. because, as a "listed" person, he was forbidden to publish under his own name. He had little formal education. From his youth he worked at menial jobs in Johannesburg. He served in World War II, after which he joined the Communist Party and became active in the labor movement. For this he was banned by the South African government. He then worked as a timekeeper with the Johannesburg Corporation until his retirement in 1977. He lives in retirement in Seabe.

Menan du Plessis (1952–). South African novelist. Menan du Plessis was born in Cape Town, had her early education there, and took a B.A. degree from the University of Cape Town, After postgraduate studies, she was cofounder and then chairperson of the National Youth Action, an organization working against racial discrimination in education. She lives in Cape Town.

Ahmed Essop (1931–). South African novelist and short-story writer. Essop was born in India but was educated in Fordsberg at the Johannesburg Indian High School. He earned his B.A. in English and philosophy in 1956 and an Honors B.A. in English in 1964 from the University of South Africa, Pretoria. He taught English in Johannesburg schools. He worked for a time in the Department of Indian Affairs.

Sir James Percy Fitzpatrick (1862–1931). South African novelist. Fitzpatrick was born in King Williamstown and educated in South Africa and England. He was a transport rider and later a clerk with the Standard Bank in the gold fields and in Cape Town. He was associated with the Jameson Raid, the attempt of the British to seize the gold fields of the Witwatersrand from the Transvaal. He was charged with treason and was banned from political activity for three years. He was a close friend of the English poet Rudyard Kipling, who encouraged Fitzpatrick to publish his various books.

Sheila Fugard (1932–). South African novelist and poet. Sheila Fugard was born in Birmingham, United Kingdom. She traveled with her family—her father was South African—to South Africa in 1937. She studied theater in Cape Town. It was there she met and married the South African playwright, Athol Fugard. Their attempt to use theater to convey the depressed state of African workers proved unsuccessful. They spent from 1957 to 1960 in England, returning to South Africa at the time of the Sharpeville massacres. Sheila Fugard remains with her husband in South Africa, but travels widely.

Reginald Perceval Gibbon (1878–1926). Gibbon was born in Wales and attended schools in London and Germany. He migrated to South Africa where he worked as a journalist for *The Natal Witness, The Rand Daily Mail,* and *The Rhodesian Times.* Like Douglas Blackburn, another expatriate, Gibbon was an exemplary advocate of a uniquely South African literature, addressing in his novels the issue of black-white relations as a continuing dominating theme in that literature.

Nadine Gordimer (1923–). South African novelist, short-story writer, and literary and political critic. Nadine Gordimer was born in Springs, a mining town near Johannesburg. Her education was in private schools and, for a short time, at the University of Witwatersrand. She has won a number of literary prizes for her writing—the James Tait Black Memorial Prize in 1972, the Booker Prize in 1974, the CNA Prize in 1979, and the Nobel Prize for Literature in 1991. She lives in Johannesburg.

Daniel Jacobson (1929–). South African novelist and short-story writer. Jacobson was born in Johannesburg, had his primary education in Kimberley, and obtained his B.A. from the University of Witwatersrand. After this he spent time on a kibbutz in Israel and in London where he began writing. He returned to South Africa in 1954 and worked for a time in business and journalism before devoting himself to full-time writing. In 1954 he returned to London where he continued writing . He was also appointed to a chair in University College London where he taught until he retired.

Alex La Guma (1925–85). South African novelist and short-story writer. La Guma was born in District Six, Cape Town, to colored parents. He worked as a clerk, factory hand, and journalist. He early joined the outlawed Communist Party. He became chairman of the South African Coloured People's Organization in 1955. He was one of 156 people charged and acquitted at the notorious 1956–60 Treason Trial. He was detained three times for alleged subversive political activity He and his family left South Africa on an "exit permit" in 1966. He worked for a time in London as a journalist. In 1978 he became the Caribbean representative for the African National Congress, based in Cuba. He died there of a heart attack in October of 1978.

Sarah Gertrude Millin (1889–1968). South African novelist. Millin was born in Lithuania, moved to South Africa as a child, and grew up near the diamond mines of the Vaal River. She was educated in Kimberley. She married Philip Millin, who became a judge of the Supreme Court of South Africa. The Millins were acquainted with some of the most influential South Africans of their day, most prominent among them Jan Christian Smuts.

Eskia Mphahlele (formerly Ezekiel) (1919–). South African novelist, short-story writer, and literary critic. Mphahlele was born in Marabsatad Township, Pretoria. He went to St. Peter's School in Rosettville, qualified as a teacher and taught in Orlando High School. He opposed the concept of "Bantu Education" and was dismissed from his teaching position. He then joined *Drum* magazine as a political editor and fiction editor. He received his M.A. from the University of South Africa for a thesis on "The Non-European Character in South African English Fiction" in 1956. He moved to Nigeria in 1957 to escape the escalation of apartheid policies. In 1958 he became director of African Programs for the Congress of Cultural Freedom in Paris. In 1963 he joined University College, Nairobi, Kenya. He left Nairobi in 1966 and joined the University of Denver where he took his Ph.D. in 1968. From 1968 to 1970 he lectured in the University of Zambia and then returned to the University of Denver. In 1974 he moved to the University of Pennsylvania. In 1977 he returned to South Africa and taught at the University of Witwatersrand until his retirement in 1987. He was awarded honorary doctoral degrees from the Universities of Pennsylvania, Natal, and Rhodes.

Lewis Nkosi (1936–). South African playwright, novelist, and critic. Nkosi was born in Durban, Natal. He received his early schooling there. He worked as a journalist on *Ilanga lase Natal, Drum,* and *Golden City* before leaving South Africa on an exit permit in 1961 to take up a fellowship at Harvard University. He was at Harvard from 1961 to 1962 and then worked in print, radio, and television journalism in London. He contributed articles and reviews in such publications as *The Times Literary Supplement, Presence Africaine,* and *The New York Review of Books.* In 1971 he was visiting regents professor in African Literature at the Irvine campus of the University of California. He was senior lecturer and the professor of literature in the University of Zambia in 1985, following periods of research and writing in London and Sussex. He was in Poland for a period beginning in 1988. In 1991 he joined the University of Wyoming as professor of English.

Solomon Tshekisho Plaatje (1876–1932). South African novelist and journalist. Plaatje was born in the Orange Free State, at that time an independent Boer Republic. Dutch missionaries gave him his early education. From them he learned Dutch, English, French, and German. Plaatje's life spans the period in South African history from the beginnings of the formal industrial colonization through the Boer War and the creation of the Union of South Africa in 1919 and the enactment of the Native Land Act in 1913, through the progressive disenfranchisement of African peoples and the coincident beginnings of formal black African political resistance. Plaatje was witness to all of these events and his acute observations of causes and consequences are reflected in his writing.

William Charles Franklyn Plomer (1903–73). South African novelist and poet. Plomer was born in Pietersberg in the Transvaal and lived alternately in South Africa and England. He was resident in England during World War I. He returned to South Africa when the war ended and worked as a sheep farmer from 1921 to 1922. He then worked with his father in Zululand in a trading store from 1922 to 1925. Whatever his occupations, Plomer was a central literary figure, associated with a number of literary movements and publication ventures, in the years when South African literature was establishing its uniqueness.

Richard Rive (1931–89). South African novelist, playwright, and short-story writer. He was born in Cape Town, District Six. His early education was in Cape Town. He took his B.A. and B.Ed. degrees from the University of Cape Town, earned an M.A. from Columbia University, and a Ph.D. from Oxford University.(His thesis topic was the writings of Olive Schreiner.) Rive traveled and lectured widely. He was head of the English Department at Hewatt Training College in Cape Town when he was murdered.

Sheila Roberts (1937–). South African novelist, short-story writer, and literary critic. Sheila Roberts was born in Johannesburg. She had her early education in Pootchefstroom and took her B.A. and M.A. degrees at the University of South Africa and her Ph.D. at the University of Pretoria. She left South Africa in 1977 and is now professor of English at the University of Wisconsin, Milwaukee.

Daphne Rooke (1914–). South African novelist, short-story writer, and journalist. Daphne Rooke was born in Boksburg, Transvaal, and grew up in Natal and Zululand. She emigrated to Australia with her husband in 1950, but returned to South Africa in the late 1950s. She remained in South Africa until 1965 when she returned to take up permanent residence in Australia.

Olive Emilie Albertina Schreiner (1855–1920). South African novelist and political writer. Olive Schreiner was born at Wittenberg mission station, Cape Colony, the ninth of 12 children. Early in her life, she rejected her parents' religious convictions and, through a process of self-education, became a free-thinker. She traveled to London in 1881, where she wrote and published *The Story of an African Farm* under the pseudonym Ralph Irons. In London she made life-long friendships with prominent and influential socialists and feminist thinkers, among them W. T. Stead, Eleanor Marx, Edward Carpenter, Havelock Ellis, and Karl Pearson. She returned to South Africa in 1889 and formed close friendships with leading politicians of the day, most prominent among them Cecil Rhodes. In 1894 she married Samuel Cronwright. After the death of her only child in 1895, she returned to England where she was associated with feminist and pacifist movements. He final years were plagued by asthma. She returned to Cape Town in 1920 and died there shortly after her return.

William Charles Scully (1855–1943). South African poet, novelist, short-story writer, and autobiographer. Scully was born in Dublin, Ireland, and went with his family to King Williamstown in South Africa's Eastern Cape in 1867. He had a rich and varied life—as a prospector for diamonds in Kimberley, and for gold in Lydenberg and Pilgrim's Rest. Later he became a magistrate and civil commissioner in the Transkei, Namaqualand, and the Transvaal.

Mongane Wally Serote (1944–). South African novelist and poet. Serote was born in Sophiatown, spent much of his life in Alexandra, and completed his schooling in Soweto. He worked as a freelance journalist and became involved in political activities. For his political activities he was jailed without charge for nine months in 1969. In 1974 he went to the United States to study at Columbia University, where he earned an M.A. in 1977. He returned to southern Africa to work in cultural affairs in Botswana. In 1986 he went to London to work for the African National Congress. In 1990 he returned to South Africa and in 1994 became head of the department of arts and culture in the newly elected government of Nelson Mandela.

Francis Carey Slater (1876–1958). South African novelist, short-story writer, and poet. Slater was born in Alice in the Eastern Cape Province. He attended Lovedale School, a multiracial and humanist institution. The school provided ideal stimulation for Slater's inquiring mind. At Lovedale he was also able to use and to perfect his use of the Xhosa language, which he learned as a youth on his father's farm. After travel in Europe, Slater became a banker for a number of years in Barkly East and Grahamstown. In 1931 he was able to retire from banking and pursue a full-time career in literature. Slater served as President of the South African Pen Club. He was awarded the honorary degree of doctor of literature in 1947.

Pauline Smith (1882–1959). South African novelist, short-story writer, and children's writer. Pauline Smith was born at Outshoorn but was sent in 1895 to Britain where she got her early education and where she lived for most of the rest of her life, making occasional visits to South Africa in 1905,

1913–14, 1926–27, 1934–35, and 1937–38. She died at Broadstone, Surrey, in England.

Wilbur Smith (1933–). South African popular novelist. Smith was born at Broken Hill, Northern Rhodesia (now Zambia) He was educated at Rhodes University in Grahamstown, South Africa. His degree was in commerce. But given the success of this first novel, *When the Lion Feeds,* in 1964, he was able to become a full-time writer of popular fiction. He divides his time between Cape Town, London, and the Seychelles Islands.

Miriam Mesoli Tlali (1933–). South African novelist. Miriam Tlali was born in Doornfontein, Johannesburg, and received her primary and secondary education there. She began her university education at the University of the Witwatersrand. When it was closed to blacks she continued and completed her education at the University of Lesotho in Roma. She attended the Iowa University Writers' Workshop. She then joined the staff of *Staffrider* and became widely known for her interviews, published as *Soweto Speaking.*

Sir Laurens Jan Van der Post (1906–97). South African novelist. Van der Post was born in Philippoles, South Africa, and educated by his parents in European culture and literature. He was, as well, educated in local schools, most notably at Grey College, Bloemfontein. Van der Post early in his life was attracted by stories about African culture, especially those of the Khoisan people and the Bushmen. He traveled to Japan in 1926. He served in World War II and was captured and interned from 1942 to 1945. He lived in England from 1948, making numerous trips to South Africa until the time of his death.

Further Readings

Each of these volumes has extensive bibliographies on the general subject of African literature and on the writing of individual authors.

Booker, M. Keith. 1998. *The African Novel in English: An Introduction*, Portsmouth, N.H.: Heinemann; Oxford: James Currey.

Gerard, Albert S., ed. 1986. *European-Language Writing in Sub-Saharan Africa: A Comparative History of Literatures in European Languages*. 2 vols. Budapest: Akademia Kiado.

Harrow, Kenneth W. 1994. *Thresholds of Change in African Literature: The Emergence of a Tradition*. London: James Currey.

Killam, Douglas, and Ruth Rowe. 2000. *The Companion to African Literatures*. Oxford: James Currey; Bloomington and Indianapolis: Indiana University Press.

Owomoyela, Okoyen. 1993. *A History of Twentieth-Century African Literatures*. Lincoln and London: University of Nebraska Press.

van Wyk, Johan. 1995. *Constructs of Identity and Difference in South African Literature*. Durban: SCCALL, University of Durban-Westville.

van Wyk, Smith. 1990. *Grounds of Contest: A Survey of South African English Literature*. Johannesburg: Jutalit.

Zanus, Chantal. 1991. *The African Palimpsest: Indiginization of Language in the West African Europhone Novel*. Amsterdam: Editions Rodopi.

Index

About the Author

DOUGLAS KILLAM was Professor of Commonwealth and African Literature at the University of Guelph, Canada. He has taught in Nigeria and Tanzania, and Sierra Leone. He is the author of several books of critical studies, including *Africa in English Literature, The Writings of Chinua Achebe,* and *An Introduction to the Writings of Ngugi.* He is co-editor with Ruth Lowe of *The Companion to African Literatures* anthologies of African fiction.